# ExtrACTION

This timely volume examines resistance to natural resource extraction from a critical ethnographic perspective. Using a range of case studies from North, Central and South America, Australia, and Central Asia, contributors explore how and why resistance movements seek to change extraction policies, evaluating their similarities, differences, successes, and failures. A range of ongoing debates concerning environmental justice, risk and disaster, sacrifice zones, and the economic cycles of boom and bust are considered, and the roles of governments, free markets, and civil society groups are re-examined.

Incorporating contributions from authors in the fields of anthropology, public policy, environmental health, and community-based advocacy, *ExtrACTION* offers a robustly argued case for change. It will make engaging reading for academics and students in the fields of critical anthropology, public policy, and politics, as well as for activists and other interested citizens.

**Kirk Jalbert** is Manager of Community-Based Research & Engagement at the FracTracker Alliance, and Visiting Research Professor in the Drexel University Center for Science, Technology and Society, USA. His work explores public participation in environmental science and policy.

**Anna Willow** is Associate Professor in the Department of Anthropology at the Ohio State University, USA. Her research spans indigenous activism and cultural responses to extraction.

**David Casagrande** is Associate Professor of Anthropology at Lehigh University, USA. His expertise is in cognition, information ecology, and policy analysis of environmental issues.

**Stephanie Paladino** is with the Center for Applied Social Research, University of Oklahoma, USA. Her research focuses on the interactions among environmental governance, equity, and sustainability.

# ExtrACTION

## Impacts, Engagements, and Alternative Futures

*Edited by Kirk Jalbert, Anna Willow,*
*David Casagrande, and Stephanie Paladino*

FOREWORD BY JUNE C. NASH
AFTERWORD BY JEANNE SIMONELLI

LONDON AND NEW YORK

First published 2017
by Routledge
2 Park Square, Milton Park, Abingdon, Oxon OX14 4RN

and by Routledge
711 Third Avenue, New York, NY 10017

*Routledge is an imprint of the Taylor & Francis Group, an informa business*

*British Library Cataloguing in Publication Data*
A catalogue record for this book is available from the British Library

*Library of Congress Cataloguing in Publication Data*
A catalogue record for this book has been requested

ISBN: 978-1-62958-469-0 (hbk)
ISBN: 978-1-62958-470-6 (pbk)
ISBN: 978-1-31522-557-9 (ebk)

Typeset in Bembo
by Out of House Publishing

We dedicate this volume to those who have struggled
against the injustices of extraction.
And to those who now work to build a more equitable future.

# CONTENTS

# FIGURES

# TABLES

# CONTRIBUTORS

**Diane E. Austin** is a research professor in the Bureau of Applied Research in Anthropology and director of the School of Anthropology at the University of Arizona. Her work focuses on community dynamics amid large-scale industrial activity, alternative technologies to address environmental and social problems, impact assessment, and community-based, collaborative research and outreach. She has maintained long-term, multisectoral partnerships in coastal communities along the US Gulf of Mexico since 1998.

**Emmanuelle Bouchard-Bastien** has a background in anthropology (BA, Laval University, 2003) and environmental studies (MEnv, University of Sherbrooke, 2011). She is Scientific Advisor in Environmental Health for the National Public Health Institute of Québec, Canada. Her work focuses on the social, psychological, and annoyance effects on quality of life related to environmental projects, as well as social representations of risk.

**Geneviève Brisson** is Professor of Regional Development at the Université du Québec à Rimouski and researcher at the National Public Health Institute of Québec. As a jurist and anthropologist, her research focuses on environmental risk, particularly risk management, citizen participation, and social impacts. She is also interested in public health actors and the relationships between citizens, experts, and decision makers.

**David Casagrande** is Associate Professor of Anthropology at Lehigh University. He has studied how humans interact with their natural environments in Latin America and the United States with support from the US National Science Foundation, National Sea Grant Program, and National Institutes of Health. He earned a PhD in Ecological Anthropology from the University of Georgia, a master's degree in

Ecology and Policy from the Yale School of Forestry and Environmental Studies, and a bachelor's degree in Geography from Southern Connecticut State University. He lives on a small farm in rural Pennsylvania where he experiments with how to live sustainably.

**Tamar Cohen** is a doctoral research student at the Centre for Mined Land Rehabilitation at the University of Queensland. She has a BSc and BA with honors in Anthropology from the University of Queensland. She has worked at the Centre for Social Responsibility in Mining and has conducted research on communities and mining processes in diverse settings, including Australia, Melanesia, and Mongolia. Her doctoral research focuses on Indigenous people's involvement in, and assessment of, mine-site rehabilitation.

**Rob Cooley** holds a doctorate in Ecological Anthropology from the University of Georgia and a bachelor's degree in Biology from Bucknell University. He joined the Pennsylvania College of Technology faculty in 2003. At UGA, Cooley focused on fisheries anthropology; in Pennsylvania, he has chosen to examine the socio-ecological impacts of the Marcellus Shale natural gas boom. Rob resides in the mountains of Northcentral Pennsylvania and enjoys spending as much time outside as possible with his family, biking, kayaking, hiking, and fishing.

**Veronica Coptis** is Executive Director of the Center for Coalfield Justice. She grew up in western Greene County near the Bailey Mine Complex and now lives in the eastern part of the county. Before joining the CCJ staff, Veronica served on the Board of Directors for CCJ and was a community organizer with Mountain Watershed Association. She received a BS in Biology from West Virginia University.

**Amelia Fiske** received her PhD in Anthropology from the University of North Carolina at Chapel Hill. She is currently a postdoctoral fellow in the Division of Biomedical Ethics at the Christian-Albrechts-Universität in Kiel, Germany. Her research addresses contests over harm resulting from oil operations in the northeastern region of the Ecuadorian Amazon, exploring questions of toxicity, uncertainty, and inequality.

**Patrick Grenter** is Senior Campaign Representative for the Sierra Club Beyond Coal Campaign, the former Executive Director of the Center for Coalfield Justice, and a licensed attorney in Pennsylvania. Patrick graduated with a BS in Political Science from Santa Clara University and a JD from the University of Pittsburgh School of Law with a certificate from the Environmental Law, Science and Policy Program.

**Kirk Jalbert** is Manager of Community-Based Research and Engagement for the FracTracker Alliance, as well as a Visiting Research Professor at the Center for Science, Technology and Society at Drexel University. He received his PhD in Science and Technology Studies at Rensselaer Polytechnic Institute and an MFA from the School of the Museum of Fine Arts, Boston. For nearly five years he investigated the emergence of citizen science groups across the Marcellus Shale that mobilized to assess shale gas extraction's risks to watersheds. His present work seeks to understand the dynamics of effective community-based research and how knowledge that stems from these efforts can be used to inform the public and influence environmental governance. He is also a member of the Pennsylvania Department of Environmental Protection's Environmental Justice Advisory Board.

**Julie Maldonado** is Director of Research for the Livelihoods Knowledge Exchange Network (LiKEN), a link-tank for sustainable livelihoods to connect communities, organizations, scholars, and policymakers. She also works as a consultant for the Institute for Tribal Environmental Professionals working with tribal communities to facilitate the development of climate change adaptation plans, is a lecturer in the Environmental Studies Program at the University of California-Santa Barbara, and co-organizes Rising Voices: Collaborative Science with Indigenous Knowledge for Climate Solutions. Her doctorate in Anthropology (American University) focused on the social and cultural impacts of environmental change in tribal communities in coastal Louisiana.

**Caitlin McCoy** is a Visiting Associate Professor of Law and Environmental Program Fellow at the George Washington University Law School where she is also pursuing an LLM in Environmental Law. She was the Legal Director of the Center for Coalfield Justice from 2014 to 2016 and is licensed to practice law in Pennsylvania. Caitlin earned her JD from Washington University School of Law in St Louis, Missouri and a BA from the University of California, Berkeley. Her interest in environmental and social justice issues around energy extraction, generation, and waste disposal has taken her across the country and around the world to learn about the effects of these industries.

**Thomas R. McGuire** is research anthropologist emeritus with the Bureau of Applied Research in Anthropology, University of Arizona. He has researched fisheries, Native American water rights, and the historic development of cattle ranching on the Fort Apache Reservation. He is currently exploring the globalization of Arizona's copper industry.

**Moriah McSharry McGrath** is Assistant Professor of Public Health in the School of Social Sciences at Pacific University in Forest Grove, Oregon. Her work centers on relationships between place and health, particularly as they relate to social stratification, sexuality, substance use, and environmental hazards. Her academic training includes degrees in urban studies and planning, sociomedical sciences, and feminist and gender studies.

**Rachel Hannah Nadelman** is a PhD Candidate at American University's School of International Service. A "Pracademic," she has spent over a decade focusing her work, scholarship, and advocacy on community-led development in Latin America and the Caribbean. Her dissertation investigates El Salvador's decision to leave its gold resources unmined at a time when most of Latin America has intensified reliance on resource extraction.

**June C. Nash** is a cultural anthropologist and Distinguished Professor Emerita at the City University of New York. She has conducted extensive field work throughout Latin America for six decades, focusing on social movements, the lives of women, and the politics of work. Her commentary on the ethics and practice of ethnography has helped shape contemporary anthropology. She is the author or editor of more than 20 books including *We Eat the Mines and the Mines Eat Us: Dependency and Exploitation in Bolivian Tin Mines* (1979), and *Mayan Visions: The Quest for Autonomy in an Age of Globalization* (2001).

**Stephanie Paladino** is an environmental anthropologist with the Center for Applied Social Research, University of Oklahoma, and co-editor of *Culture, Agriculture, Food and Environment*. She researches sources of conflict and collaboration around the environment, and how environmental governance strengthens equity and sustainability, most recently in the areas of carbon forestry offset markets, oil spill response, ecologically protected areas, and currently, water management in the Rio Grande basin. She is also co-editor of *The Carbon Fix: Forest Carbon, Social Justice and Environmental Governance* (Routledge).

**Andie Diane Palmer** is Associate Professor in the Department of Anthropology at the University of Alberta. She is a linguistic and legal anthropologist. In her research project, *Making Treaties Matter*, she draws on her experiences as an international observer at the Waitangi Tribunal hearings to study relationships between the Crown and Indigenous Peoples of New Zealand and British Columbia. She has provided expert testimony for the Canadian Environmental Assessment Agency on behalf of the Esketemc First Nation.

**Tristan Partridge** is a postdoctoral researcher at the University of California, Santa Barbara (based in Anthropology, and in the Center for Nanotechnology in Society), currently working on a collaborative National Science Foundation-funded project, *Energy, Risk and Urgency*. He received his PhD in Social Anthropology in 2014 from the University of Edinburgh, and has carried out research in Ecuador, the UK, India, and the USA. His research explores how communities reorganize to address environmental injustice and intersecting social inequalities.

**Dana E. Powell** is a cultural anthropologist who works with environmental justice movements in indigenous North America. Her research focuses primarily on energy development on the Diné (Navajo) Nation in the US Southwest, where she has studied the cultural politics of coal production in the context of debates over sovereignty, economic development, and expertise. She serves as Assistant Professor of Anthropology at Appalachian State University in Boone, North Carolina, where she directs the undergraduate program in Social Practice and Sustainability and teaches courses in political ecology, critical development, environmental justice, and the anthropology of energy.

**Daniel Renfrew** is Associate Professor of Anthropology at West Virginia University. He received his MA and PhD from Binghamton University-SUNY. Drawing from political ecology and social movement theory, his Uruguay-based research has focused on environmental justice and the urban health politics of toxic exposure, as well as environmental movements and conflicts related to mega-development and extractivism.

**Carlos Santos** is Instructor in Social Sciences and Extension at the Universidad de la República (UDELAR-Uruguay) and a PhD candidate in Social Sciences at the Universidad Nacional General Sarmiento (UNGS-Argentina). He received an Anthropology *Licenciatura* from UDELAR and a MA in Social Science from UNGS. He has researched and published extensively on the politics of development and conservation, environmental movements, and social conflicts related to the advancement of Uruguay's agro-industrial frontier.

**Jeanne Simonelli** is a recently retired applied anthropologist, writer, and activist. Her published books include: *Uprising of Hope* (2005), *Crossing Between Worlds* (2008; 1997), *Too Wet To Plow* (1992), and *Two Boys, A Girl, and Enough!* (1986)—as well as a recently released co-edited volume entitled *Artisans and Advocates in the Global Market: Walking the Heart Path*. She has spent summers as an interpretive park ranger, worked with a rebel organization in southern Mexico, guided tours at an historic silver mine in Leadville, CO, and now volunteers in New Mexico parks while also working with communities facing hydraulic fracturing and its infrastructure. An independent consultant, she claims academic affiliation with Wottsamotta U.

**Anna Willow** is Associate Professor in the Department of Anthropology at Ohio State University. She is the author of *Strong Hearts, Native Lands: The Cultural and Political Landscape of Anishinaabe Anti-Clearcutting Activism* (SUNY Press, 2012), which documents First Nation members' struggle to protect the boreal forest from industrial clearcutting. For the past decade, Anna Willow has been learning and writing about cultural and political dimensions of environmentally transformative natural resource extraction. More recently, she has conducted qualitative research concerning Ohio residents' experiences of and responses to shale energy extraction. Her present project seeks to shed light on cumulative cultural effects and environmental decision-making in the context of concurrent oil and gas extraction, coal mining, and hydroelectric energy development in northeastern British Columbia, Canada.

**Amanda E. Wooden** is Associate Professor in the Environmental Studies Program at Bucknell University in Pennsylvania and the 2015–2020 David and Patricia

Ekedahl Professor in Environmental Studies. Her research explores environmental politics, protests, extractive industries, and narratives about environmentalism, waterways, nationalism, and nature. Her long-term field work and most recent publications are about environmental protests, mining, glaciers, and hydroenergy disputes in Kyrgyzstan.

# FOREWORD

## Extractive Industries in Global Economies

*June C. Nash*

Extractive enterprises represent the quintessential basis of globalization processes. In the eighteenth and nineteenth centuries, mining operations provided the resource base for development and production catering to local and regional markets. Today, extraction industries support such activities everywhere.

Extractive enterprises represent the following characteristics that dominate global production: Firstly, returns to investment accrue to a decreasing number of capitalists as profits are increasingly concentrated at the top level. Secondly, new strategies of capital redistribution are invented, such as the inversion of capital development in nations and localities with low tax policies where high earnings are easily hidden. Thirdly, migrant workers attracted to these enterprises experience pressure from lowering wages, resulting in increasing inequality between capitalists and labor. Lacking investment opportunity, entrepreneurs cannot develop secondary industries in these sites to compete with economies dominated by established extractive enterprises. Even in the United States, local economies remain dependent on external demand.

In 1967, I chose to study one such industry in Bolivia. There, the 1952 Revolution had succeeded in nationalizing the mining industry, ending European control that had failed to invest profits within the country. I read newspaper accounts of how Bolivian miners rejected the militarization of the mines following a US-backed 1964 coup. Arriving in Oruro, Bolivia, I learned that the San José mine was paralyzed because workers rejected a work reorganization plan proposed by the Interamerican Development Bank (IDB). IDB's capital loan to the Nationalized Mining Corporation of Bolivia (COMIBOL) required that several hundred workers be dismissed. Among these were disabled workers whose only form of compensation was employment in lighter tasks such as being watchmen at the surface of the mine and women who worked to concentrate metals. I spoke to a few people—a teacher in the mine school who sympathized with the workers, a woman in *chola* dress selling candy and fruit, and a gate-keeper who could no longer work inside the mines due to silicosis. All of them spoke bitterly of the government and the nationalized COMIBOL administration. Slogans on the walls of company buildings called for "*la lucha contra imperialismo*" (the fight against imperialism) and "*muerte a los asesinos militares y parasíticos*" (death to the military assassins and parasites), signed with the initials of the political parties and unions.

I returned to Bolivia in summer 1969. Like most nations whose economies were limited to extractive industries, the government served the interests of elites. President Barrientos had died two months before in an airplane crash. His successor, Siles Suazo, lacked what American journalists called a "charisma" for holding the people under a repressive military regime. Che Guevara was still trying to muster a revolutionary brigade in the jungles of Santa Cruz.

The resistance against the government was led by highland miners, not peasants, who had gained lands in the national territories of the Santa Cruz region. Many of the mines were running at a loss. Pensioned workers were not receiving subsistence checks, and even when forthcoming, these checks could not cover food costs. Government-employed teachers had not received their paychecks for months. Mining police received more pay than the production workers to catch "*jucos*," unauthorized workers who entered deserted shafts and "stole" left-behind minerals, which they considered to be their national right to extract. Union leaders were still in hiding or in exile, and "yellow" union agents were serving as spies for the mining administration.

Based on this preliminary visit, I requested a Title V grant, which made it possible for me to return in January, 1970, to begin a year of research on the work process and community life in Bolivian mining centers. During my stay, I learned how community solidarity developed and was reinforced in the face of mining disasters, miserable living conditions, and unjust rewards that benefited distant owners at the expense of human life. This solidarity bred forms of cooperation that enabled miners to survive and resist the injustice they suffered daily.

During the seventeen months that I lived in Oruro between June, 1969, and July, 1971, I witnessed an extraordinary explosion of political forces in the country, combined with an implosion of the mining economy. The dynamic energies of a people who had endured the most extreme forms of economic exploitation and political repression emerged from a limited opportunity for democracy during my research period. This experience enabled them to resist, but not overthrow, the subsequent seven years of dictatorship.

In my early interviews with workers, I found more than the answers to my questions about myths stemming from historic events prior to and following the Spanish conquest. I also learned of massacres in the mines and the disastrous Chaco War in which they were forced to enlist; also where they learned military strategies that enabled them to reject the mining industry's repressions. They made clear their views on the future of their country and their families, both affected by corrupt political leaders.

I was particularly impressed with two of the older workers who seemed to have transformed their hard and often bitter experiences working from an early age into a meaningful and rewarding life. The urgency of their claims about life and self-expression that I experienced during the Feast of the *Compadres* was repeated many times that year, often at events commemorating the deaths of miners. I also learned how carnival epitomized their collective experience. When people conversed about daily difficulties, they often changed the conversation abruptly, asking me if I had ever been there for carnival. They would follow this with a description of the lavish costumes and the enormous expenditure of effort and wages that went into the magnificent display. In carnival of February of 1971, miners—including all the men, women, and children of the community—watched or joined processions of underground workers, devil dancers, milkmaids, and *chicheros*, asserting a profound respect for their work and lives; a momentary denial of their impoverishment.

My work pivoted to study the family members of underground workers and their assessment of the miners' consciousness. One of the young workers asked me if I thought that miners were alienated by their arduous work and living conditions. My first response was to deny it as a dominant sentiment, despite its significance in Marxist theory. It was only after I lived in the mining community for months that I was able to understand it in the context of their life circumstances. In my interviews with workers they articulated their decision to work in the mines as a sacrifice for a better life for their children. The mining school had good teachers and ample supplies compared to public schools in town. Furthermore, the hospital and doctors affiliated with the mines were superior to any medical attention available in the city.

I also documented autobiographies, including those of a mine union leader, a first class driller, his wife, and a "*palliri*" (women who salvage mineral from the slag pile) (Nash and Rocca 1976; Rojas and Nash 1976). We decided to use pseudonyms due to fear of reprisals. From these individuals I gained an understanding of the basic dialectic between personal opportunism and collective action that emerges in the family, something that also played out in their strategies for living in the mining community. Wives are a necessary complement to preserve the honor of the family while ensuring that it meets the daily needs of all members. The family instills the basic rules of getting along with others, for minimizing conflict while still maximizing individual benefit. This demonstrated a need for cooperation while providing some minimal effort for realizing collective action.

Throughout this process I learned that, in Bolivia, the mines are a synonym for the modern age of industrialization. Their history encompasses the international expansion of capitalist economies that exported capital and machinery from metropolitan centers to remote corners of the world, absorbing labor and national resources. In the structure of global economic accumulation there were no margins set aside for workers caught up in the transitions of declining production. The slag piles, which workers relied upon as a resource after a mine's interior was exhausted, were being leased to US companies in a transition period that threatened to close nationalized mines.

In countries like Bolivia where mining accounts for the majority of gross domestic product, the old dichotomies of traditional and modern no longer made sense.

People maintain alliances with the old and the new as they strive for a better future for themselves and their children. Each of the generations that experienced major historical changes shaping the twentieth century—from the first organized strike in Uncia in 1916, to the Chaco War in the 1930s, to a democratic turn in the 1940s, to the organization of the *Movimiento Nacional Revolucionario*—are assessed in terms of the progressive advances made by unionizing, as well as by their development as politically conscious miners.

## Exploitation, Resistance, and Extraction

The failure of nationalized mining in Bolivia was not due to a lack of class consciousness, as Marx would warn, nor was it due to the restriction of national borders, as Trotsky, whom the miners favored, advised. Engineers I knew in Bolivia marveled at the miners' knowledge of strategies used by industrial nations to stockpile resources and force prices below market norms as they took advantage of capital control in a global network. However, the working classes lacked access to, and control over, market conditions that were essential to challenging managerial domination. Their unique power was to withhold labor but, lacking alternative sources of income, they were unable to survive. Therein lies the tragic significance of the phrase uttered by a miner who summed up his life and that of his comrades in stating, "we eat the mines and the mines eat us," the title of the book I later wrote about Bolivian mines. Lacking alternative economic opportunities, Bolivian miners could not muster the political power to affect their destiny until the 1952 Revolution.

*ExtrACTION: Impacts, Engagements, and Alternative Futures* is a contemporary discussion of how similar conflicts play out today. The chapters that follow span countries with distinct cultural and economic conditions, providing the comparative examples we need to draw conclusions about how to advance the struggle from all sides. The cases, drawn from the USA, Canada, El Salvador, Ecuador, Uruguay, Australia, and Kyrgyzstan, document boom and bust trajectories of scarcity in world resources, from oil to minerals to water. They show the wide range of risks and opportunities determining the success or failure of labor resistance in extraction operations. They demonstrate how the global market that extraction serves evades attempts by marginal national or local economies in producer countries to plan their own future. They bear witness to environmental degradation resulting from extraction industries and how these lead to the destruction of alternative economic activities. Technological advances promoted by the industry are a constant competitor to labor power that defeats militant action from the start.

This book is also a meeting point of social theory and activist insights into how consciousness can be translated into societal change. Marxist ideas on class conflict provide a base for identifying exploitation of workers in production processes where surplus value is created and extracted. But, as in Bolivia, the cases within demonstrate how this can only be translated into social change when those who are caught in the capitalist cycle are aware of how their actions can bring about political revolution. Many authors demonstrate what they have learned from playing an activist role in the movement alongside community leaders. This provides us with a view of those who are making history in their daily struggle for survival despite formidable odds. In this context of globally connected industrialized capitalism, the only way of ensuring justice is by forging unity among the diverse societies affected by extraction at local, national, and international levels. We are privy to some of these incipient maneuvers in this book, a remarkable summation of the experiences and actions of extraction populations.

## References

Nash, June C., and Manuel Maria Rocca. 1976. *Dos mujeres indígenas: Basilia [y] Facundina.* Mexico City: Instituto Indigenista Interamericano.

Rojas, Juan, and June C. Nash. 1976. *He agotado mi vida en la mina: Autobiografía de un minero boliviano.* Buenos Aires: Nueva Visión.

# PREFACE

## A Critical Mass of Engagements

This volume is an outgrowth of the ExtrACTION Topical Interest Group—first convened by Jeanne Simonelli at the 2012 meetings of the Society for Applied Anthropology (SfAA) to support multidisciplinary research and dialogue on natural resource extraction. However, SfAA is unique among professional anthropological associations in its diverse membership; the group attracts social scientific professionals who work in a wide range of settings—ranging from academia, business, law, public health, nonprofit organizations, and governmental agencies—and who are committed to making a positive impact on the quality of human life. Expanding from only a few sessions in its first year, a special conference track dedicated to ExtrACTION at the 2015 SfAA meetings in Pittsburgh, Pennsylvania (in the heart of rich coal deposits and the natural gas fields of the Marcellus Shale), brought together more than 100 presenters on 20 panels. This overwhelming response indicated that a critical mass of work was underway to make sense of natural resource extraction within the anthropology community and far beyond.

In compiling this book, the editors were particularly interested in presenting this research community's unique perspective to a wide audience of practitioners. For social scientists who work with populations dealing with the first-hand impacts of extractive industries, this has entailed documenting the experiences of those affected by extraction—and sometimes even participating in movements to counter extraction projects. Authors in this text have a range of backgrounds and provide diverse theoretical perspectives on the social phenomena they observe. Many authors use contemporary political ecology as a lens to examine intersections of environment, culture, and political power in which extraction is embedded. Others employ historical ecology and political economics to understand what enables or constrains viable alternatives to extraction. Still others draw from the field of science and technology studies (STS). Some of the frequently overlapping frameworks represented in the volume include environmental justice, risk and disaster studies, resource sacrifice zones, the economic cycles of boom and bust, and transitional social movements. We hope that our audience includes activists, policy analysts, and legal scholars who can use these contributions to the dialogue of activism in responding to the daily challenges of extreme extraction.

# ACKNOWLEDGEMENTS

Many people deserve recognition for bringing this volume together. First and foremost, we thank the engaged researchers—our contributors and others—whose tireless work reveals how extraction is experienced on the ground and the complex global and political processes that shape its trajectory. We acknowledge the members of the ExtrACTION Topical Interest Group in encouraging this work, and in particular thank those who participated in panels at the 2015 meetings of the Society for Applied Anthropology from which the volume arose. The editors also wish to express gratitude to a number of individuals who were instrumental in crystalizing the ideas and content of the volume. These include Jeanne Simonelli, for donating many hours of assistance throughout the editing and peer review process as well as for her insightful afterword; June Nash, for reflecting on her many years of ethnographic engagements with extraction; Donna Gayer, for collaborating with the volume's contributors to create rich and detailed maps in the chapters; Rommy Torrico, for designing the volume's cover in partnership with Kentuckians For The Commonwealth (KFTC); Richard Bargielski of the University of South Florida, for generating the volume's index; and Mitch Allen of Left Coast Press for seeing the importance of this volume. We acknowledge the financial contributions of Ohio State University and the FracTracker Alliance for underwriting the cost of the volume's maps and graphic design needs. The editors also thank our friends and families for the love and support they consistently offer, without which such projects would be impossible. Finally, we recognize those whose stories are told in this volume. It is through their experiences that we learn of extraction's true costs, but also of the possibilities that exist for a more equitable future.

# ACKNOWLEDGEMENTS

# INTRODUCTION

## Confronting Extraction, Taking Action

*Kirk Jalbert, Anna Willow, David Casagrande,*
*and Stephanie Paladino*

When Chevron's LANCO 7H shale natural gas well exploded in rural Bobtown, Pennsylvania, one worker died and another was injured. The well burned for nearly a week before a Texas-based emergency response company arrived to extinguish the fire (Colaneri 2014). Chevron launched a local public relations campaign, mailing gift certificates to every township resident for a free pizza and two-liter bottle of soda. The accompanying letter read:

> Chevron recognizes the effect this has had on the community. We value being a responsible member of the community and will continue to strive to achieve incident-free operations. We are committed to taking action to safeguard our neighbors, our employees, our contractors and the environment.
>
> *(Colaneri 2014)*

Angry Bobtown residents responded in kind, taking pop and pizza of their own to Chevron's local command center. According to one frustrated citizen:

> Chevron thought we were some kind of radical group. We brought them a thumb drive with 11,000 names of people who don't want their damn pizza. They physically closed the door in front of us and held it shut so we couldn't enter. So that's what they think about us.[1]

Far to the north, in Canada's boreal forest, extreme extraction has taken a different form as trees are shipped to distant mills for processing and profit. For the region's indigenous peoples, industrial logging destroys productive hunting and trapping grounds, reduces local game populations, and literally wipes away emplaced memories and sacred sites. An activist leader from Grassy Narrows First Nation—the site of the longest anti-logging blockade in Canadian history—was once asked what he thought motived the logging companies to wreak havoc on portions of his northwestern Ontario homeland. What they want, he surmised, is "every available log in our territory."[2] Clearcutting poses a threat to traditional land-based cultures and exemplifies the global crisis caused by extraction. It is as socially unjust as it is ecologically destructive. To provide the paper for the letters we write, the tissues we use, and the beams that support our structures, forests around the world are being destroyed.

On November 5th, 2015, a dam broke in Brazil's southeastern state of Minas Gerais ("Large Mines"), unleashing 13 billion gallons of mining waste into the city of Mariana, destroying homes and killing at least a dozen people (Damsgaard 2016). The dam—which had held back decades of discarded tailings, chemicals, and wastewater—was part of a major iron ore mine co-owned by the Brazilian company Vale (originally an economic development venture of the Brazilian Federal Government) and BHP Billiton (the single largest mining company in the world). In the days that followed, a flow of toxins would cut off drinking water for a quarter of a million people and destroy much of the aquatic life in the Rio Doce. It is estimated that the spill will cost more than $1 billion to clean up (Eisenhammer 2015). Brazil's Environment Minister told reporters, "It is not a natural disaster, it is a disaster prompted by economic activity, but of a magnitude equivalent to those disasters created by forces of nature." BHP answered with claims that the spill did not pose any threat to the people of Minas Gerais (Australian Associated Press 2015).

A young boy in the Democratic Republic of the Congo toils under dangerous conditions to mine coltan. He works for a warlord. He has no choice. His family's farm has been destroyed by a brutal civil war financed by his own labor. Coltan is a mineral source of tantalum, which is essential for manufacturing electronic devices. Most of the tantalum used in the world comes from the Democratic Republic of the Congo (DRC), where it has been linked to violence, murder, corruption, rape, and child labor (Amnesty International 2013). Coltan could be mined in other countries, but weak property rights and poor regulatory oversight make it less expensive to produce in the DRC (Nest 2011). Small-scale mining of coltan is still common, but industrial mining is on the rise as Chinese companies and other multinationals have come to dominate mining in the DRC. While these companies may be easier to regulate and hold accountable, continuing human rights tragedies are driven by an unscrupulous industry eager to include low-cost tantalum in consumer products. This substance is present in the electronic devices we use every day, from our laptop computers to our mobile phones.

## Legacies of Exploitation

Humans have a long record of extracting resources from our environments. Excavations of early settlements in modern day Mongolia suggest that mining of coal for fuel dates back as far as 2,000 BC (Dodson et al. 2014). Ancient Greek metal workers listed coal in their fifth century BC accounting of labor and materials needed for the manufacture of bronze (Mattusch 1988). One of the oldest known gold mines, Sakdrisi, in southern Georgia, is estimated to be 6,000 years old

(Hauptmann and Klein 2009). While this kind of artisanal-scale mining has been carried out at relatively low rates for the benefit of local populations for millennia, modes of extraction changed dramatically with the fifteenth century dawn of the European Renaissance. Natural resources became tied to nation-state expansions, with mass exploitation enabled by modern technologies and large capital investments. As Lewis Mumford (1934, 74) observed of the birth of industrial-scale mining:

> The deepening of the mines, the extension of the operations to new fields, the application of complicated machinery for pumping water, hauling ore, and ventilating the mine, and the further application of waterpower to work the bellow in the new furnaces—all these improvements called for more capital than the original workers possessed. This led to the admission of partners who contributed money instead of work: absentee ownership: and this in turn led to a gradual expropriation of the owner-workers and the reduction of their share of the profits to the status of mere wages.

Due to historical processes of European conquest and colonization, this history of extraction-dependent economies is now mirrored across the Americas, Africa, and Asia. In the past century, extraction has produced yet another unprecedented level of social and environmental transformation—one that is inextricably bound to new "extreme" forms of extraction evidenced by mountain-top removal for coal, hydraulic fracturing for natural gas, and deep-water exploration for oil. Modalities of extraction are extending to regions and resources once considered unreachable in order to extract more dilute, more remote, and significantly deeper deposits to fuel global energy consumption and manufacturing markets. Today, the US Energy Information Administration (EIA) estimates that, globally, more than 8.5 billion tons of coal, nearly 30 billion barrels of oil, and 150 trillion cubic feet of natural gas are extracted annually from beneath the earth's surface (US EIA 2015). Meanwhile, the British Geological Survey estimates that nearly 3 billion metric tons of iron ore, 150 million metric tons of aluminum, 40 million metric tons of copper, 6 million metric tons of lead, 29 million kilograms of silver, 3 million kilograms of gold, and 3 million kilograms of mercury were mined to fuel the growing demands for metals and minerals (Brown et al. 2015).

As staggering as these numbers appear, they are abstractions that fail to capture the brute realities of extraction so commonly regarded as "externalities"—impacts experienced by places and people typically (and conveniently) left out of industrial accounting. Along with new mining technologies also come chemicals and processes with unknown human and environmental health effects. Fragile ecosystems are being subjected to unprecedented levels of irreversible destruction. These impacts are often multiple and cumulative, and they are shaped (and reshaped) by local land use histories and rooted in socioeconomic patterns of vulnerability. The story of the Bobtown well blowout, clearcutting in Canada, the Minas Gerais dam failure, and coltan mining in the DRC are only a few of the countless real-world cases demonstrating how natural resource extraction rearranges physical landscapes and transforms people's lives, often unnoticed.

Yet, even as populations and landscapes are subject to extreme extraction's ever-increasing hazards, regulatory oversight and corporate accountability remain weak and fragmented as a result of the enormous economic and political influence exerted by extractive industries. Decisions that determine the fate of extraction projects often emerge from amorphous national and transnational corporate networks that operate beyond the controls of any single legal jurisdiction or national boundary. The roots of these entanglements can be found in free market policies initiated by the International Monetary Fund (IMF) and the World Bank, as well as in countless trade agreements pushed through by neoliberal agendas that favor accumulation of power and resources. As Pramod Parajuli (2004, 239) reflects, "Globalization is a phase in which 'capital' is naturalized, while simultaneously 'nature' is capitalized."

Many citizens of developed countries have been prevented from witnessing the long history of natural resource exploitation from which they benefit. This is in part due to the geographic distances that often exist between sites of extraction and markets of consumption, but is compounded by sophisticated greenwashing campaigns financed by extractive companies. In short, extraction's growing demands on nature and people have not been accompanied by a concomitant recognition of its true costs. The very industries on which modern technology and living standards so heavily depend—and which have such profound environmental, cultural, and economic consequences—are also those over which we seemingly have little control.

Nevertheless, indiscriminate acceptance of extreme extraction is changing in an era of rapid global communication, reflections brought on by the climate change crisis, political revolutions in regions oppressed by resource wars, and increasing instability in a global market hopelessly tied to the value of fossil fuels. High-profile actions are sowing the seeds for a critical new consciousness. A different reality is coming in to view in which at-risk communities are challenging systemic injustices, questioning the false promises of economic growth guided by a blind eye to public health and environmental sustainability, and looking for solutions to realize a post-extraction world. This is occurring not only in regions historically associated with extractive economies, but also within the borders of wealthier nations as people reflect upon the legacies that led to accumulations of wealth and power. It is evidenced in the wide popularity of authors like Bill McKibben (2012) and Naomi Klein (2014). As more regions of the world encounter the realities of extraction's impacts, the possibilities for political resistance and diversely imagined alternatives to an extraction-dependent world will continually expand.

It is into this terrain of unprecedented extraction dependencies and struggles that this volume steps. *ExtrACTION: Impacts, Engagements, and Alternative Futures* is a book about extraction, but it is also a book about ACTION. Its title indicates a concurrent focus on the human and ecological impacts of extractive agendas as well as on resistance movements that seek to break the bonds that tie extraction to economic and political trajectories. Significant cultural transformations are underway that reexamine the role of extraction in contemporary society. While these

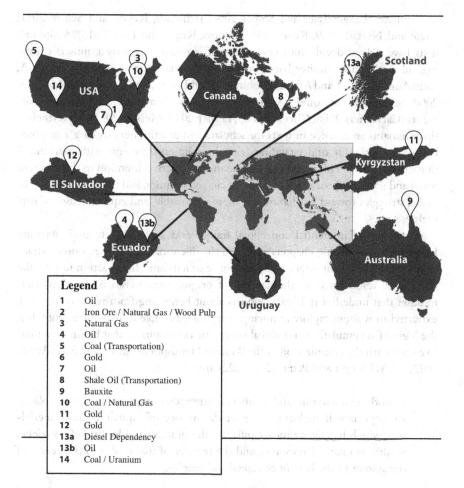

**FIGURE 0.1** The common experiences that structure and define emerging anti-extraction movements on a global scale are represented by the diversity of countries in which the authors of this volume are working and resources are being extracted. The numbers on the map represent chapter numbers of this volume. Map by Donna Gayer, Artasaverb.

responses may seem place-based and specific, common experiences structure and define emerging anti-extraction movements on a global scale (Figure 0.1). Given the capacity that exists within these spaces to diminish the power of extractive policies that now threaten the very survival of humankind and our planet, we believe that understanding the scope of public dissent and the nature of their activism is critical.

## Situating ExtrACTION

Monographs and edited volumes predating this text have thus far examined extraction within narrow conceptual windows, including global energy politics, capitalism, and climate change (Baer and Singer 2008; Behrends, Reyna, and Schlee 2011; Crate and Nuttall 2009; Kirsch 2014; Strauss, Rupp, and Love 2013). Additional texts have delved deeply into geopolitics of regional ecotourism, minerals mining, oil exploration, timber harvesting and industrial waste hazards in the USA, Latin America, Asia, and Africa (Bebbington and Burry 2013; Sawyer 2004; Zerner 2000). Still others have offered valuable case studies of environmental justice movements (Carruthers 2008; Checker 2005; Lerner 2010; McNeil 2011). Nevertheless, there remains an absence of texts for scholars and practitioners seeking a comprehensive resource for understanding critical public engagements with extraction's impacts writ large. This volume is unique in its collective attention to the different scales and scopes of extractivist social policies, economies, and the explosive rise of global struggles toward less hazardous, more sustainable, and equitable uses of natural resources.

A number of influential conceptual frameworks are critical to understanding how authors of ensuing chapters approach the dilemmas raised by resource extraction. Perhaps most important is the idea of "extractivism." If extraction implies the removal of resources from their points of origin, extractivism is the ideological mindset that underlies it. If extraction is about benefiting from resource removal, extractivism is about rapidly removing everything possible to maximize profit. It is the logic of accumulation and global economic development that began on a massive scale with the colonization of the Western Hemisphere, Africa, and Asia (Acosta 2013, 62). Veltmeyer and Petras (2014, 222) argue:

> …both extractivism and primary commodity exports have long played an important if inglorious role in the history of capitalism and imperialism, which has always meant pillage—the plunder and looting of a society's wealth and natural resources, and the transfer of this wealth to the center of the system to the benefit of capital and empire.

As it transfigures environments, extractivism concurrently transforms community structures, cultural fabrics, and political interactions.

While the scale of extraction is now greater than at any time in the past, today's extractive industries reproduce these entrenched patterns: wealth and power are reaped by the few, while local populations are forced to contend with degraded environments, lost subsistence opportunities, and social upheaval. Complicating matters, governments often bind natural resource extraction to economic development platforms intended to improve quality of life in impoverished communities, particularly in Latin America. These interdependencies have created a modern crisis in governance and accountability as whole nations weigh the benefits of extraction-based modernization against growing dissent by their citizens (Sawyer 2004). Even in developed regions of the world, local populations are made to feel reliant upon the charity of industrial capitalists who use a small portion of their wealth to create company towns; building schools and playgrounds that then legitimize their social license to operate.

Part I of this volume, "Histories & Trajectories," provides insight into how extractive industries came to dominate these global political and economic systems. The section opens with the rise of American oil companies and their relationship to the international hydrocarbon complex in Chapter 1—Diane Austin's and Tom McGuire's "The Great Crew Change? Structuring Work in the Oilfield." Readers are introduced to the "supermajors," such as Shell and ExxonMobile, and learn not only how these corporations developed strategies to accumulate global oil reserves, but also how they become susceptible to the "boom and bust cycle" of supply and demand. Austin and McGuire use this history to show how the oil industry has found ways to structure its workforce in order to adapt to changing economic times. They tell this story through the voices of workers who have witnessed the emergence of an increasingly risky industry, now reliant on webs of dispensable and less dependable contractors.

Daniel Renfrew and Carlos Santos' "Mega-Mining Sovereignty: Landscapes of Power and Protest in Uruguay's New Extractivist Frontier," Chapter 2, throws us headlong into the roots and implications of extractivism in Latin America, viewed through the lens of Uruguay's leftist government, which utilizes extraction as a means to support national social progress agendas. Here, extractivism is shown in its ideological form, known as the "Uruguay Productive" model, now considered necessary for creating a post-colonial, post-neoliberal nation. Under this new model, Uruguay has partnered with private industry to develop large-scale timber extraction and iron ore mining projects. However, increasing environmental impacts, and the perception that the state prioritizes economic growth over the public health, have created deep political divides among Uruguay's people.

Chapter 3, "Marcellus Shale as Golden Goose: The Discourse of Development and the Marginalization of Resistance in Northcentral Pennsylvania," by Rob Cooley and David Casagrande, examines why people who live with the daily realities of extraction often fail to question its ostensible indispensability. They suggest that the powerful oil and gas industry is able to structure public discourse in order to create support for gas development while discouraging opposition. By tapping into regional sensitivities surrounding decades of economic decline, extraction companies promise growth, national energy independence, and the return of working-class jobs. In doing so, the industry polarizes residents who must either support extraction or be considered anti-patriots who threaten the American way of life.

## Framing Impacts

The meaning of "impacts" varies greatly across the chapters in this volume. For some, whose lives are affected by the experiences of extraction, impacts refer to infrastructural changes such as road building, railway extensions, or earth removal. Others define impacts as the deterioration of water and air quality, or dangers to public health. Impacts can also take shape as cultural displacements brought on by changing personal relationships to space, or by disruptions in the social fabric of a community. In all of these instances, impacts alter the well being of human and environmental systems, with secondary and tertiary impacts of unknown consequence.

This volume addresses the complexity of impacts in two ways. The authors first interrogate how the "risks" of impacts are imagined and planned for. Risk assessment weighs relative costs and benefits, but more often than not also relies on the judgment of experts. In many cases, political institutions may even limit democratic participation by a broader citizenship in order to expedite decision-making. The results can be a systematic exclusion of stakeholders with less power, and thus an elimination of alternative ways of understanding impacts. As sociologist Brian Wynne (1996, 57) argued:

> Through their rationalist discourses, modern expert institutions and their "natural" cultural responses to risks in the idiom of scientific risk management, tacitly and furtively impose prescriptive models of the human and the social upon lay people, and these are implicitly found wanting in human terms.

Part II of the volume, "Risks & Rights," explores how risks are made acceptable when evaluating the efficacy of extraction. It begins with Amelia Fiske's "Bounded Impacts, Boundless Promise: Environmental Impact Assessments of Oil Production in the Ecuadorian Amazon" in Chapter 4. Many nations require companies to conduct environmental impact assessments (EIAs) in order to evaluate and mitigate the potential negative effects of industrial development. As Fiske demonstrates in the case of Ecuadorian mining laws, these assessments are obfuscated when impacts are reduced to quantitative figures and scientific analysis. Such appraisals allow mining companies to establish and then justify tolerable thresholds of degradation while the very question of whether or not a project should proceed on ethical or cultural grounds is left unquestioned.

Moriah McSharry McGrath addresses the topic of risk assessment from a public health perspective in Chapter 5, "The Power and Politics of Health Impact Assessment in the Pacific Northwest Coal Export Debate." In this chapter, readers learn about expanding coal export terminals in the US Pacific Northwest and the political processes that are used to determine their viability. McGrath suggests that by conducting more holistic Health Impact Assessments that focus on the values of health and well being, rather than on technical measures of risk, communities can reinsert a human rights-based approach to evaluating extraction projects.

The meaning of risks and rights can also change over the lifetime of extraction endeavors when legal, regulatory, and economic patterns reorganize, as Andie Palmer highlights in Chapter 6, "Contingent Legal Futures: Does the Ability to Exercise Aboriginal Rights and Title Turn on the Price of Gold?" British Columbia's interior, home to the Tsilhqot'in and Secwepemc First Nations, has a long history of gold mining dating back to the late nineteenth century. Palmer suggests that, over the course of history, there has been a direct correspondence between how Canadian legal bodies, mining companies, and First Nations define tribal rights depending on the rise and fall in the price of gold. Even today, Canadian economic objectives, combined with recently enacted federal environmental legislation, threaten to invalidate newly recognized rights to exclusive Aboriginal use, occupancy, and control of land.

The second way this volume contends with the nature of risk is by evaluating what happens when impacts are deemed acceptable for certain geographies and populations. Communities with relatively little political and economic capital often lack the ability to resist damaging extractive industries. As a result, they disproportionately face the detrimental byproducts of industrial development. Social scientists refer to these areas, dismissed as necessary losses for the benefit of economic development, as human and environmental "sacrifice zones" (Bullard 1993; Fox 1999; Hooks and Smith 2004; Kuletz 1998; Lerner 2010).

Julie Maldonado, in Chapter 7, concludes Part II by providing a succinct example of how economic, political, and discursive patterns set the stage for employing disproportionate risks to communities deemed expendable. "Corexit to Forget It: Transforming Coastal Louisiana into an Energy Sacrifice Zone" offers insights into the consequences of the 2010 *Deepwater Horizon* blowout experienced by Native American and Acadian residents of coastal Louisiana. Using the sacrifice zone concept to ground her analysis, Maldonado documents how government–corporate partnerships, and their decision to use toxic dispersants following the spill, threatened local subsistence practices. The effects of the disaster are intensified by sociopolitical structures that rejected transparency and democratic participation, while ensuring that the financial burdens of industrial accidents were borne by local communities rather than corporations.

## Building Resistance

The stories of Part I and II bring us to a topic of central importance to this volume—environmental justice. The environmental justice (EJ) movement first emerged in the early 1980s when predominantly African-American communities protested against toxic-waste disposal in the southern United States (Bullard 1990; Checker 2005). In the ensuing decades, the EJ movement expanded to encompass scores of multi-ethnic grassroots groups in North America and beyond. United in a struggle to overcome the patterns that place the burdens of industrial development on the shoulders of those who benefit least, EJ activists have refused to allow their communities' sacrifices to pass unnoticed. In doing so, they have sought greater transparency and public participation in decisions that impact their way of life (Adamson 2001; Schlosberg 2007).

Part III in the volume, "Struggles & Opportunities," considers how communities cope with the disproportionate impacts of extractive industries but, more importantly, how they seek ways to transcend their legacies as victims. Chapter 8, "With or Without Railway? Post-catastrophe Perceptions of Risk and Development in Lac-Mégantic, Québec," by Geneviève Brisson and Emmanuelle Bouchard-Bastien, describes the aftermath of the oil train explosion that destroyed the downtown core of the small municipality of Lac-Mégantic, Québec, in July

2013. Brisson and Bouchard-Bastien suggest that formerly latent tensions between the risk of the railroad and the risk of economic decline that surfaced in the aftermath of the disaster were, in fact, as serious as the initial blast and compounded its impacts. Noting that the train that wreaked havoc on Lac-Mégantic was carrying shale oil from North Dakota, the piece also encourages broader reflection on the hazards of commodity transport in an era of expanding infrastructural interconnections.

Chapter 9, "Bringing Country Back? Indigenous Aspirations and Ecological Values in Australian Mine-Site Rehabilitation," by Tamar Cohen, illustrates how companies rehabilitate post-mining landscapes to meet regulatory guidelines requiring the re-settlement of native ecosystems. Presenting a case study of bauxite mining on the Cape York Peninsula of Queensland, Australia, Cohen calls attention to ongoing processes of remediation wherein industry uses rehabilitation to promote social responsibility and to safeguard future extraction opportunities. At the same time, however, Aboriginal Alngith citizens use rehabilitation as a tool to recapture uses and cultural significances of traditionally native lands.

"Harmonizing Grassroots Organizing and Legal Advocacy to Address Coal Mining and Shale Gas Drilling Issues in Southwestern Pennsylvania," Chapter 10 in the volume, explores how communities responded to the cumulative effects of extreme forms of coal mining and shale gas extraction. Written by Caitlin McCoy, Veronica Coptis, and Patrick Grenter of the Center for Coalfield Justice (CCJ), readers learn of their organization's strategies for mobilizing citizens historically disempowered over generations of living with extractive industries. This chapter is important as it illustrates how grassroots oppositional groups develop legal tactics rooted in community-based activism to fight seemingly overwhelming and entrenched political and economic structures produced by legacies of extraction.

## Toward Post-Extractivism

The fourth and final part of the volume, "Alternative Futures," confirms that visions for a post-extraction world are possible. Each of the four chapters deals with different ways of imagining and enacting this future. In Chapter 11, "Images of Harm, Imagining Justice: Gold Mining Contestation in Kyrgyzstan," Amanda Wooden maps the discourses of anti-mining activists and how they are shaped by the media devices of photography and film. As Kyrgyzstan faces the realities of melting glaciers, these documents have become fundamental artifacts connecting minerals mining in glaciers to topics of climate change, thus creating a national dialogue about what justice means for Kyrgyzstan's people.

Rachel Hannah Nadelman continues the discussion about framing alternative futures in Chapter 12, "El Salvador's Challenge to the Latin American Extractive Imperative." As the only nation in the world that has effectively banned metals mining (while neighboring countries like Guatemala and Honduras continue to follow an extractivist path), El Salvador's recent political history demands close attention. Nadelman argues that the success of this ban pivoted on situating anti-extraction rhetoric as emphasizing protecting water rather than one that opposed development. El Salvador's anti-mining movement was successful in building partnerships with powerful institutions like the Catholic Church, which was concerned about the moral importance of preserving natural resources, as well as with domestic businesses that depended on clean water. This tactic ultimately prevented international mining companies from gaining a political foothold in El Salvador.

Visions for alternative futures are also emerging in spaces where people are choosing to reduce their dependencies on the incentives and commodities of extraction. In Chapter 13, "Unconventional Action and Community Control: Rerouting Dependencies Despite the Hydrocarbon Economy," Tristan Partridge details how this is occurring in two vastly different communities. The Isle of Eigg, off the coast of Scotland, has installed an island-wide electricity micro-grid based on renewable sources, thus reducing its need for diesel-fuel based generators. Meanwhile, in the Ecuadorian Andes, the indigenous community of San Isidro reduced its dependency on oil extraction-based income by building additional capacity for agricultural production. In both instances, readers discover that these movements succeed by negotiating for greater control over local land management and governing processes. While small in their impact compared to the systems of power they seek to disrupt, Partridge argues that these cases demonstrate how we can loosen the hold that fossil fuel industries have over our lives.

"Toward Transition? Challenging Extractivism and the Politics of the Inevitable on the Navajo Nation," the fourteenth and final chapter in the volume by Dana Powell, reminds readers that transition to a post-extraction world will not be a single event but an ongoing process. For those living in the Navajo Nation, this means untangling generations of colonialism where coal mining has largely been controlled by external political power. Navajo activists now contend with a political environment where the Diné are gaining greater control over mining operations, but simultaneously questioning their long-term future as a society bound to the economics of coal. These two competing energy futures illustrate the difficult choices that are made as people redefine their relationships to centuries of natural resource extraction.

Collectively, the chapters in this volume encourage readers to consider the root causes of industrial-scale extraction along with its environmental, cultural, and political consequences. The authors call into question the complicit role of governments, as well as their responsibility to protect the people they are meant to serve. The picture these chapters paint is one that suggests we are in desperate need of a new way of life. There is perhaps no other issue that threatens humankind as does unchecked industrial-scale resource extraction, and it is this dilemma that "extrACTIVISTs" seek to resolve. Local communities, activist coalitions, and forward thinking governments are seeking to alter their fate as victims of extraction. These people are indeed leading the way to a post-extractivist future. The ultimate goal of this text is to share their stories and to encourage others to follow their path in building a world driven by principles other than those tied to legacies of exploitation and injustice.

## Notes

1 Kirk Jalbert, Marcellus Shale research fieldnotes; March 19, 2014.
2 Anna Willow, Asupbeeschoseewagong research fieldnotes; October 9, 2004.

## References

Acosta, Alberto. 2013. Extractivism and neoextractivism: Two sides of the same curse. In *Beyond development: Alternative visions from Latin America*, edited by Miriam Lang and Dunia Mokrani, 61–86. Amsterdam: Transnational Institute.

Adamson, Joni. 2001. *American Indian literature, environmental justice, and ecocriticism: The middle place.* Tucson: University of Arizona Press.

Amnesty International. 2013. *Profits and loss: Mining and human rights in Katanga, Democratic Republic of the Congo.* London: Amnesty International.

Australian Associated Press. 2015. Brazil to sue mining companies BHP and Vale for $5bn over dam disaster. *The Guardian*, November 27. www.theguardian.com/world/2015/nov/28/brazil-to-sue-mining-companies-bhp-and-vale-for-5bn-over-dam-disaster (accessed January 5, 2016).

Baer, Hans, and Merrill Singer. 2008. *Global warming and the political ecology of health: Emerging crises and systemic solutions.* Walnut Creek, CA: Left Coast Press.

Bebbington, Anthony, and Jeffrey Bury, eds. 2013. *Subterranean struggles: New dynamics of mining, oil, and gas in Latin America.* Austin: University of Texas Press.

Behrends, Andrea, Stephen P. Reyna, and Gunther Schlee, eds. 2011. *Crude domination: An anthropology of oil.* New York: Berghahn Books.

Brown, Teresa Jane, C. E. Wrighton, E. R. Raycraft, R. A. Shaw, E. A. Deady, J. Rippingale, T. Bide, and N. Idoine. 2015. *World mineral production 2010–2014.* Nottingham, UK: British Geological Survey. www.bgs.ac.uk/mineralsuk/statistics/worldArchive.html (accessed January 5, 2016).

Bullard, Robert. 1990. *Dumping in Dixie: Race, class, and environmental quality.* Boulder, CO: Westview Press.

Bullard, Robert. 1993. *Confronting environmental racism: Voices from the grassroots.* Boston, MA: South End Press.

Carruthers, David V., ed. 2008. *Environmental justice in Latin America: Problems, promise, and practice.* Cambridge, MA: MIT Press.

Checker, Melissa. 2005. *Polluted promises: Environmental racism and the search for justice in a southern town.* New York: New York University Press.

Colaneri, Katie. 2014. Chevron pizza "scandal" leaves small town divided. *National Public Radio*, March 25. www.npr.org/2014/03/25/293875192/chevron-pizza-scandal-leaves-small-town-divided (accessed February 27, 2017).

Crate, Susan A., and Mark Nuttall, eds. 2009. *Anthropology and climate change: From encounters to actions.* Walnut Creek, CA: Left Coast Press.

Damsgaard, Nina. 2016. The forgotten tragedy: Revisiting Brazil's 'worst ever' environmental disaster. *The Argentina Independent*, April 7. www.argentinaindependent.com/currentaffairs/analysis/revisiting-brazils-worst-ever-environmental-disaster/ (accessed February 27, 2017).

Dodson, John, Xiaoqiang Li, Nan Sun, Pia Atahan, Xinying Zhou, Hanbin Liu, Keliang Zhao, Songmei Hu, and Zemeng Yang. 2014. Use of coal in the Bronze Age in China. *The Holocene* 24, 5:525–530.

Eisenhammer, Stephen. 2015. Brazil mine disaster could devastate ecosystem for many years. *Insurance Journal*, November 16. www.insurancejournal.com/news/international/2015/11/16/389012.htm (accessed January 5, 2016).

Fox, Julia. 1999. Mountaintop removal in West Virginia: An environmental sacrifice zone. *Organization & Environment* 12, 2:163–183.

Hauptmann, Andreas, and Sabine Klein. 2009. Bronze Age gold in southern Georgia. *ArcheoSciences* 33:75–82.

Hooks, Gregory, and Chad L. Smith. 2004. The treadmill of destruction: National sacrifice areas and Native Americans. *American Sociological Review* 69, 4:558–575.

Kirsch, Stuart. 2014. *Mining capitalism: The relationship between corporations and their critics.* Berkeley: University of California Press.

Klein, Naomi. 2014. *This changes everything: Capitalism vs. the climate.* New York: Simon and Schuster.

Kuletz, Valerie. 1998. *The tainted desert: Environmental and social ruin in the American West.* New York: Routledge.

Lerner, Steve. 2010. *Sacrifice zones: The front lines of toxic chemical exposure in the United States.* Cambridge, MA: MIT Press.

Mattusch, Carol C. 1988. *Greek bronze statuary: From the beginnings through the fifth century* BC. Ithaca, NY: Cornell University Press.

McKibben, Bill. 2012. Global warming's terrifying new math. *Rolling Stone,* July 19. www.rollingstone.com/politics/news/global-warmings-terrifying-new-math-20120719 (accessed January 5, 2016).

McNeil, Bryan T. 2011. *Combating mountaintop removal: New directions in the fight against Big Coal.* Urbana: University of Illinois Press.

Mumford, Lewis. 1934. *Technics and civilization.* Chicago, IL: University of Chicago Press.

Nest, Michael Wallace. 2011. *Coltan.* Cambridge, UK: Polity.

Parajuli, Pramod. 2004. Revisiting Gandhi and Zapata: Motion of global capital, geographies of difference and the formation of ecological ethnicities. In *In the way of development,* edited by Mario Blaser, Harvey A. Feit, and Glenn McRae, 235–256. London: Zed Books.

Sawyer, Suzana. 2004. *Crude chronicles: Indigenous politics, multinational oil, and neoliberalism in Ecuador.* Durham, NC: Duke University Press.

Schlosberg, David. 2007. *Defining environmental justice: Theories, movements, and nature.* Oxford: Oxford University Press.

Strauss, Sarah, Stephanie Rupp, and Thomas Love, eds. 2013. *Cultures of energy: Power, practices, technologies.* Walnut Creek, CA: Left Coast Press.

US Energy Information Administration (US EIA). 2015. *International energy statistics.* www.eia.gov/cfapps/ipdbproject/IEDIndex3.cfm (accessed January 5, 2016).

Veltmeyer, Henry, and James Petras. 2014. *The new extractivism: A post-neoliberal development model or imperialism of the twenty-first century.* London: Zed Books.

Wynne, Brian. 1996. May the sheep safely graze? A reflexive view of the expert–lay knowledge divide. In *Risk, environment, and modernity: Towards a new ecology,* edited by Scott Lash, Bronislaw Szerszynski, and Brian Wynne, 44–83. London: Sage Publications.

Zerner, Charles, ed. 2000. *People, plants, and justice.* New York: Columbia University Press.

# PART I

# Histories & Trajectories

# 1

# THE GREAT CREW CHANGE?

## Structuring Work in the Oilfield

*Diane E. Austin and Thomas R. McGuire*

> When the oilfield crashed [in the 1980s, people in the industry] never recovered. They got real, real, real leery. Nobody thought it would ever end, and when it did, a lotta people lost a lotta money. People came to a[n] abrupt halt, and after I guess four or five years, they saw it wasn't gonna come back like they thought it would. So then they even got more cautious. From that point in time, I found a lot more of the [oil] companies went to contract help. Contract helped cut their expenses. They don't have to insure 'em, they just give 'em so much an hour, and the [contract] companies take care of that. And that's how it pretty much wound up to where it is today, where it's probably ninety percent contract. And, at one time, you know, in the sixties and seventies, it was ninety percent, you know, the company. They were all company employees.
>
> *(Parish Council Member, Plaquemines Parish, LA, July 23, 2003)*

## Introduction

In June 2008, the Cushing, Oklahoma, spot price for a barrel of oil climbed above $133; in January of the following year it was just above $41. A similar pattern played out in 2014, from a high of almost $106 a barrel in June to just over $47 a barrel in January 2015. In 2015, as in earlier times, the industry's response was quick. Brock Pronko (2015), writing in *Pennsylvania Business Central and Marcellus Business Central* in March, discussed the loss of 21,000 oil and gas industry jobs in January alone and the impending loss of tens of thousands more, especially in service companies that support oil and gas field operations on a contractual basis and are therefore particularly sensitive to price changes. *The Wall Street Journal* underscored the magnitude of the workforce volatility, reporting that energy companies announced plans to lay off more than 100,000 workers worldwide; 91,000 layoffs had materialized by April 2015 (Molinski 2015).

The oil and gas industry has a history of booms and busts, imbalances in supply and demand, "crewing up" in expansive times, then retrenching and downsizing in bad times. The 2015 situation heralded something more, reflecting the cumulative effects of this history. Many in the industry labeled the early twenty-first century workforce turnover as "The Great Crew Change" and expressed concern that the skilled workers being laid off would be supplanted by inexperienced replacements or—given yet another episode of industry volatility—not replaced at all.

In this chapter, we examine the nature of work in the oilfield and the context within which it takes place, focusing on the offshore sector in the US Gulf of Mexico where we have carried out a number of studies sponsored by the US Department of the Interior's Minerals Management Service (MMS), retitled the Bureau of Ocean Energy Management (BOEM) in the wake of the *Deepwater Horizon* explosion on April 20, 2010 (Figure 1.1). The studies have covered a number of field sites, from Brownsville, Texas, through south Louisiana and Mississippi, to Gulf Shores, Alabama. Topics ranged from baseline histories; the impacts of the industry on individuals, families, and communities; oral histories of oil and gas workers, company executives, and scientists and engineers; and the ongoing effects of the 2010 disaster on the people of the Gulf coast. Throughout, we have talked with thousands of people and seen through their eyes an industry that both attracts and repels its workforce: high wages, overtime pay, opportunities for innovation, pride, excitement, and company loyalties draw people in. Layoffs, occupational hazards, and bosses who put profits before safety push them out. We address the conundrum of repulsion and attraction in the second section of this chapter.

These conditions, however, are shaped by a larger complex of global hydrocarbon extraction, which we address first. We discuss the highlights of this complex, which has changed the conditions of access to global oil reserves as oil-rich countries invite and expel international oil companies and force oil exploration to move to expensive and risky prospects in deepwater and ultradeepwater areas and hostile environments such as the Arctic. Industry restructuring of the major oil companies into the cast of "supermajors"—ExxonMobil, Shell, BP, and other well known entities—also has played a significant role in structuring labor in two significant ways. Directly, thousands of mid- and upper-level employees become redundant as companies merge. At the same time, the oil companies have been increasingly contracting out the actual work of finding and extracting hydrocarbons to drilling and service companies such as Transocean, Halliburton, and Schlumberger, and innumerable smaller outfits. When the *Deepwater Horizon* rig blew up in the Gulf of Mexico, only eight of the 126 on board were employed by BP, the company financing the operation (Juhasz 2011, 6). Finally, oil producers face difficult investment decisions, which directly affect the level of activity and the size of the workforce throughout all sectors of the industry: do we spend money to drill for new oil, do we buy companies that have reserves in hand, or do we satisfy our shareholders with dividends? These are the primary elements of the hydrocarbon industry that shape what happens on the ground and in the water.

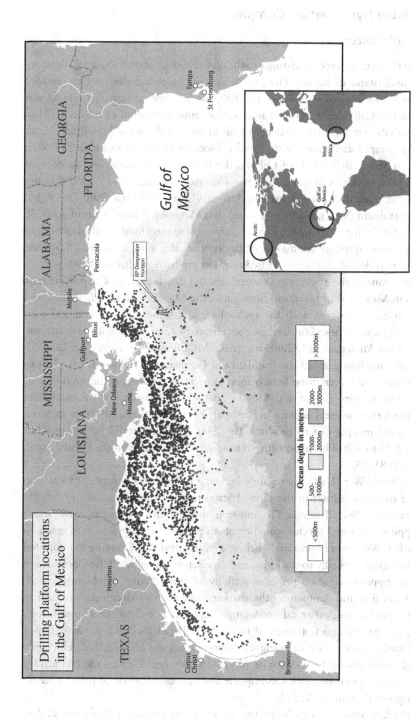

**FIGURE 1.1** The shift from relative price stability to volatility and nationalization of developing oil production have forced multinational oil company exploration into expensive and technologically risky deepwater and ultradeepwater areas, hostile environments such as the Arctic, and politically unstable nations such as countries along the west coast of Africa. This has been accompanied by downsizing and outsourcing the workforce, which decreases job security and increases safety risks for oil workers. Map by Donna Gayer, Artasaverb.

## The Global Hydrocarbon Complex

### Historical Context

To grasp the extent of recent changes to the global hydrocarbon industry it is important to understand its history. The first successful use of a drilling rig to produce
oil occurred in Pennsylvania, USA, in 1859, and the first commercial oilfield was
discovered in California in 1875. Large-scale commercialization of oil occurred in
the twentieth century after discovery of oil in the salt domes at Spindletop, Texas,
followed in rapid succession by the nearby discovery of several major fields (Olien
and Olien 1986). In 1901, Gulf Oil was the first company established to develop
the region's oilfields; next came the Texas Company (Texaco) in 1902. Within ten
years, these companies were joined by Union Oil of California, Pure Oil, Royal
Dutch Petroleum (Shell), Humble (Exxon), and Magnolia (Mobil) (Austin 2008, 2).
Though the California oilfields would continue to foster technological advances and
industry "firsts" through the middle of the century, the states of Texas, Oklahoma,
and Louisiana dominated domestic hydrocarbon production into the 1960s.

Internationally, the twentieth century saw the development of major oil production in Mexico, Venezuela, and throughout the Middle East. Dutch, British, and
American oil companies, with the technology and know-how to find and produce oil, typically worked on foreign concessionary agreements with host nations.
The Arabian American Oil Company (ARAMCO) was the archetype. In 1933,
the Saudi Kingdom granted the Standard Oil Company of California the right to
explore for oil in its territory. Texaco soon joined the concession, followed by two
of the other majors, Exxon and Mobil (Vitalis 2009). The major oil companies
were drawn into overseas activity in large part because oilfields, especially in Saudi
Arabia, were inexpensive to produce. By 1960, Saudi oil could be produced at
roughly $.05 to $.20 a barrel, compared to some $1.75 a barrel in the United States
(Prindle 1981, 75).

After World War II, the discrepancy between foreign and domestic production
costs led to two measures in the United States that kept the price of oil relatively
stable. First, the Texas Railroad Commission, in its regulatory role over the state's
vast supplies, instituted production controls to prevent oversupplies from reaching
the market. Wells were "prorated" below capacity and the Commission adjusted
these allocations annually to track demand. In essence, this allowed the Commission
to put an upper control on prices as well, by allowing "spare" production capacity back on line and dampening the market. Given Texas's dominant position in
domestic production, other oil producing states had to follow the Commission's
pricing and production initiatives (Prindle 1981, 41–44). Second, the Eisenhower
administration, in the face of rising oil imports from the Middle East, reluctantly
acceded to the demands of domestic producers and signed off on the Mandatory
Oil Import Program in 1959. Oil imports were curtailed at 9% of total domestic
consumption (Yergin 1991, 538).

In the late 1960s and early 1970s, the global hydrocarbon landscape under-
went drastic changes. Oil production in the United States was in decline as fields

matured. Under pressure from domestic consumers and foreign oil-producing allies, President Richard Nixon rescinded the import quotas in 1969. In 1971, the Texas Railroad Commission ended its proration program. Simultaneously, the Organization of the Petroleum Exporting Countries (OPEC), founded in 1960, supplanted the United States as the arbiter of oil prices (Yergin 1991, 589). Years of relative price stability would be replaced by a new normal of drastic geopolitical and market volatility. The United States had fully joined the world oil market.

The decade of the 1970s was particularly unstable. The 1973 Yom Kippur War led to the Middle East oil embargo against Israel's allies and a cutback of five million barrels per day of OPEC production, with prices quadrupling through 1974. Prices remained relatively high until 1980, when the Iranian Revolution, and Iraq's invasion of that country, led to further price spikes and curtailed supply on the global market (Yergin 1991, 710–711). Two significant trends played out through the decade. Domestically, despite a period of price controls imposed on US producers in an effort to moderate price spikes, drilling activity expanded rapidly—particularly in the offshore waters of the Gulf of Mexico and, after the approval of the Alaska Pipeline, on the state's North Slope in 1973 (Levi 2013, 8). Internationally, under a regime of high prices, and as part of a broader effort to take control over their raw materials, countries that heretofore were eager to have foreign companies and expertise exploit their national resources through concessionary agreements promptly nationalized their oil. By the end of the 1970s, Libya, Iran, Iraq, Venezuela, Kuwait, Nigeria, Algeria, Qatar, and the United Arab Emirates had pursued this path. Saudi Arabia completed its full takeover of ARAMCO by the mid-1980s (Juhasz 2008).

In the United States, the boom of the 1970s went bust in the 1980s. Saudi Arabia's oil minister warned OPEC members that the rapidly increasing oil prices in 1979 and 1980 would lead to a reduction in demand. This occurred as consumers heeded US President Jimmy Carter's calls for conservation. The Saudis attempted to get fellow OPEC members to observe production quotas to stabilize prices and rebuild demand. Few complied, and by mid-decade Saudi Arabia tired of playing the role of price setter by controlling its own production. The country ramped up its output from two million barrels per day to five million. By mid-1986, prices crashed to $10 a barrel, and US producers curtailed their activity (Mitchell 2011; WTRG Economics n.d.).

Prices spiked again in the early 1990s with Middle East supplies cut by Iraq's invasion of Kuwait and the ensuing Gulf War, then steadily declined into 1994, reaching their lowest level since 1973. Demand through the decade increased with a strong US economy and an economically booming Asia Pacific region, only to spiral back down as the rapid expansion of Asian economies came to a halt (WTRG Economics n.d.). Volatility continued in the new millennium in the wake of global responses to terrorist attacks, wars and revolts, strikes against Venezuela's national oil company, the "Great Recession" of 2008, and the increasing influence of commodity futures trading in the global market. This volatility, and its relationship to national and global economies, established the conditions under which oil companies and their employees had to operate.

## Seeking Economic Viability: Accessing and Replacing Reserves

All sectors of the "industry"—including the myriad specialized companies that service the oil companies and the yards fabricating rigs, platforms, and vessels for the expanding offshore sector around the globe—had to adapt through these decades of volatility. However, the major international oil companies faced unique problems: decreased access to the world's hydrocarbons and the conundrum of replacing reserves while maintaining shareholder value. Many developing countries nationalized their resources in the 1970s, but this trend was reversed abruptly in the 1980s, allowing one leading analyst to proclaim confidently that, by the 1990s, "[r]esource nationalism has practically disappeared from the discourse of international relations" (Morse 1999, 14). While the oil price drop in 1986 may have spurred the shift, it occurred in a context of neoliberal reforms and privatization, often referred to as the "Washington consensus" orchestrated by Ronald Reagan and Margaret Thatcher. Nationalized reserves were thus reopened to international oil companies. Oil-exporting states required state of the art exploration and production technology, as well as the expertise of international oil companies and their contractors. These states offered major oil companies opportunities to work in their oilfields, although under less profitable arrangements than the deals made during the era of concessions, such as those made by the Saudi Kingdom in the 1930s (Morse 1999, 19; Vivoda 2009, 2).

However, with a rise in oil prices in the new millennium, oil-rich countries once again began to reassess their dealings with foreign multinationals, revising contracts, blocking foreign direct investments (FDI), and reinstating national control over hydrocarbon resources. Vlado Vivoda, an Australian political scientist, places this resurgent resource nationalism into the political context of post-neoliberalism: the privatization of national patrimony sectors in the 1990s generated a backlash as foreign takeovers mounted (Vivoda 2009, 3–4). Beginning in the mid-2000s, the national oil companies, which included state enterprises such as Petrobras in Brazil, Lukoil in Russia, and the China National Offshore Oil Corporation (CNOOC), took control of roughly 80% of the world's proven hydrocarbon reserves. Major independent oil companies thus confronted the realities of having access to fewer and fewer places to explore and produce.

The access problem was compounded by the ever present need to replace reserves as existing oil and gas wells become depleted. A time-honored method to replace reserves is to buy other companies. When Reagan succeeded Carter as president in 1980, a relaxed antitrust environment followed. The US Justice Department showed signs that it might approve vertical combinations such as Conoco and the chemical giant DuPont, as well as horizontal mergers between major oil producers. Mobil and Gulf tested this new environment: Mobil acquired Marathon and Gulf bid for Cities Service. Neither move was challenged, and major oil producers quickly acquired Superior, Gulf, and Getty (Jaffe and Soligo 2007). An additional flurry of corporate reorganization took place at the end of the millennium. Between 1998 and 2001, the major integrated oil companies went through a succession of mergers that resulted in only a handful of "supermajors": British Petroleum (BP), ExxonMobil, Chevron, ConocoPhillips, and Royal Dutch Shell (Jaffe and Soligo 2007; Priest 2007, 275). Analysts and participants in these mergers offered a number of rationales, such as increased efficiencies through a reduction of duplicate management teams and facilities, and size advantages in approaching complex frontier areas with high technological and management demands. In addition, size increases through mergers and acquisitions could generate greater lobbying power. For companies still operating in the international arena where profits depend on political stability and the benevolence of national and local politicians, companies "strive for size in order to raise market shares and sales, but also to increase investment possibilities and political influence" (Neubecker and Stadler n.d., 7).

Other than mergers and acquisitions, the primary means to replace reserves is to hunt for and develop new oilfields. This method of replenishing reserves is often at odds with increasing obligations to maximize shareholder value given that new exploration requires huge capital expenditures. Company managers and their boards of directors must balance these conflicting imperatives. One approach to satisfying shareholders is to repurchase stock (which raises the value of individual shares). Another is to increase dividends to shareholders (Osmundsen et al. 2007). The investment decisions of the supermajors have taken a toll on reserve replacements. Due to reduced exploration expenditures, companies with operations in the United States have gradually depleted their reserves, with an average replacement ratio of only 82% since 1999 (Jaffe and Soligo 2007, 25).

When investment imperatives, driven by a need to find oil and to satisfy shareholders, are coupled with the increasing political difficulties in accessing the world's potential oil reservoirs, one consequence is that major oil companies are forced to work in hostile arenas—environmentally risky regions of the Arctic, politically unstable nations such as countries along the west coast of Africa, and the technologically risky spaces of deepwater and ultradeepwater extraction. The majors also invested in the environmentally problematic "fracking revolution," the hydraulic breaking of tight shale formations to extract oil and gas (Zuckerman 2013). The bounty from the major shale plays—the Marcellus in Pennsylvania, Bakken in North Dakota, Eagle Ford in south Texas, and many others—has helped redraw the hydrocarbon landscape of the United States. Oil and natural gas prices plunged, pressures built to overturn long-standing Congressional restrictions on the export of crude oil, and facilities approved in the early 2000s to import liquefied natural gas (LNG) received permits in 2014 and 2015 to export surplus natural gas to European and Far Eastern markets (Kolb 2014).

The decisions by the majors and supermajors to search for oil and gas under risky conditions, for which the *Deepwater Horizon* has become iconic, have created special challenges for, and furthered the development of, highly complex and dangerous oilfield service sectors. The fracking revolution, too, has taken its toll on these sectors. Though the oil companies make investment decisions about exploration, production, and acquisition of oil and gas, and about management of profits, the service companies provide much of the innovation to support these decisions and often absorb the brunt of employment expansions and contractions. These, in turn, shape the "culture" of local communities (cf. McGuire and Austin 2013). While the supermajors that emerged from the mergers of the late 1990s may have achieved some workforce stability in their expensive deepwater projects,[1] the service companies operate under a different set of rules, and many are highly sensitive to price fluctuations. The next section provides a look at how this history of volatility and the increasing risk associated with oil and gas development has been experienced by people most intimately involved in day-to-day operations of the industry—the workers.

## Operating in the Oilfield: Companies and Workers

### Labor Expansion and Divestment

The early commercialization of oil in the United States relied on investors, wildcatters (individuals who drilled exploratory wells), as well as workers who would lay board roads, construct platforms, and operate the machinery required for drilling. As oil exploration and development came under the control of major companies, the number and type of workers expanded to include administrative and office personnel, geologists and engineers, as well as the "roustabouts" and "roughnecks" who had quickly become associated with the oil and gas industry. As the needs of exploration and production grew, so, too, did the variety of tasks undertaken by oil companies themselves. Thus, the companies came to own trucks and planes, drilling rigs, and barges.

Over time, oil companies began divesting various functions, starting with exploration and drilling. With investors willing to take a gamble on potentially high returns, many entrepreneurs found their niche in providing services to the oil companies. In 1921, for example, Ludger Mintrop, a German scientist, founded Seismos Gesellschaft, a company that used seismic technology to search for oil in eastern Texas and the Texas Gulf Coast from 1923 to 1925. Gulf Oil employed one of the Mintrop crews in 1924, resulting in the first seismic discovery of a salt dome along the Texas coast (Petty 2010). As seismic technologies became standard in oil exploration, some oil companies created seismic divisions while others continued to rely on contracting. Seismic crews evolved from a few people operating equipment from the back of a wagon to trained crews operating from the decks of specially designed seismic vessels.

In another example of a developing service sector, Rowan Drilling Company formed in 1923 to provide contract drilling rigs and services. By 1940 there were enough independent drilling companies to warrant the formation of the International Association of Drilling Contractors (IADC) to represent the worldwide oil and gas drilling industry. The oil companies also supplemented their labor force with contractors who had specialized skills and would remain employed only during the phase of operations that required those skills, spurring the development of oilfield service companies and sectors. Technological advances and industry reorganization served to open up new opportunities for innovation, leading to alternating periods of expansion and divestment of labor and capital for oil companies as they rode the wave of fluctuating markets.

## Adapting to Changing Circumstances

The quality of jobs, level of responsibilities, and associated risks of oilfield work can vary tremendously. Nevertheless, oilfield workers, from office staff to roughnecks to drilling superintendents, are lured by the prospect of working in a profitable industry. Many workers make their money in overtime rather than direct wages, and though the rapid wage hikes and bonuses of the 1970s have never returned, working in the twenty-first century oilfield has offered a way to make money quickly. However, the global shift from relative price stability to volatility, and the trend away from oil company employment to contract work, has created challenges for people seeking an oilfield career. Some consequences of the shift to contract work—both short and long term—are illustrated in the following profiles of two individuals whose oilfield careers began in 1949 and ended in the 1980s bust.

### Melvin Blanchard

Melvin Blanchard was born in southern Louisiana in 1930. His father farmed and hauled sugarcane, and by high school Melvin decided to work in the oilfield because it paid at least twice as much as any other work in southern Louisiana. In 1949, he began working as a roustabout for a contract company, carrying supplies to and from the rigs and repairing pipelines laid across the bottom of shallow lakes. After serving two years in the US Army, he returned to Houma, Louisiana and began working for an oilfield service company seven days a week because there was "no such thing as time off." He left that job to take a position with Magnolia Oil Company (which became Mobil in 1959) where he experienced better working conditions and received higher pay and insurance benefits. He was laid off after six months when the oil industry slowed in 1954. The following year he got a job with another drilling contractor and stayed 12 years, working his way up to driller, the individual in charge of the drilling operation. He attributed his rapid advancement to the higher employee turnover rates in contract companies, compared to the rates within oil companies. Melvin moved between contract companies as markets and work fluctuated until 1979 when he took a job as drilling foreman with a small, independent oil company. He was laid off in 1986 with severance pay and six months of insurance benefits; he had not been with the company long enough to qualify for retirement. Reflecting on his career in the industry, Melvin remarked:

> It's been good to me, until it fell apart, you know. Other than that, it's been good, 'cause when it fell apart, I was at the wrong age. No one would hire you back. No one was gonna hire you … It's not always easy, and nobody

said it was gonna be fair. Did anybody ever promise you that life was gonna be fair?

(Interview, 3-25-02)

## R.J. Cheramie

R.J. Cheramie was born in 1929 and remembers when oil companies moved into his southern Louisiana hometown in the 1930s in the search for oil—they even moved his house so they could place a drilling rig on its original location. R.J. joined the Marines out of high school and attended college until 1949 when he started working with drilling contractors. He moved from one company to another to make more money, and was eventually hired by Exxon in 1952 to work on one of the company's drilling rigs. He sought the job with an oil company because, instead of the seven days per week and no benefits that he had experienced when working for drilling contractors, he had at least two days off per week and a place to live near the drilling rig when he was at work. He received his first raise less than a year after he started work. Exxon sold its drilling rigs in the mid-1950s, but R.J. was fortunate to get transferred into production. He remained with the company the rest of his career, spending seven of his 34 years in Burma and Singapore. Like many men of his generation, R.J. retired in 1986 when, in the wake of the bust, the oil companies were giving their longtime employees retirement packages. He proudly declared:

> I'll never, never say anything bad about Exxon because I'm Exxon. Just like I'm a Marine all the way, I'm Exxon all the way … I can honestly say, I've had more good times with them than I've had bad times. 'Cause I always thought Exxon treated me very, very well.

(Interview, 7-19-01)

Since the end of the twentieth century, few workers in any industry have experienced the long-term stability or compensation that R.J. Cheramie described. The oil and gas industry has drawn people in for other reasons. Along with the money to be made in the oilfield, workers cite excitement, entrepreneurial options, and chances for advancement. Such opportunities have not been unlimited, though, and the global trends toward more challenging environments and increasingly complex, expensive technologies have favored large companies with massive capital and extensive liability coverage and have reduced the attractiveness of participating in this industry for many workers and company owners. In these changed circumstances, contracting companies often provide services to multiple oil companies at any one time, ameliorating some of the financial risk.

The volatility that pushed companies into new frontiers and created opportunities also put workers in risky situations. An oilfield diver who began diving in 1964 and saw his diving assistant perish in an accident in 1969 explained why, a few years later, he helped organize a union for Gulf of Mexico divers.

## Paul Woodhall

The depth got deeper and we didn't use bail out bottles, so we used to dive a lot with what they call bounce gas diving. You'd be outside the bell, they'd shut your gas off, and you would have to run back to the bell in order to get a breath of breathing medium, but that's the way the industry was. I mean it wasn't just where I was working, but it was across the industry. It was just growing in such leaps and bounds that we outran ourselves in regard to safety ... I guess a lot of us felt that we were being human guinea pigs or whatever ... One of our goals was to try to make it safer, make everybody safer and have the union play a role in that as well. ... It was not entirely just for benefit of wages or whatever, I mean we truly wanted to help the contractors with the plight that they had as well ... Particularly back in those days where there was a majority of the people [who] were sort of floating from one company to another.

*(Interview, 8-1-03)*

The divers union was short-lived. Across the Gulf of Mexico oil fields, layoffs, company mergers, and reorganization, along with resistance from company owners and some workers, have prevented labor unions from ever gaining more than a temporary toehold in any sectors dominated by the offshore oilfield (Austin et al. 2006). Responding to concerns about rapidly rising insurance costs and fear of government intervention, as well as the divers' labor organizing efforts, a group of diving companies organized the Association for Diving Contractors to develop industry standards and address safety concerns. With the continuing march of the oil companies into deeper and riskier water, the limits of even the most technologically advanced commercial oilfield divers were exceeded, and their tasks were increasingly assumed by remotely operated vehicles (ROVs). Many divers were replaced by ROV operators, or moved into divisions of companies where diving was just one of an array of underwater services (Austin 2003). By the upturn of the 2000s, large companies that offered diving and ROV services dominated the service sector, and small entrepreneurs were limited to working on pipeline repairs or decommissioning projects in shallow waters.

As illustrated by the example of oilfield divers, the increasing volatility and complexity of the industry has necessitated social and technological innovation. This need has lured hundreds of thousands of people into the industry to work for oil and service companies, or to start their own businesses. It also has led to changes in the skills and educational requirements of the workforce. While entry-level positions still require little education, advances in technology require highly trained workers who can operate and repair sophisticated equipment. These workers, in turn, require ongoing training, liability insurance, and policies and practices that prioritize their safety. Unfortunately, as illustrated most recently following the *Deepwater Horizon* explosion, changes in industry practices have frequently come only as a result of disaster. As both the cost of entry and the risks increase, will the factors pushing workers away from the industry exceed those pulling them in?

## The Great Crew Change?

Given the ongoing demand for crude oil and its refined products, the oil industry is unlikely to collapse in the foreseeable future, but it will be required to persist with a labor force that awaits the next round of pink slips. This leads us to a rhetorical—and perhaps heretical—question: will the hydrocarbon complex collapse from within? Will the evolving structure of the industry—the volatility of crude prices; the oil producers finding it harder and riskier to replace their portfolios of oil and gas; the myriad service companies responding to the spending vagaries of the oil producing companies by controlling what they do have control over: their own employees and out-sourced labor—ultimately drive potential workers away from the industry in even larger numbers?

For more than a half century, oil and service companies operating in the Gulf of Mexico, as in other regions with significant oil and gas activity, have repeated a pattern of hiring and layoffs, followed by labor shortages and widespread recruitment and training efforts (see, e.g., Austin et al. 2006). Companies reacted to the bust of the 1980s with retirement packages and layoffs; they retained many of their younger employees and did very little hiring through the 2000s. They increased labor contracting as they tried to respond more effectively to fluctuations in demand. The fracking revolution further increased demand for labor, some of which was met by the relocation of companies and workers from the Gulf of Mexico in the wake of the *Deepwater Horizon* disaster. When that boom fizzled out due to the oversupply of natural gas and then oil, followed by a rapid decline in prices in 2014, frantic efforts to recruit and train workers ended abruptly. Even with large numbers of labor contractors to slough off first, service companies again responded with retirements and layoffs. An employee with one of the large oilfield service companies that had become a major supplier of labor and equipment to oil companies involved in fracking, and who had survived the downturn of the 1980s, shared his story:

> I was four days away from my thirty-ninth anniversary with the company when I was called in to meet with management. I thought they were going to give me an award. Instead, they told me I was being laid off. At least they gave me 24 hours to get my things and did not escort me directly off the property. It has been hard, but I know a lot of people and have been doing some contract work. I think I may be offered a position with another company but am not sure I want to take it.
>
> *(Interview, 5-4-15)*

Money matters, and it certainly explains why many people get into the industry—and why they often feel they cannot get out. However, it is not just money. Though industry restructuring, bureaucratization, and fear of lawsuits have tamed the wildness of the early days of oil and gas (Olien and Olien 1986), the yearning for unlimited opportunity remains. Some people are still drawn in by the risk, the excitement, and the challenge of finding and developing large reservoirs of oil and gas. And, for all the devastation and chaos it caused in the past and continues to cause today, the industry's presence is also a source of pride. From tours of Pennsylvania Oil Country to the Shrimp and Petroleum Festival of Morgan City, Louisiana, local communities, companies, and households communicate and celebrate their historic and present ties to oil and gas. Despite efforts to diversify household, community, regional, and even national economies, people facing economic hard times and few employment alternatives struggle to resist the lure of another possible industry upturn.

Nevertheless, industry leaders and observers cite a multitude of factors—retirements of experienced workers, limited hiring, and fewer opportunities for entrepreneurship—as having contributed to their rising concerns about the industry. Some fear the difficulties attracting younger workers, exacerbated by uncertainty, potential danger, and a negative public image, are creating a major crisis across the industry. Of particular concern are the effects on safety due to high levels of turnover and the influx of large numbers of inexperienced workers. The prospects for a stable industry, a secure work environment, and a satisfied labor force in the Great Crew Change are dismal.

## Note

1 However, a 2015 report from the consulting firm, Wood Mackenzie, noted that major oil and gas companies deferred more than $200 billion worth of investments in deep and ultradeep projects due to the oil price slump that year (Rigzone 2015).

## References

Austin, Diane E. 2003. Moving offshore in the Gulf of Mexico: People, technology, and the organization of work in the early years of oilfield diving. *Oil-Industry Journal* 4:87–105.

Austin, Diane E. 2008. *History of the offshore oil and gas industry in southern Louisiana. Volume III: Morgan City's history in the era of oil and gas: Perspectives of those who were there*. OCS Study MMS 2008–044. US Department of the Interior, Minerals Management Service, Gulf of Mexico OCS Region, New Orleans, LA.

Austin, Diane E., Thomas R. McGuire, and Rylan Higgins. 2006. Work and change in the Gulf of Mexico offshore petroleum industry. *Research in Economic Anthropology* 24:89–122.

Jaffe, Amy Myers, and Ronald Soligo. 2007. *The international oil companies*. Houston, TX: James A. Baker III Institute for Public Policy, Rice University.

Juhasz, Antonia. 2008. *The tyranny of oil: The world's most powerful industry—and what we must do to stop it*. New York: Harper.

Juhasz, Antonia. 2011. *Black tide: The devastating impact of the Gulf oil spill*. Hoboken, NJ: Wiley.

Kolb, Robert W. 2014. *The natural gas revolution: At the pivot of the world's energy future*. Upper Saddle River, NJ: Pearson.

Levi, Michael. 2013. *The power surge: Energy, opportunity, and the battle for America's future*. New York: Oxford University Press.

McGuire, Thomas, and Diane Austin. 2013. Beyond the horizon: Oil and gas along the Gulf of Mexico. In *Cultures of energy: Power, practices, and technologies*, edited by Sarah Strauss, Stephanie Rupp, and Thomas Love, 298–311. Walnut Creek, CA: Left Coast Press.

Mitchell, Timothy. 2011. *Carbon democracy: Political power in the age of oil*. London: Verso.

Molinski, Dan. 2015. Oil layoffs hit 100,000 and counting. *The Wall Street Journal*, April 14. www.wsj.com/articles/oil-layoffs-hit-100-000-and-counting-1429055740 (accessed February 1, 2016).

Morse, Edward L. 1999. A new political economy of oil? *Journal of International Affairs* 53, 1:1–29.

Neubecker, Leslie, and Manfred Stadler. n.d. In hunt for size: Merger formation in the oil industry. Department of Economics, University of Tübingen. http://econpapers.repec. org/paper/zbwtuedps/258 (accessed February 1, 2016).

Olien, Roger M., and Diana Davids Olien. 1986. *Life in the oil fields.* Austin: Texas Monthly Press.

Osmundsen, Petter, Klaus Mohn, Bård Misund, and Frank Asche. 2007. Is oil supply choked by financial market pressures? *Energy Policy* 35:467–474.

Petty, O. Scott. 2010. Oil exploration. *Handbook of Texas Online.* Austin: Texas State Historical Association. www.tshaonline.org/handbook/online/articles/doo15 (accessed May 25, 2015).

Priest, Tyler. 2007. *The offshore imperative: Shell's search for petroleum in postwar America.* College Station, TX: A&M Press.

Prindle, David F. 1981. *Petroleum politics and the Texas railroad commission.* Austin: University of Texas Press.

Pronko, Brock. 2015. Layoffs hit field services companies as drillers cut production. *Pennsylvania Business Central and Marcellus Business Central*, March 16. www.pabusiness-central.com/layoffs-hit-field-services-companies-as-drillers-cut-production/ (accessed May 25, 2015).

Rigzone. 2015. Wood Mac: Deep-sea projects make up most of $200B deferrals. www.rigzone.com/news/oil_gas/a/139817 (accessed July 28, 2015).

Vitalis, Robert. 2009. *America's kingdom: Mythmaking on the Saudi oil frontier.* London: Verso.

Vivoda, Vlado. 2009. Resource nationalism, bargaining and international oil companies: Challenges and change in the new millennium. *New Political Economy* 14, 4:517–534.

WTRG Economics. n.d. Oil price history and analysis. www.wtrg.com/prices.htm (accessed July 15, 2015).

Yergin, Daniel. 1991. *The prize: The epic quest for oil, money and power.* New York: Simon & Schuster.

Zuckerman, Gregory. 2013. *The frackers.* New York: Portfolio/Penguin.

# 2

# MEGA-MINING SOVEREIGNTY

## Landscapes of Power and Protest in Uruguay's New Extractivist Frontier

*Daniel Renfrew and Carlos Santos[1]*

At the 2012 Rio+20 international environmental summit, Uruguay's Frente Amplio (or "Broad Front"—a leftist political coalition) President José "Pepe" Mujica, the former Tupamaro guerrilla fighter-turned-horticulturalist-turned-politician, gave a stirring speech that went "viral" on the Internet. Mujica strongly condemned hyper-consumerism, market society, and humanity's progressive path toward planetary suicide, while evincing a common-sense vision of economic development tailored to the basic and enduring human needs of shelter, family, love, and the humble, modest "good life." In his own words:

> We have created this civilization we find ourselves in: child of the market, child of competition that has offered us a portentous and explosive material progress. But the market economy has created market societies ... Are we governing globalization or is globalization governing us? Is it possible to speak of solidarity and that we are all "in it together" within an economy based on merciless competition? ... Development cannot go against happiness. It has to be on the side of human happiness; based on love upon the Earth, on human relations, on the care of our children, on having that which is most essential.
>
> *(Mujica 2012)*

Along with his unpretentious and neo-Luddite public persona as the world's "poorest president," the speech cemented a growing cult following among domestic and international leftists, progressives, and alter-globalization activists. Uruguay's Frente Amplio party joined Latin America's "pink tide" of recent leftist governance. Along with other leftist and center-left governments in South America (most notably Argentina, Bolivia, Brazil, Chile, Paraguay, and Venezuela), the Frente Amplio came to power in 2005 largely based on the elusive promise of transcending neoliberalism's so-called "Washington Consensus." Along with strong job growth and anti-poverty measures that dramatically reduced the rampant unemployment, poverty, and indigence that characterized the neoliberal administrations of the late 1990s and early 2000s, Uruguay, under a leftist regime, was harkening back to its early twentieth century reputation as one of Latin America's most enlightened and progressive nations.[2] For some, it had become a model of how to create a strong and viable post-neoliberal social state in the midst of global neoliberal dominance.

For others, however, job growth and development have come at the cost of growing and urgent threats to quality of life and the environment. Much of Uruguay's recent economic success, and the fiscal basis of the state's renewed social agenda, is driven by the so-called "Productive Uruguay" political-economic model. Under this model, economic growth centers on new large-scale resource extraction and mega-development projects including the pulp mill/commercial forestry complex, export-oriented genetically modified (GM) soy and rice agriculture, and a proposed massive open pit iron ore mine. The Uruguayan state has partnered with private capital in developing large-scale energy and infrastructure projects to facilitate the extraction, processing, and export of these resources and commodities. New energy projects include expansion of the biofuels industry, the rapid enlargement of wind farms, onshore and offshore oil and gas prospecting, and the construction of a Liquified Natural Gas (LNG) processing facility in semi-rural western Montevideo (Figure 2.1). Planned infrastructure projects have included an Atlantic deep-water port, as well as bridges, highways, and "hydro-ways" to access regional and global markets.[3]

The potential environmental fallout of mega-development and "extractivism"—a political economic development model founded on large-scale resource extraction for export—has become one of the Achilles heels of Uruguay's three successive leftist governments, which have otherwise enjoyed widespread popular support. On the eve of the Frente Amplio's first national electoral victory in 2004, environmentalist scholar Eduardo Gudynas (2004) warned of the "return of the chimney dreamers"—bearers of that classic leftist development strategy based on smokestack industries, rendering environmental concerns as bourgeois "luxuries" secondary in importance to job growth and social equity. In Immanuel Wallerstein's characterization, the Frente Amplio conforms to Latin America's "modernizing" Left and, like other "official" leftist governments and parties of the region, is rooted in extractivism. This means of development finds itself in opposition to an alternative leftist project based on the conservation of traditional lifeways. This "second" Left is exemplified by the indigenous concept of "buen vivir" (living well) and reflects values found in various indigenous, afro-descendent, and rural worker (peasant) anti- or alter-capitalist initiatives across the region (Wallerstein 2015).

As Fernando Coronil (2011) reminds us, however, Latin American governments of *both* the Left and the Right have turned to the accumulation of capital through the development of nature-intensive resource based economies as a primary source of foreign exchange (Svampa 2013). Composto and Navarro (2014) refer to this

**FIGURE 2.1** The leftist government of Uruguay has pursued energy and mineral resource extraction policies across the country in order to finance expansive social programs. This has created a new wave of environmentalism within the country that cuts across traditional political alliances. Map by Donna Gayer, Artasaverb.

relatively unified regional process as a shift away from the neoliberal Washington Consensus that was largely based on speculative and finance capital, to a post-neoliberal "Commodity Consensus" based on the large-scale export of primary resources.

Around the time Mujica was gaining international fame for his progressive eco-friendly messages, new environmental conflicts surged, targeting the very heart of the Left's political economic strategy. Unprecedented grassroots actions have been remapping Uruguay's political landscape, tilting established relations of power and political relevance from political parties to grassroots coalitions, and from the capital to the gradually depopulating and long taken for granted countryside. They involve the defense of land, coasts, and traditional ways of life linked to farming, harvesting, and artisanal fishing. They also promote the protection of bohemian lifestyles associated with new eco-conscious rural dwelling and intentional communities (Chouhy 2013). Finally, they have drawn together people and communities directly contaminated or displaced by Uruguay's new mega-development and extractivist enterprises.

The primary catalyst of Uruguay's new environmentalism was the planned $3 billion Aratirí open pit iron ore mine led by the Indian corporation Zamin Ferrous and slated to begin in 2011. Taking advantage of historically high commodity prices that quintupled the value of iron between 2008 and 2011, the Aratirí project was designed to extract ore quickly over a twelve-year period, and at the highest possible volume. The mining area was to span three departments (the equivalent of US states) and would include a pipeline reaching hundreds of kilometers, while necessitating the construction of a new deep-water port to facilitate mineral exports, mostly to China. Complementing these mega-projects of extraction (iron ore mine) and infrastructure (pipeline and deep-water port), the government pushed forward the construction of an energy facility in the capital, Montevideo, through an offshore LNG plant.

Our chapter begins with an examination of the Frente Amplio's Productive Uruguay economic model as an example of the country's turn to the Commodity Consensus through its promotion of mega-development and extractivism. We key in on the political-economic continuities and the socio-environmental consequences and legacies located at the intersection between ostensibly neoliberal (Natural Uruguay) and post-neoliberal (Productive Uruguay) models. We argue that on the one hand, the Productive Uruguay model has garnered strong popular support of the state through the Left's poverty reduction, job growth, and social justice agendas, thereby leading to a virtual end of the "neoliberal protest cycle" (Santos et al. 2013) that characterized popular movements of the past few decades. On the other hand, Productive Uruguay's extractivist program has generated and multiplied environmental conflicts, leading to the creation of new environmental subjectivities and the rise of a post-neoliberal and "post-Left" New Environmentalism.

We examine Uruguay's New Environmentalism expressed through three emblematic movements that have contested the Left's political economic model: the anti-mine Uruguay Libre movement, the broader anti-extractivist Permanent National Assembly coalition, and the anti-LNG Western Montevideo Neighbors Coordinate. These three interconnected movements have mirrored the government's triangulation of extraction (iron ore mine), infrastructure (pipelines and deep-water port), and energy (LNG plant), while forging a seldom seen unification of territorial struggles emerging from the interior, the coast, and the capital.

## From a Natural to a Productive Uruguay

"Natural Uruguay" (or Uruguay Natural Country) traces its roots to political and economic trends started in the early 1990s, and later implemented by the neoliberal administration of Jorge Batlle (1999–2004). Finance and services came to rival the respective contributions of livestock and manufacturing to Uruguay's gross national product (GNP). Furthermore, with tourism becoming the largest foreign currency earner, and the rising popularity of global environmental governance ideologies, Natural Uruguay became the business and political elite's premier project for economic promotion and country branding.

According to the Natural Uruguay vision, the country would become a service center of regional and global finance, conferences, tourism, and a general "gateway to Mercosur" (the regional trade bloc), while establishing and promoting a series of carefully crafted "showcase ecology" sites. Protected coastal areas, wetlands, and other ecological zones were meant to both lure tourists as well as shape Uruguay's international image as a "serious" country that was "ready for business" and "open for growth" (Campomar and Andersen 1999; Renfrew 2009). Showcasing clean and pristine ecological zones promoted an image of order and lawfulness. It synchronized with corporate social responsibility principles in the global North, paving the way for what corporate shareholders presumed to be politically uncontested projects spawned by foreign direct investment. Meanwhile, constitutional amendments and new environmental protection laws enacted in 1994 and 2000 declared the environment of "general interest." These initiatives established the legal and institutional mechanisms to create Uruguay's modern environmental regulatory framework. They also arguably helped facilitate the growth of a broader environmental consciousness among the citizenry, laying the groundwork for some of the country's first sustained environmental struggles (Renfrew 2009; Santandreu and Gudynas 1998).

Under the Frente Amplio's Productive Uruguay model (2005–present), the government has continued an economic development strategy based on foreign direct investment favorable to transnational capital, one that we argue has not fundamentally altered the legal and macroeconomic frameworks of the neoliberal era. Commodity exports have fueled rising gross domestic product (GDP), with a manifested state goal to generate and maintain a "positive investment climate" by containing inflation, maintaining flexible exchange rates, and reducing the fiscal deficit (Santos et al. 2013, 15).

One of the key differences between neoliberalism and leftist extractivism is the role of "compensatory social policies," or the strategic expansion of the state (back) into the social realm, counter to neoliberal prescriptions of reduced welfare provisioning and the dismantling or outsourcing of the public sector (Grugel and Riggirozzi 2012; Gudynas 2009; Santos et al. 2013). Upon coming to power in 2005, the Frente Amplio created the Ministry of Social Development, and launched the National Social Emergency and Equity Plans. Similar to regional initiatives such as Brazil's "Fome Cero" (Zero Hunger) or Argentina's "Plan Jefes y Jefas de Hogar" (Head of Household), these plans included economic direct payments and food subsidies to the nation's most destitute in order to palliate the dramatic socio-economic crisis of the early years of the millennium.

Taking advantage of a favorable global economic climate, including strong Chinese demand for commodities, GNP growth rates exceeded 6% per year and real wages increased 36% between 2005 and 2012. Meanwhile, poverty fell from 40% to 13%, indigence from 4% to 0.5%, and unemployment from a historic high of 20% in 2002 to a historic low of 6% by 2010 (Santos et al. 2013, 20). These measures fostered strong popular support for the Frente Amplio, marking an end to the anti-neoliberal "protest cycle" that had characterized organized labor and popular movements since the 1980s (Diaz Estévez 2013; Santos et al. 2013).

In spite of many social advances, however, the extractivist model based on large-scale multinational corporate investment has precipitated a foreign "land grab" through land concentration and foreign property holdings, raising political concerns over compromises to national sovereignty. According to one estimate, up to 33% of arable land was sold or leased between 2000 and 2010, mostly to foreign investors, and the Uruguayan share of landholdings during this period declined from 90.4% to 53.9% (Oyhantçabal 2013, 90–91). Due to Uruguay's continuing reliance on a political economic strategy of "accumulation by dispossession"—the extension of capital markets through the appropriation of public goods, services, land, and common resources (Harvey 2005)—the Frente Amplio's economic model has not significantly altered the long-term structural problems of national dependency and domestic income inequality. As a result, this has opened up new political opportunities for post-neoliberal social struggles oriented around the social and environmental disarticulations of the extractivist productive model (Santos et al. 2013).

## Early Challenges to the Productive Uruguay Model

The first major environmental conflict related to the Productive Uruguay model occurred during the Frente Amplio's first term under President Tabaré Vázquez (2005–2010) in response to the installation of massive billion dollar pulp mills along the Uruguay River bordering Argentina, financed primarily by Finnish, Swedish, and Spanish capital. This was the largest private investment project in Uruguayan history. Environmental critics pointed to the risks of chemically intensive pulp industries and their threat to biodiversity and small-scale agriculture. Other concerns related to threats to national and territorial sovereignty posed by the creation of the so-called "green deserts" of ecologically uniform mono-cultivation, and the extensive land grabs on the part of large-scale transnational corporate investors. Through plantation forestry, hundreds of thousands of hectares of exotic non-native tree species were planted that eventually encompassed 70% of the country's total forested area (Oyhantçabal 2013, 89).

A major pulp-mill facility in Fray Bentos, known as the Botnia project, catalyzed the first environmental movement specifically targeting the negative consequences and contradictions of the Productive Uruguay model. What began as a local issue turned into a major international environmental and diplomatic standoff, however, as activists from Gualeguaychú, Argentina, the city across the river from Fray Bentos, led the opposition (Reboratti and Palermo 2007). The transnational growth of the conflict, reaching all the way to The Hague's World Court, fueled an anti-environmentalist backlash in Uruguay. Leftists as well as those on the Right, however, framed the defense of Botnia as a nationalist cause to protect sovereignty. To be an environmentalist became equated with foreign and anti-patriotic ideology, effectively stalling the emergence of an independent environmentalist political force in the country.

Enrique Viana, called Uruguay's "green prosecutor" for his years long, nearly singlehanded legal campaign in favor of environmental protection, referred to the chilling and internalized disciplining of the judiciary following this conflict as the "Botnia effect," which he argues impeded subsequent court decisions potentially favorable to environmental protection. Viana filed multiple lawsuits against the Uruguayan government for establishing bilateral free trade agreements that facilitated large-scale resource exploitation.[4] The state, according to Viana, had acted as an "interested" investment partner profiting from, and guaranteeing market freedoms to, foreign firms engaging in real or potential environmental harm. This went against the state's mandate under constitutional law to act as guarantor of environmental wellbeing.

Under Frente Amplio governance then, Uruguay became engaged in contradictory mandates simultaneously promoting conservation (Natural Uruguay) and development (Productive Uruguay). The process reflects what James O'Connor (1994) has termed the "second contradiction" or "cost crisis" of capitalism—the process of degradation that compromises the very conditions of capitalist production. For example, the Natural Uruguay model's previously established zones of showcase ecology, such as relatively pristine coastal areas and protected wetlands, became threatened by mass scale mega-development projects introduced by the Productive Uruguay model.[5] As natural resources and the environmental commons became central to both capitalist accumulation strategies and to Uruguay's insertion into global markets, the environment emerged as a central site of resistance and as a generator of new environmental and political subjects.

## The Rise of Uruguay's New Environmentalism

With the Left now in its third consecutive term in power, and with multiple environmental problems and conflicts sweeping across the territory, the "Botnia effect" has held less sway than in the past and grassroots coalitions are in the process of forging a new wave of post-neoliberal protest. As elsewhere in the geopolitical South, increasingly fractious public debates in Uruguay have focused on the real and potential socio-environmental risks of mega-development and resource extraction. Activists have called attention to the risks of environmental contamination, threats to biodiversity and water quality, the concentration of land ownership, and the loss of territorial and food sovereignty. At stake too are competing ideologies of Uruguay as a country-model, and of the rural countryside as embodying on the one hand a space of harmonious and pastoral tradition, or on the other an untapped basin of seemingly endless resources and riches.

Uruguayan social movements have historically been dominated by labor and student activism. These were joined in turn by movements promoting human rights and collective memory during the dictatorship period (1973–1985) and its aftermath. In the 1990s and early 2000s—under the Natural Uruguay development model—most popular movements crystalized in one way or another into the struggle against neoliberalism.[6] Uruguay's social movements were in dialogue with or inspired by regional anti-neoliberal struggles such as the Argentine factory occupation movement, the Zapatista uprising in Mexico, the Movement of Landless Workers in Brazil, the Bolivarian Revolution in Venezuela, the Bolivian "Water Wars," and the World Social Forums. However, as noted above, the Frente Amplio's electoral victory in 2004 signaled the end of the anti-neoliberal protest cycle, leaving a relative political vacuum for popular movements and social activism.

The growing Uruguayan opposition to extractivism and mega-development has similarly emerged in dialogue with regional movements, particularly the popular assemblies against mega-mining in Argentina.[7] Both the Argentinean and Uruguayan anti-extractivist movements are ideologically diverse, poly-classist, "horizontal" and assembly-based in political organization, as well as mostly independent of the political party system (c.f. Colectivo Voces de Alerta 2011). Journalist and activist Victor Bacchetta, one of the founders of the Uruguayan anti-extractivist movement, has described this new brand of environmentalism as "transversal" to the political party system in that it crisscrosses the ideological spectrum and established party lines. The Uruguayan movement has drawn together a loose and variegated, often colorful, coalition of small- and medium-scale ranchers, agricultural workers, artisanal fishermen, tourism operators, organic farmers, and beekeepers. New age hippies, surfers, musicians, actors and celebrities, ecological activists, new indigenous collectives, anarchists, Trotskyists, and other leftist "ultras" can be found. In sum, thousands of concerned citizens from small towns and the capital fill their ranks. In the remainder of this chapter we highlight three emblematic anti-extractivist movements built by these many parties that have contested the government's mega-development prongs of extraction, infrastructure, and energy.

## Uruguay Libre

In 2010 rural producers of Cerro Chato, a small town in the interior, began mobilizing against the Aratirí iron ore mega-mining project. At the same time, coastal residents of Rocha organized to fight a port expansion project in La Paloma. Lacking information, and suspicious of the claims and promises of the mining company and the government, the Cerro Chato residents contacted the Uruguayan Environmental non-governmental organization (NGO) network, a collection of NGOs and activists that share knowledge and plan actions. Environmental journalist Bacchetta and the

NGO network offered information and technical assistance, serving as a bridge between the burgeoning activism of the interior and the Atlantic coast. From there the Movement for a Sustainable Uruguay (*Movimiento por un Uruguay Sustentable—MOVUS*) was born, later expanding into what is known as Uruguay Libre, the Uruguay Free of Open Pit Metallic Mining Movement (*Movimiento Uruguay Libre de Minería Metalífera a Cielo Abierto*).[8]

MOVUS/Uruguay Libre developed a diverse and sophisticated tactical repertoire. They created the "Mining Observatory of Uruguay," an online blog and information clearinghouse that investigated the activities of the Indian corporation Zamin Ferrous, and connected Uruguay's experiences to regional and worldwide struggles against mega-mining (Bacchetta 2015; Mining Observatory of Uruguay n.d.). They created a strong social media presence, particularly through Facebook and Twitter. They held press conferences, released press statements, visited Parliament, and hosted a debate on mega-mining and extractivism with presidential candidates on the eve of Uruguay's 2014 elections. Uruguay Libre also assembled "technical teams" to counter official documents, studies, or statements, drawing on the expertise of national academic allies and international experts. For instance, Uruguay Libre assembled an "environmental team" to issue a point-by-point rebuttal of the government's first environmental impact assessment of the proposed Aratirí mine. An "economic team" contested government and corporate claims of the economic and job growth benefits.

Uruguay Libre used a range of legal channels as well. Its "legal team" dissected and critiqued the new Mining Law, ultimately suing for injunctions and utilizing the 2008 Public Access to Information Law to obtain government documents. It helped over 200 rural producers file legal actions against the government's attempts to grant land prospecting titles, thereby stalling company incursions for almost two years as the title dispute wound its way through the judicial appeals process. It also organized signature drives to authorize plebiscites at both the departmental and national level. Residents of the rural departments of Tacuarembó, Lavalleja, and San José successfully organized plebiscites that declared moratoria on mass open pit metallic mining projects as well as fracking. As of June 2015, a national plebiscite campaign to ban open pit metallic mining had gathered 100,000 signatures.

The movement's actions also targeted Zamin Ferrous' international credit rating by contesting its "social license to operate." Bacchetta explained:

> What we created is a morass of situations that cause uncertainty … The grades of international investment risk each year are based on ten indicators of highest risk for investment. There is a category called, "social license to operate," [which] refers to whether a project has the support and consent of the neighboring communities. So as all of this was unfolding we wrote articles and spread information internationally … and Uruguay, which had never been a significant site of mining conflicts in the register of mining conflicts in South America, now started to appear.[9]

### The Permanent National Assembly

Uruguay Libre collaborated with the 50 or so organizational members of the ANP, the Permanent National Assembly in Defense of Land, Water, and Natural Resources (*Asamblea Nacional Permanente en Defensa de la Tierra, el Agua, y los Recursos Naturales*). The ANP has hosted eight national marches in the capital, Montevideo, drawing a diverse group of organizations and activists. Urban residents contemplated the quixotic scenario of dozens of gauchos on horseback descending upon the city, leading the unorthodox coalition of rural ranchers, disaffected leftists, various rural workers and activists, urban ecological activists, and environmental NGOs. Guitars, trumpets, and drums animated the marches. In the 2013 march, estimated to have drawn between 10,000 and 15,000 participants, people wore skull masks and others carried a giant inflatable turtle. Highlighting the intersections and contradictions between the Natural and Productive Uruguay models, a common theme at these protests, activists hoisted a fake coffin with the slogan "Natural Uruguay, RIP" (*Uruguay Natural, QEPD*) (Acosta 2013). While protest marches are ubiquitous in Montevideo, those who participated in these ANP marches found them entirely different from "typical" protests. Bacchetta noted the unprecedented nature of the marches' socio-economic, generational, geographic, and political heterogeneity. Student activist Guidahí Parrilla, of the Federation of University Students (FEUU) CELTA commission (*Comisión en Lucha por la Tierra y el Agua*/Commission in the Struggle for Land and Water), emphasized the particular energy and passion at the protests: "It was amazing. The people *screamed!* You could feel how they were really fighting against something."

At the end of the fourth march, held in 2013, an official proclamation by the ANP highlighted their broad understanding of resource extraction's link to the reigning political economic development model and its social, environmental, and economic effects. The proclamation read that beyond being merely an "environmental struggle," they also rejected:

> the development model, looter and contaminator that has been imposed in this territory, which does not diversify production, which "re-primarizes" the economy [reprimariza la economía] and perpetuates us as exporters of primary resources, which exhausts the earth, which contaminates the water, which threatens to deprive us of non-renewable natural resources, which empties the countryside, and which, contrary to what they say, eliminates jobs.

### The Western Montevideo Neighbors Coordinate (CVOM)

The LNG processing plant was the only project of the extraction–infrastructure–energy triad we examine here that actually commenced construction. The facility, located in a picturesque and tranquil coastal working class corner of western Montevideo, has generated direct action protest, a hunger strike, and heated debate and opposition. The floating natural gas reconversion facility was designed through a joint venture under the newly created company Gas Sayago, forged between the Uruguayan state (through its electric and energy utility UTE and its petroleum, gas, and cement utility ANCAP), the French multinational energy conglomerate GDF-Suez, and the Japanese corporation Marubeni. The gas was slated for both domestic consumption and export, and to supply the energy needs of the Aratirí mega-mine. The project was granted environmental impact assessment approval in record time, with the National Environmental Director admitting strong government pressure to endorse it quickly (Tiscornia 2015). Neighborhood activists denounced the approval process, associated with what they referred to as the "dark mud of this mega-business" that acts against the "exploited, forgotten and dismissed of always."[10]

The government held the legally mandated public hearing in a remote, hard to reach rural area, but it nevertheless drew 600 concerned citizens. The Western Montevideo Neighbors Coordinate (*Coordinación de Vecinos del Oeste de Montevideo—CVOM*), also affiliated with the ANP, organized the opposition. In an astute tactical intervention they negotiated with the government for the exclusion of law enforcement at the meeting and instead coordinated their own security, training twelve local women who successfully defused a tense standoff between neighbors in favor of and opposed to the project. In response to growing local opposition, the company flew a dozen neighbors to Brussels, Belgium, to tour a similar LNG facility and convince them of the project's environmental and safety credentials, thereby advancing further division among some members of the community.

In addition to major concerns over safety and contamination in the case of an industrial accident or sabotage of the floating plant, activists also called into question a wide range of topics: the economic benefits of the project, both locally and nationally; the contracted construction company's haphazard and reckless building of roads and infrastructure; the forfeiture of productive land due to gas pipeline construction; biodiversity loss and the decimation of the local artisanal fishing industry; environmental health risks from heavy metals contamination caused by dredging the River Plate; the erosion and pollution of local beaches; and increased risks of child and adolescent sexual exploitation. Unfortunately, protestors claimed that most government officials and company representatives dismissed, and even ridiculed, their concerns. In a poignant example, activists highlighted how some officials referred to the "stupid neighbors" who don't want to sell their farmland to make room for the pipeline, because it has a "rock where grandpa used to sit."

## Discussion

At the 2015 Conference of the Parties (COP) 21 climate talks in Paris, Uruguay once again garnered international environmental accolades, this time for the "green energy" initiatives that expanded renewables within the country's energy grid to 95% (Graham-Harrison 2015). It should be evident, as we have examined throughout this chapter, that evaluation of environmental quality depends upon perspective and scale of analysis, and often harbors simultaneous and contradictory tendencies. Five years into the Productive Uruguay model, several major mega-projects have stalled. Following sharply declining iron ore commodity prices, as well as widespread and growing public opposition, newly elected Frente Amplio President Tabaré Vázquez in 2015 froze the Aratirí and deep-water port mega-projects. Uruguay Libre and the ANP remain vigilant, preparing for an eventual increase in commodity prices that might encourage a project relaunch, while continuing their legal, national plebiscite, and public information strategies. The construction of the LNG plant also stalled. The government rescinded its contract following a corruption scandal involving Brazilian state petroleum enterprise PETROBRAS, parent of the now bankrupted construction company OAS. The government nevertheless is bidding for new contracts. CVOM activists continue to demand information sharing and transparency as well as a meaningful consultative, democratic, and participatory process. In a recent case, they launched an ongoing public "Ethics Hearing" against Gas Sayago.

By drawing together diverse interests and employing sophisticated tactical coordination, Uruguay Libre, the ANP, the CVOM, and the broader coalition of organizations involved in Uruguay's New Environmentalism have mobilized political capital in innovative ways. The movement's organizational capacity has allowed it to adapt to new political developments and emergent environmental conflicts. For instance, in light of the recent stalling of Uruguay's mega-projects, the ANP expanded its agenda to the defense of the Guaraní Aquifer and the rejection of the possible use of hydraulic fracturing drilling techniques in any future hydrocarbon exploitation.

What we find interesting about these new developments is the way local and regional issues turn into national causes, generating new mechanisms for mobilizing citizens. Activists are connecting for the first time diverse socio-environmental issues across the national territory, unifying experiences from the interior, the coast, and the capital, and drawing political lessons from each conflict and movement. Activists have also connected processes and experiences internationally by building far reaching grassroots networks. They are in dialogue with indigenous Andean conceptualizations of *buen vivir* (the good life) and the rights of nature, while forging political alliances with the growing anti-mega-mining movements of Argentina, Chile, and Peru. Their actions are founded upon an understanding of the triangulation of extraction, infrastructure, and energy projects at home, and of the transnational and global re-dimensioning of capital, nature, and politics across the region and world.

## Conclusion

Uruguay's New Environmentalism is a response to both the real policies and the actual and projected impacts of the Frente Amplio's embracing of the Commodity Consensus. It has also emerged in response to political opportunities opened through the end of the anti-neoliberal protest cycle and the subservience of traditional popular movements to the official Left. As CELTA student activist Verónica put it, although mobilizing independently against officialism has been fraught with challenges over the past few years, "at least we won the right to take the floor."

Not so long ago, conflicts over the pulp-mill mega-projects positioned environmentalism as a foreign ideology and a threat to national sovereignty. Now the environment has emerged as a succinct symbol of opposition, unifying diverse actors transversally across the political spectrum. For biologist Daniel Panario, "To be a leftist today is to be an environmentalist." At the same time, as student activist Guidahí told us in relation to the right wing sectors of the movement, "To be conservative today is to be against the multinationals." It remains to be seen whether Uruguay's five-year-old New Environmentalism will have lasting political impacts, and how the ANP umbrella organization will continue to successfully navigate its internal social, tactical, and ideological heterogeneity. For the CVOM's Ruben Bouza, the continuous challenge is how to successfully "unify struggles" while productively "working within diversity."

Uruguayan activists have both consciously and unwittingly joined a growing Latin American environmentalist movement and thought led by a new generation of coalitions consisting of indigenous *campesinos*, urban youth, independent leftists and intellectuals, environmental NGOs, and cultural collectives.[11] Largely deploying horizontal and autonomous organizational and political strategies, these movements are calling for a vision that looks beyond the limited frame of the extractivist paradigm and the continued "el Dorado" view of Latin America as a fount of endless resources. In doing so they question and expand discourses around long taken for granted understandings of democracy, development, sustainability, human rights, and sovereignty (Svampa 2013, 42–46). Until these debates are meaningfully addressed, the environment is poised to remain a central and unpredictable yardstick of the potential success of leftist experiments in post-neoliberal reform.

## Notes

1 Daniel Renfrew's 2015 summer research in Uruguay was generously funded by West Virginia University's Faculty Senate, the Eberly College of Arts and Sciences, and the Department of Sociology and Anthropology. He would also like to thank Javier Taks and the University of the Republic's Environmental Studies Network for the opportunity to present some of this work as an invited guest in the public seminar, "The Environmental Question in Uruguay." The authors would like to thank the students of the FEUU's CELTA group for research data, interviews, and the invitation to attend their meeting, Victor Bacchetta of Uruguay Libre, and the CVOM's Ruben Bouza and Marcela Jubin for their most gracious hosting of us in western Montevideo. Kirk Jalbert and David Casagrande provided invaluable editorial guidance. Any remaining errors or omissions are our responsibility.

2 Marquee social legislation enacted by the Mujica administration (2010–2015) included the legalization of gay marriage, the decriminalization of abortion, a legalized and state-regulated marijuana industry, expanded rights for transgendered persons, and an affirmative action law for the afro-descendent community.

3 Most of Uruguay's large-scale energy and infrastructure projects constitute nodes within the Mercosur–Chile axis of the ambitious and controversial continent-wide Initiative for the Integration of South America's Regional Infrastructure, now called COSIPLAN.

4 The judiciary reassigned Viana from his public prosecutor position in 2015 in what he and his supporters have suggested was a politically motivated move to silence him.

5 To cite some examples, Uruguay is undergoing a water contamination crisis from the pollution of waterways and drinking water sources by the expanding and chemically intensive agro-industrial activities of GM soy and corn cultivation and dairy production. The country's most pristine Atlantic coastline, central to Natural Uruguay's tourism and country branding strategies, is threatened by the deep-water port and mineral pipeline. Environmentally protected areas and native forests are continuously threatened by the territorial incursions of commercial forestry.

6 There are many other social movements in Uruguay, including for instance those oriented around gender and sexuality, the afro-descendent community, drug legalization, animal rights, fair and cooperative housing, and right wing law and order campaigns. We only highlight those that most strongly characterized particular historical periods.

7 Although carrying distinct and sometimes diametrically opposed political histories, the neighboring countries of Argentina and Uruguay have also shared a great deal of cultural, political economic, and social movement traditions.

8 Unless otherwise noted, personal information and quotes in this section are drawn from participant observation and interviews with the authors in June and July 2015.

9 Interview with first author, June 9, 2015 (our translation).

10 Information about the LNG plant opposition is drawn from interviews, participant observation, and documents made available by movement referent Ruben Bouza.

11 Maristella Svampa (2013) and others have referred to this process as Latin America's "eco-territorial turn."

## References

Acosta, Inés. 2013. Y se fue la cuarta …, *La Diaria*, May 13. www.observatorio-minero-del-uruguay.com/2013/05/y-se-fue-la-cuarta/ (accessed December 6, 2015).

Bacchetta, Victor L. 2015. *Aratiri y otras aventuras: Las soberanias questionadas*. Montevideo, Uruguay: Doble Clic Editores.

Campomar, Andres, and Brian M. Andersen. 1999. *Uruguay: Open for growth*. Coventry, UK: Euromoney Publications.

Chouhy, Magdalena. 2013. Cabo Polonio, área protegida: Conservacionismo en diálogo con cosmovisiones salvajes. In *Anuario de Antropología Social y Cultural del Uruguay*, edited by Sonnia Romero Gorski, 87–102. Montevideo, Uruguay: FHCE-Nordan-UNESCO.

Colectivo Voces de Alerta. 2011. *15 mitos de la megaminería transnacional*. Montevideo, Uruguay: Librería de Humanidades-Konopios-De la Mancha.

Composto, Claudia, and Mina Lorena Navarro. 2014. Claves de lectura para comprender el despojo y las luchas por los bienes comunes naturales en América Latina. In *Territorios en disputa. Despojo capitalista, luchas en defensa de los bienes comunes naturales y alternativas emancipatorias en América*, edited by Claudia Composto and Mina Lorena Navarro, 33–75. Mexico City: Bajo Tierra Ediciones.

Coronil, Fernando. 2011. The future in question: History and utopia in Latin America (1989–2010). In *Business as usual: The roots of the global financial meltdown*, edited by Craig Calhoun and Georgi Derluguian. New York: New York University Press.

Díaz Estévez, Pablo. 2013. El hierro y la resistencia "de a caballo" en la Cuchilla Grande. *Contrapunto* 2:73–80.

Graham-Harrison, Emma. 2015. Where Uruguay leads, the rest of the world struggles to keep up. *The Guardian*, December 5. www.theguardian.com/commentisfree/2015/dec/06/uruguay-climate-change-reform-progress (accessed December 6, 2015).

Grugel, Jean, and Pia Riggirozzi. 2012. Post-neoliberalism in Latin America: Rebuilding and reclaiming the state after crisis. *Development and Change* 43, 1:1–21.

Gudynas, Eduardo. 2004. Regresaron los soñadores de chimeneas. *La Insignia*. www.lainsignia.org/2004/junio/econ_005.htm (accessed December 6, 2015).

Gudynas, Eduardo. 2009. Diez tesis urgentes sobre el nuevo extractivismo. In *Extractivismo, política y sociedad*, edited by Francisco Dávila. Quito, Ecuador: CAAP and CLAES, 187–225.

Harvey, David. 2005. *A brief history of neoliberalism*. Oxford: Oxford University Press.

Mining Observatory of Uruguay. n.d. *Observatorio minero del Uruguay*. www.observatorio-minero-del-uruguay.com/ (accessed December 6, 2015).

Mujica, José A. 2012. *Rio + 20 speech*, June 6. United Nations Conference on Sustainable Development, Rio de Janeiro. Translation by the authors.

O'Connor, James. 1994. Is Sustainable Capitalism Possible? In *Is capitalism sustainable? Political economy and the politics of ecology*, edited by Martin O'Connor. New York: The Guilford Press.

Oyhantçabal, Gabriel. 2013. Los tres campos en la cuestión agraria en Uruguay, *Revista NERA* 16, 22:82–95.

Reboratti, Carlos, and Vicente Palermo, eds. 2007. *Del otro lado del río. Ambientalismo y política entre Uruguayos y Argentinos*. Buenos Aires: Edhasa.

Renfrew, Daniel. 2009. In the margins of contamination: Lead poisoning and the production of neoliberal nature in Uruguay. *Journal of Political Ecology* 16:87–103.

Santandreu, Alain, and Eduardo Gudynas. 1998. *Ciudadanía en movimiento. Participación y conflictos ambientales*. Montevideo, Uruguay: Ediciones Trilce.

Santos, Carlos, Ignacio Narbondo, Gabriel Oyhantçabal, and Ramón Gutiérrez. 2013. Seis tesis urgentes sobre el neodesarrollismo en Uruguay. *Contrapunto* 2:13–32.

Svampa, Maristella. 2013. "Consenso de los Commodities" y lenguajes de valorización en América Latina. *Nueva Sociedad* 244:30–46.

Tiscornia, Fabián. 2015. Los 10 aspectos más cuestionados sobre la planta regasificadora. *El País*, January 26. www.elpais.com.uy/economia/noticias/aspectos-mas-cuestionados-planta-regasificadora.html (accessed January 26, 2015).

Wallerstein, Immanuel. 2015. La izquierda latinoamericana se mueve a la derecha. *La Jornada*, July 10. www.jornada.unam.mx/2015/07/10/opinion/023a1pol (accessed August 15, 2015).

# 3

# MARCELLUS SHALE AS GOLDEN GOOSE

## The Discourse of Development and the Marginalization of Resistance in Northcentral Pennsylvania

*Rob Cooley and David Casagrande*

### Extraction, Discourse, and Marginalization

Pennsylvania's modern history of natural resource production began in the nineteenth century, when timber and coal industries fueled the US industrial economy. It continues today with development of Marcellus Shale gas reserves through hydraulic fracturing. Thousands of wells have been drilled in Pennsylvania since drilling began around 2005 (Olmstead et al. 2013). Shale gas extraction has been linked to numerous environmental impacts, including methane migration into aquifers (Osborn, Vengosh, and Warner 2011), impacts on surface water quality (Olmstead et al. 2013), airborne contaminants (Field, Soltis, and Murphy 2014), and habitat disturbance and fragmentation (Drohan et al. 2012). Evidence of negative human health impacts led the state of New York to ban hydraulic fracturing for natural gas (NY DOH 2014) in stark contrast to the drilling bonanza that blanketed neighboring Pennsylvania.

Since the mid-twentieth century, rural Pennsylvania has been experiencing a slow economic decline comparable to other Appalachian and east coast industrial regions as local manufacturing and extraction are increasingly outsourced. It is this context of economic decline that pervades regional public discussions focusing on themes like economic growth, national energy security, and jobs. These themes have been used to promote development and marginalize opposing views that link it with boom and bust economic cycles, environmental hazards, and health risks.

Why do so few residents of Pennsylvania publicly oppose shale gas development given the environmental and health risks? Many fear offending friends, family, and other community members perceived to benefit economically from the gas industry's activities. Economic, personal, and political factors all contribute to the industry's regional *hegemony*—the term used by Gramsci, Hoare, and Nowell-Smith (1971) to describe a situation where behavioral norms are defined as common sense by powerful actors and imposed on less powerful groups. In this chapter, we focus on discourse (the way people talk about things), because it is a formidable political tool (Hudgins and Poole 2014; Willow 2015). We seek to answer two questions: first, how has discourse been framed to favor shale gas development, and second, how do cultural norms, legal practices, and social institutions marginalize citizen opposition? The Marcellus Shale gas industry places Pennsylvania residents in a conundrum analogous to Aesop's fable of the golden goose:

> One day a countryman going to the nest of his goose found there an egg all yellow and glittering … he took it home … and soon found that it was an egg of pure gold … he grew rich by selling his eggs. As he grew rich he grew greedy; and thinking to get at once all the gold the goose could give, he killed it and opened it only to find nothing.
>
> *(Aesop 2005)*

The discourse set in motion by the politically and economically powerful Marcellus Shale oil and gas industry mirrors this classic narrative. A previously unknown resource—invisible and thousands of feet below the earth's surface—suddenly becomes valuable. This discovery and its impacts on Northeastern Pennsylvania's communities and ecology—described well in Seamus McGraw's 2012 *The End of Country*—enabled the industry to establish a powerful narrative: if impeded, it will leave, taking the region's last chance for economic growth with it. Unimpeded, it will produce "golden eggs" for everyone. Those who oppose the industry face negative consequences. The industry group Energy from Shale (a media outlet supported by state, national, and multinational groups profiting from the industry) summarizes this conundrum on their website:

> Fracking has emerged as a contentious issue in many communities … there are only two sides in the debate: those who want our oil and natural resources developed in a safe and responsible way; and those who don't want our oil and natural gas resources developed at all.
>
> *(Energy from Shale n.d.)*

Gas development discourse in Pennsylvania could focus on fairness, equality, justice, and a democratic decision-making process. Instead, industry promoters have established a dichotomous choice for regional residents: one can either support gas and be an asset to one's community and country, or one can oppose it and by extension threaten the American way of life.

All discourse occurs within what cognitive linguist George Lakoff (2005) calls a *discourse frame*. These frames define what is "right" about an issue, why it is considered to be so, and which words, metaphors, or cultural expectations are used to communicate about it. Regardless of how attitudes and perceptions change over time, all discourse is framed by cultural rules. US citizens tacitly agree on acceptable topics and what domains of supporting information are considered relevant.

How different people interpret these facts and act on them is unpredictable and individualized, but a cognitive frame must be shared for conversation to occur. Our research goal is to describe that discourse frame and examine how it is employed in Northcentral Pennsylvania's shale gas extraction zone.

In general, local, state, and federal entities in the USA assume economic development to be desirable *unless* individual health or property is damaged. Drivers of economic growth are privileged because creating wealth, jobs, energy, and other values is accepted unconditionally and because they possess financial and legal resources to contest unfavorable regulations (de Rijke 2013). The current discourse frame is based on the assumption that economic growth, jobs, and energy independence will result from development, but negative consequences must be proven. This shifts the responsibility of identifying negative impacts away from industry and toward citizen groups with far fewer resources. Industry and its supporters exploit these assumptions. As we will see, industry proponents reproduce narratives that cast state regulations as onerous and detrimental to profitable gas production and job creation, while promoting fear that individual rights to benefit from development might be threatened by environmental protection.

## Extraction and the "Company Town"

Pennsylvania's nineteenth century coal towns were isolated communities of laborers built adjacent to the coalmines in which they toiled (Bartoletti 1996). The mining company owned the towns' houses, schools, and stores, and controlled nearly every aspect of workers' lives. Working and living conditions in "company towns" were grim. Geographic and communication isolation enabled coal companies to control labor and maximize profitability (Metheny 2007, 62). For many residents, coal companies provided the only source of employment, so they tolerated the industry's control. This example of industry hegemony sets a precedent for today's industry-controlled shale gas discourse.

The notion of the "company town" also characterizes realities faced by stakeholders in Pennsylvania's shale gas boom. Instead of corporate ownership and explicit control, today's company town exists as a regional association of non-unionized workers and other residents who profit (albeit at different levels) from the industry, reside in a wide geographic region, and are drawn together by the promise of economic opportunity. Some benefit by employment or leasing their property, but many do not. Ostensibly, residents can move if they feel that the detriments of gas development outweigh its benefits. The reality, though, is that mobility is often limited by economic and social factors, as well as by declining property values in the Marcellus region (Muehlenbachs, Spiller, and Timmins 2015).

By manipulating information, the industry and its supporters have created a social environment that behaves like a company town, paralleling the physical and economic isolation that constrained nineteenth century coal and timber communities. Corporate interests have convinced residents that shale gas is a vital resource, contribution to shale gas production is important to society as a whole, and that individual sacrifices made to facilitate gas production will benefit everyone at local and national levels (see Maldonado, Chapter 7, on the concept of the sacrifice zone). Perceived opportunity in the face of scarcity motivates people to endure inconvenience and accept risk. Brasier et al. (2013) found that shale region residents are willing to tolerate gas-related risks if the benefits were perceived to be "worth it." And Perry (2012) describes how one Pennsylvania resident took her to see "the great American Industry that will save our nation from foreign dependence on oil."

Throughout Pennsylvania, in towns created by timber or coal extraction a century ago, the message of the new gas industry is pervasive. Pro-industry narratives seek to justify or reframe the industry's permanent social, economic, and ecological transformations (Finewood and Stroup 2012). Packaged as television ads, billboards, and vehicle stickers, they celebrate the new extractive chapter of Pennsylvania's history. Pro-gas media define fossil fuels as a patriotic solution to economic stress, normalizing the negative impacts of gas development as necessary for the greater good (Finewood and Stroup 2012; Perry 2012; Willow and Wylie 2014). It may be that the region's company town heritage enables the acceptance of environmental sacrifice through landscape transformation, ecological degradation, and health risks. Or perhaps the extractive history promotes a regional feeling of resignation regarding fracking. Whatever the reason, locals, having lived with extraction and its environmental impacts for generations, appear able to accept its social and environmental transformations, so long as it somehow contributes to the American way of life.

## Energopower and Extraction Discourse

Political ecology examines the unequal distribution of costs and benefits of environmental change (Bryant and Bailey 1997). We apply this perspective by examining how local people perceive the benefits and impacts of shale gas development in Pennsylvania. In Pennsylvania's historic coal and timber company towns, laborers were disenfranchised by economic and geographic boundaries. Contemporary corporate-driven shale discourse may be seen as a tool to sculpt a perception of opportunity, encouraging local residents to support an industry that might, ultimately, benefit a select few. Stakeholders benefiting from gas development produce discourse attempting to legitimize benefits that were clearly generated at the expense of neighbors, family, or friends. In this section, we focus on the patterns of discourse framing that makes this possible.

Given the health risks, ecological impacts, and imbalance in economic benefits generated by the shale gas industry, one would expect to find Marcellus region residents demanding greater government oversight of the industry. Examples of government oversight could include prohibition of development near schools, greater setback distances from houses, mandatory water-monitoring, health impact studies, limits on truck travel, light, or noise, or a registry of chemicals used in development processes.

Most opposition to Marcellus Shale development has come from outside development zones. Shale energy's best-known opponent is Josh Fox, a Northeastern

Pennsylvania native who attracted national attention through his "Gasland" documentaries. Other nationally recognized people like Ethan Hawke, Robert Redford, Yoko Ono, and Mark Ruffalo have also vocally opposed shale extraction. Staff of environmental organizations like the Sierra Club and Food and Water Watch in Pennsylvania's larger cities have opposed shale gas development in general or called for greater regulation. Yet very few people within the Northern Tier oppose shale gas development outright. The Responsible Drilling Alliance, a grassroots group of citizens from Lycoming County, and Wyoming County's Connection for Oil, Gas and Environment in the Northern Tier (COGENT) have advocated for greater oversight and regulation. But without celebrities to draw attention to their cause, they have not enjoyed Fox's level of exposure. And, while Fox and other celebrity opponents have received public criticism from pro-industry interests, local activists have experienced negative responses from industry supporters in their own communities and on a much more personal level.

Perceptions of risk and risk tolerance among stakeholders appear in this case to be heavily influenced by the attraction of instantaneous or future wealth and the observed benefits associated with "boomtowns," where new restaurants, hotels, stores, park equipment, fire and rescue equipment, and local event sponsorship are obvious and immediate. But numerous studies have shown that the optimism that accompanies early stages of extractive development wanes over time. As the industry matures in a locale, the reality of the costs sets in, and people become less likely to favor it or desire it in their community (Anderson and Theodori 2009; Brasier et al. 2011; Theodori 2009). Therefore, the industry promotes energy extraction as a patriotic obligation, which supersedes individual concerns, vilifying resistance as a threat to these once-in-a-lifetime economic opportunities. The industry has propagandized itself into a golden goose—a "last chance" for regional economic salvation (Brasier et al. 2013; Jacquet and Stedman 2013; Willits, Luloff and Theodori 2013).

Boyer's concept of *energopower* (an adaptation of Foucault's *biopower*) helps explain how discourse eclipses individual rights and environmental health to favor more politically malleable concepts like "job creation." Biopower refers to a benign governmental focus on efficiency and optimization, responsibility and rigorousness, all with the intention of improving statistical measures of biological characteristics of mass populations as opposed to individual well-being (Foucault 1978). From this definition, Boyer (2011) derived the term "energopower" to describe government–industry collaboration designed to maximize efficiency, optimization, and output of energy supply and demand. In an energopolitical system, power concentrates in the hands of those best able to demonstrate capacity for energy production and job creation. Energopower represents a redirection of the goal of governance away from the development of individual quality of life, focusing instead on energy for economic growth (Boyer 2014) and shifting the perceived role of government to the facilitation of private industry's ability to harness energy to create jobs. The effects on individuals who disproportionately bear the costs and perceive significant degradations of their personal quality of life are discounted in favor of statistical outcomes of energy development perceived to contribute to the greater societal good.

## Research Methods

We conducted research between January 2014 and December 2015 to address two questions: how is Pennsylvania's shale discourse framed to favor oil and gas development and how do cultural norms and social institutions marginalize citizen opposition to such development? We inferred that economic beneficiaries would favor themes promoted by industry (Perry 2012) while opponents would focus on negative impacts on quality of life (Willow 2015). We used a household survey of five counties in Pennsylvania's Northern Tier to quantify distribution of economic benefits and negative impacts (Figure 3.1). We also analyzed interviews, focus groups, and mass media to identify discursive themes and their usages.

We audio-recorded 19 semi-structured interviews and two focus groups conducted in Lycoming, Susquehanna, and Wyoming counties. Recordings were transcribed verbatim. Interviewees included government planners and elected officials, activists, and economic beneficiaries of gas development. One focus group was composed entirely of property owners who had leased property for gas operations and the other had no lessors. Transcriptions were coded in QSR NVivo for general discursive themes used by supporters, opponents, economic beneficiaries, and non-beneficiaries and for factors that made people reluctant to speak about shale gas issues. During interviews and focus groups, we asked about positive and negative impacts on quality of life and about which media channels interviewees found most useful for obtaining information.

We developed a household survey to document disparities in economic benefits and quality of life impacts among households, identify respondents' primary sources of information on shale gas development, and solicit voluntary comments that could be thematically coded. We mailed letters of invitation to participate in an online structured survey to 2,130 households randomly selected from 14 townships distributed across five counties (Bradford, Lycoming, Sullivan, Susquehanna, Wyoming). Potential respondents were offered a $20 gift card. We asked whether a respondent benefited from development by leasing property, being employed directly by the industry, or having employment that supports the industry. On a scale of 1 (negative) to 5 (positive) respondents rated how gas development impacted their overall quality of life. They rated the importance of 19 specific impacts identified from interviews, focus groups, and relevant literature (e.g., noise, traffic congestion, social relationships, financial status, cost of living, health). Respondents also rated the perceived usefulness of sources of information about shale gas development (e.g., internet, local newspapers, friends and neighbors) and were asked to name the source they found most useful (e.g., a specific television station or newspaper). The survey response rate was 13.5% (n = 287). We then thematically coded industry messages from the most important sources of information identified by

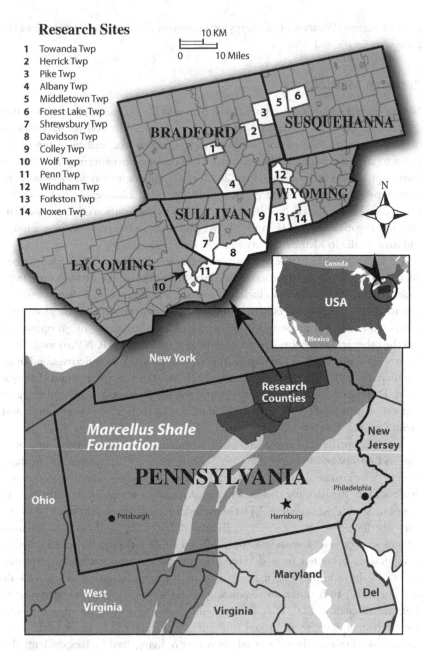

**Research Sites**

1 Towanda Twp
2 Herrick Twp
3 Pike Twp
4 Albany Twp
5 Middletown Twp
6 Forest Lake Twp
7 Shrewsbury Twp
8 Davidson Twp
9 Colley Twp
10 Wolf Twp
11 Penn Twp
12 Windham Twp
13 Forkston Twp
14 Noxen Twp

**FIGURE 3.1** Surveys and interviews conducted in 14 townships in five counties within Pennsylvania's Marcellus Shale play revealed how development discourse privileges government, industry, and elite stakeholders, marginalizes those likely to experience negative, uncompensated impacts, and influences local behavior. Map created by Donna Gayer, Artasaverb.

survey respondents. Respondents were also given an open-ended option to enter any comments about shale gas development.

## Social Inequality and the Energopower Discourse Frame

Our first research question required us to document inequality of development impacts and to elucidate a discourse frame and how it's used. Survey respondents who gain direct economic benefits from leasing their property for gas development and/or working for the industry indicated that gas development improved their quality of life (mean = 3.38). Those experiencing no direct economic benefit indicated development lowered their quality of life (mean = 2.85). This difference was significant (t [285] = 4.49, p <0.001). Respondents indicated the greatest negative impacts were increased traffic congestion, traffic accidents, cost of living in general and cost of housing in particular. Respondents relied heavily on local television and newspapers, the internet, and personal relationships for information about shale gas development (Table 3.1). National news and opinion outlets were far less important.

Given respondents' emphasis on local television, we included television commercials in our analysis of industry messaging. We selected ten industry sources for thematic content analysis: four television commercials produced by the American Petroleum Institute that were heavily rotated on local television stations; four industry websites named by survey respondents (Chevron, Marcellus Shale Coalition, Energy from Shale, Anadarko); and two educational brochures widely distributed throughout local communities (one from Chesapeake Energy and one from Cabot Oil & Gas). Dominant themes were economic growth, jobs, patriotism, clean energy, safety, energy independence, and responsible development (Table 3.2). The industry's discourse frame can be summarized as follows: "America needs energy and jobs. There are massive resources available for development in the Marcellus Shale. The industry can safely and responsibly develop Marcellus gas while also building stronger communities, making America energy independent, and reducing greenhouse gas emissions."

**TABLE 3.1** Relative importance of information sources indicated by survey respondents in the Marcellus Shale region of Northern Pennsylvania

| Source | Rank |
| --- | --- |
| Local television or newspapers | 1 |
| Internet (unspecified) | 2 |
| Family, friends, and neighbors | 3 |
| Industry websites, publications, or direct conversations | 4 |
| Television (unspecified) | 5 |
| Government websites and public fora (including Penn State extension, the Department of Environmental Protection, and elected officials) | 6 |
| National news outlets (e.g., Fox News, National Public Radio) | 7 |

**TABLE 3.2** Ten most common themes identified in ten Marcellus Shale industry media sources

| Theme | No. sources including theme | Frequency themes referenced |
|---|---|---|
| Economic benefit | 10 (100%) | 16 |
| Jobs | 8 (80%) | 18 |
| Patriotism | 8 (80%) | 20 |
| $CO_2$ emissions | 8 (80%) | 12 |
| Local community | 6 (60%) | 6 |
| Clean energy | 6 (60%) | 18 |
| Safety | 6 (60%) | 8 |
| Energy independence | 6 (60%) | 14 |
| Truth/facts | 6 (60%) | 6 |
| Responsible development | 5 (50%) | 8 |

America's energy needs, jobs, patriotism, and independence are themes used by industry proponents in interviews, focus groups, and survey comments to justify development:

> People here recognize gas as an interim fuel to help get us off the Middle East oil and get us out of there. I can tell you personally, my son did two tours in Iraq with the army, and anything we can do to get out of that mess in the Middle East, we need to do.
>
> *(Lycoming County, appointed public official)*

These same themes were used to stigmatize opponents:

> The landman put his hand on my pro-gas neighbor's shoulder and said, "Ed I'm sorry you have to live next to this woman who wants us to remain dependent on foreign oil."
>
> *(Lycoming County, retired small-business owner)*

Survey results showed that increased traffic congestion, traffic accidents, cost of living, and cost of housing impacted economic beneficiaries and non-beneficiaries equally. In interviews, focus groups, and survey comments these issues were emphasized by development opponents, but downplayed as inevitable costs of progress by supporters. They were never mentioned in industry messaging.

## Cultural Norms of Censorship

Our second research question focused on how social norms and institutional behavior marginalize opposition to development. Interviews and focus groups revealed a cultural taboo against challenging the industry's themes. No one would say we don't need jobs or that our children should be sent to war. No one wants to be perceived as un-American. These values are widely shared and fundamental to American identity. Many Pennsylvania residents engage in self-censorship to avoid controversy engendered by the polarized "for it or against it" discourse frame:

> Gas development is very polarizing. It cost my wife two of her friends. We stopped talking about it.
>
> *(Sullivan County, anonymous survey respondent)*

Some residents are frustrated that cultural taboos and environmental risks are in conflict and that this conflict leads to self-censorship:

> I know people need jobs around here. Kids are leaving and farmers are struggling. But should we poison the water? It's to the point where you can't talk about it at dinner with family. I just don't talk about it anymore.
>
> *(Lycoming County, college student)*

In addition to self-censorship, some industry supporters attempt to control discourse through intimidation. Several interviewees who did criticize the industry or questioned the lack of government oversight stated they were threatened or harassed:

> A number of us have had death threats, and others had tires slashed ... dogs killed ... just this past year, second dog killed of one of my friends who's another outspoken person.
>
> *(Susquehanna County, political activist)*

Others were afraid to speak out because they observed others being harassed:

> The industry are corporate bullies. They will stop at nothing to get what they want. There's a fear in me of getting involved in any kind of protest ... fearing that I may personally be harmed by gas industry goons.
>
> *(Tunkhannock Focus Group, retired medical doctor)*

> You can be targeted of course ... and maybe labeled a terrorist if you are an activist.
>
> *(Tunkhannock Focus Group, retired schoolteacher)*

## Energopower and the New Company Town

> Energy has to come from somewhere. The needs of the many may outweigh the inconvenience of the few who live near the exploration efforts. This is not an ideal situation for all residents, but it is the reality.
>
> *(Sullivan County, anonymous survey respondent)*

The above quote embodies energopower: societal energy needs, as defined by the interests that supply them, supersede the rights of individuals. Macro-level statistics like Marcellus Shale productivity are imbued with value while reduced quality of life, as documented in our survey, is downplayed. Dehumanized statistics that state how many jobs the industry has generated dominate mainstream media and conversations. But discussion of individual worker quality of life is notably absent. Only in confidential conversations does one hear statements like "I quit, because they required too many hours to leave time for family." Of course, some industry employees are happier with their jobs than others, but in the energopower discourse, only the number of jobs matters. Negative impacts are dismissed as irrelevant or as acceptable costs of progress. The industry and its proponents refuse to acknowledge statements like the following that challenge the discourse frame:

> We moved here for the quiet life, to escape the industrial landscape. We expected our grandchildren to live here. The gas industry has stolen our dreams.
>
> *(Lycoming County, retired small-business owner)*

In the old company town, the company controlled the mode of production and owned every resource. Philanthropy legitimized the company and the unequal social structures it produced, while also intensifying reliance on the company for crucial social services (Metheny 2007). The current Marcellus Shale case is little different. Interviews, focus groups, and reviews of news sources and industry communications suggest that the gas industry has purchased the allegiance of critical social institutions. Hospitals, the United Way, technical schools, art centers, and tourist bureaus all accept industry funding. Townships are now obligated to rely on industry impact fees for critical road improvements and services. The authors could not identify one social institution in three counties that had not received financial support from the industry.

In every interview with representatives of these institutions (or during failed attempts to interview them), interviewees stated that industry contributions had increased their ability to fulfill their missions, and that this outweighed any negative impacts on the community. A local United Way director told us she "would not be able to do her job without the industry." In some cases, organizations have become reliant on industry funding to manage problems caused by shale gas development itself, like domestic violence, drug abuse, traffic, crime, and negative impacts on tourism. Nevertheless, the message of philanthropy resonates with the general public:

> Gas industry donations built hospitals, school buildings, playgrounds, and many other things that everyone uses. No one can deny this.
>
> *(Susquehanna County, anonymous survey respondent)*

Dissenters find themselves isolated in opposition to social institutions like hospitals, law enforcement, the arts, and schools, which are socially imbued with respect and moral value in this part of America. This is highly effective for marginalizing anyone opposed to development. Thus, institutional behavior interacts with social norms to silence opposition to development. Industry hegemony is legitimized because the industry alone provides the golden goose.

## Conclusion

> So here we are now … instead of coal it's gas … but we are a company town because you don't speak against them. Things have somewhat settled down … I'm not sure I feel less hostility, but I am not really rocking the rig these days either.
>
> *(Susquehanna County, retired schoolteacher and activist)*

The dominant discourse of American capitalism promotes fossil fuel extraction as a patriotic act that generates jobs, creates energy independence, and normalizes negative impacts as necessary for the greater good (Finewood and Stroup 2012; Perry 2012; Willow and Wylie 2014). Our research in rural Pennsylvania shows how this worldview is framed and exploited by the industry. By its very nature, extraction pits those who benefit against those who bear negative impacts without gain. In our survey, economic beneficiaries said shale gas development improved their quality of life, while non-beneficiaries said their quality of life had diminished. The industry needs public support to repel public oversight of development through federal and state regulations and local ordinances. To garner this support, it has promoted a discourse frame emphasizing core American values, making it immune to criticism while simultaneously justifying decisions of economic beneficiaries.

Such framing diverts attention from individual well-being by emphasizing dehumanized statistics like numbers of jobs created, dollars donated, or units of gas produced. Negative impacts identified as most important in our survey are absent from industry propaganda and downplayed as "part of progress" by development supporters. The frame is intentionally polarizing—one is either for or against core American values like independence, hard work, and economic growth—and is used by the industry and its supporters to stigmatize critics. In Pennsylvania, most residents seek to avoid the social conflict inherent in such polarizing discourse and self-censorship occurs because opposing core American values is a cultural taboo.

The oil and gas industry has delivered an irresistible golden goose, dressed in red, white, and blue, fomenting the desire to grasp wealth without regard for current or future repercussions. But the golden goose is a fable, which brings us to one of our most important implications. The message that economic growth *alone* is the key to well-being is also a fable. Well-being tends to increase with income, but only when starting income is insufficient to meet basic human needs or provide a sense of security (Kahneman and Deaton 2010). Beyond that point, the ability for income to enhance well-being is superseded by one's quality of social relationships, sense of place, and ability to commune with nature, which are often compromised by rapid and intensive economic development of extraction (Higginbotham et al.

2006; Theodori 2001; Willow 2015). The fable of economic growth as salvation persists because the industry has shifted attention away from negative local impacts by framing discourse around patriotic propaganda and creating a point of view that justifies sacrificing local quality of life.

Our focus on the role of values in framing discourse has implications for critiques of extractivism in general. Intentionally changing core cultural values is nearly impossible, but Lakoff (2005) explains that discourse framing is accomplished by emphasizing only a few shared core values out of many. Politically powerful interest groups choose to emphasize the core values and beliefs that conform best to facts, statistics, and emotional messaging that they can produce and promote. Once these core values are "owned" by a group, attempts by others to provide contradictory facts or information usually serve to legitimize the point of view of the powerful rather than sway opinion against them. For example, in the global climate debate, the fossil fuel industry promotes the fact that oil and gas extraction provides millions of jobs globally. Those defending the status quo—in this case a fossil fuel-based economy—always have an advantage.

No one can contradict the fact that fossil fuel development has created millions of jobs and the industry has the financial resources to saturate the media with examples of jobs created in the past. Arguments that alternative energy can produce the same number of jobs are based on projections and lack tangible evidence. Thus, arguments that alternative energy *could* create jobs psychologically reinforce that claim that fossil fuel extraction *has* created jobs. As a result, the argument that renewable energy would create enough "green" jobs to offset those lost in the fossil fuel industry has had little impact on the global climate discourse outside the environmentalist community. In the Northern Tier of Pennsylvania, as in much of Appalachia, arguments that tourism, sustainable forestry, or other non-extractive forms of economic development could provide as many jobs as extractive industries have in the past are inherently less persuasive.

We suggest that instead of contradicting themes and statistics promulgated by the energopower system, activists who oppose extraction might constructively reframe the debate around other core values (e.g., Nadelman, Chapter 12). In America, these might include fairness, justice, and democracy—all themes conspicuously absent in the shale gas discourse. Wherever extractivist hegemony has stifled opposition, it is likely that some core values and beliefs have been emphasized by extractivist proponents to frame discourse at the expense of other values and beliefs.

## References

Aesop. 2005. *Aesop's fables.* Translated by Vernon Jones. Whitefish, MT: Kessinger.

Anderson, Brooklynn J., and Gene L. Theodori. 2009. Local leaders' perceptions of energy development in the Barnett shale. *Southern Rural Sociology* 24, 1:113–129.

Bartoletti, Susan Campbell. 1996. *Growing up in coal country.* Boston, MA: Houghton Mifflin Company.

Boyer, Dominic. 2011. Energopolitics and the anthropology of energy. *Anthropology News* 52, 5:5–7.

Boyer, Dominic. 2014. Energopower: An introduction. *Anthropological Quarterly* 87, 2:309–333.

Brasier, Kathryn J., Matthew R. Filteau, Diane K. McLaughlin, Jeffrey Jaquet, Richard C. Stedman, Timothy W. Kelsey, and Stephan J. Goetz. 2011. Residents' perceptions of community and environmental impacts from development of natural gas in the Marcellus Shale: A comparison of Pennsylvania and New York cases. *Journal of Rural Social Sciences* 26, 1:32–61.

Brasier, Kathryn J., Diane K. McLaughlin, Danielle Rhubart, Richard C. Stedman, Matthew R. Filteau, and Jeffrey Jacquet. 2013. Risk perceptions of natural gas development in the Marcellus Shale. *Environmental Practice* 15, 2:108–122.

Bryant, Raymond L., and Sinead Bailey. 1997. *Third world political ecology*. New York: Routledge.

de Rijke, Kim. 2013. Hydraulically fractured: Unconventional gas and anthropology. *Anthropology Today* 29, 2:13–17.

Drohan, Patrick J., James C. Finley, Paul Roth, Thomas M. Schuler, Susan L. Stout, Margaret C. Brittingham, and Nels C. Johnson. 2012. Perspectives from the field: Oil and gas impacts on forest ecosystems: Findings gleaned from the 2012 Goddard forum at Penn State University. *Environmental Practice* 14, 4:394–399.

Energy from Shale. n.d. www.energyfromshale.org/ (accessed August 23, 2015).

Field, Robert. A., Joseph Soltis, and S. Murphy. 2014. Air quality concerns of unconventional oil and natural gas production. *Journal of Environmental Monitoring* 16, 5:954–969.

Finewood, Michael H., and Laura J. Stroup. 2012. Fracking and the neoliberalization of the hydro-social cycle in Pennsylvania's Marcellus Shale. *Journal of Contemporary Water Research & Education* 147, 1:72–79.

Foucault, Michel. 1978. *The history of sexuality, Vol. 1: The will to knowledge.* London: Penguin.

Gramsci, Antonio, Quintin Hoare, and Geoffrey Nowell-Smith. 1971. *Selections from the prison notebooks of Antonio Gramsci.* New York: International Publishers.

Higginbotham, Nick, Linda Connor, Glenn Albrecht, Sonia Freeman, and Kingsley Agho. 2006. Validation of an environmental distress scale. *EcoHealth* 3, 4:245–254.

Hudgins, Anastasia, and Amanda Poole. 2014. Framing fracking: Private property, common resources, and regimes of governance. *Journal of Political Ecology* 21, 303–319.

Jacquet, Jeffrey B., and Richard C. Stedman. 2013. Perceived impacts from wind farm and natural gas development in northern Pennsylvania. *Rural Sociology* 78, 4:450–472.

Kahneman, Daniel, and Angus Deaton. 2010. High income improves evaluation of life but not emotional well-being. *Proceedings of the National Academy of Sciences* 107, 38:16489–16493.

Lakoff, George. 2005. *Don't think of an elephant! Know your values and frame the debate.* White River Junction, VT: Chelsea Green.

Metheny, Karen Bescherer. 2007. *From the miners' doublehouse: Archaeology and landscape in a Pennsylvania coal company town.* Knoxville: University of Tennessee Press.

Muehlenbachs, Lucija, Elisheba Spiller, and Christopher Timmins. 2015. The housing market impacts of shale gas development. *American Economic Review* 105, 12:3633–3659.

New York Department of Health (NY DOH). 2014. *A public health review of high volume hydraulic fracturing for shale gas development.* www.health.ny.gov/press/reports/docs/high_volume_hydraulic_fracturing.pdf (accessed August 23, 2015).

Olmstead, Sheila M., Lucija A. Muehlenbachs, Jhih-Shyang Shih, Ziyan Chu, and Alan J. Krupnick. 2013. Shale gas development impacts on surface water quality in Pennsylvania. *Proceedings of the National Academy of Sciences* 110, 13:4962–4967.

Osborn, Stephen G., Avner Vengosh, and Nathaniel R. Warner. 2011. Methane contamination of drinking water accompanying gas-well drilling and hydraulic fracturing. *Proceedings of the National Academy of Sciences* 108, 20:8172–8176.

Perry, Simona L. 2012. Development, land use, and collective trauma: The Marcellus Shale gas boom in rural Pennsylvania. *Culture, Agriculture, Food and Environment* 34, 1:81–92.

Theodori, Gene L. 2001. Examining the effects of community satisfaction and attachment on individual well-being. *Rural Sociology* 66, 4:618–628.

Theodori, Gene L. 2009. Paradoxical perceptions of problems associated with unconventional natural gas development. *Southern Rural Sociology* 24, 3:97–117.

Willits, Fern K., Albert E. Luloff, and Gene L. Theodori. 2013. Changes in residents' views of natural gas drilling in the Pennsylvania Marcellus Shale, 2009–2012. *Journal of Rural Social Sciences* 28, 3:60–75.

Willow, Anna J. 2015. Wells and well-being: Neoliberalism and holistic sustainability in the shale energy debate. *Local Environment* 21, 6:768–788.

Willow, Anna, and Sara Wylie. 2014. Politics, ecology, and the new anthropology of energy: Exploring the emerging frontiers of hydraulic fracking. *Journal of Political Ecology* 21, 222–236.

# PART II
# Risks & Rights

# 4

# BOUNDED IMPACTS, BOUNDLESS PROMISE

## Environmental Impact Assessments of Oil Production in the Ecuadorian Amazon

*Amelia Fiske*[1]

A presentation of the Environmental Impact Assessment (EIA) for a new set of wells that the Andes Petroleum Company proposes to drill in the northeastern corner of the Ecuadorian Amazon has just concluded. One of the wells is sited near the community center and school, as well as several residents' homes. A woman stands, attempting to appeal to the officials' humanity rather than their technical expertise. She expresses concern that noise from the drilling will be unbearable, given the proximity of the well to her home. Would the company consider moving the platform or at least agree not to run the drilling equipment at night so that her family might sleep? The company engineer is visibly tired of hearing about the well's location, which people have raised repeatedly during the question and answer period. He informs her that her comment has been recorded, but that changing the platform location will be an option only if it proves technically feasible because the sites that were selected are "geologically optimal." The company's Community Relations Officer steps in, but the engineer cuts him off before he can say anything: *The company's first interest regarding this platform is to extract hydrocarbons.* He pauses. *Then we will get to other concerns. The EIA lists the permissible limits, so please inform yourselves. We will take two more comments.*[2]

An "EIA" refers to two things: it is a set of scientific practices and a document that characterizes and evaluates the potential Impacts[3] to the environment and local community of a proposed project, and analyzes risks and proposes means of preventing and managing potential negative impacts. EIAs are required by law for every step of oil exploration and production. Teams of experts turn terrains into a set of facts that takes many forms—numbers, lists, charts, statistical evaluations, and narratives within a several hundred-page document—which enable this particular place to be compared to others. This categorization, measurement, and community presentation solidifies certain impacts as important, and others as irrelevant. Such technologies of quantification predispose the representation of the places and phenomena toward certain kinds of "objective" knowledge that reifies the information in the EIA as neutral (McGrath, Chapter 5). By defining Impact as something that can be positive or negative, the document makes manageable all conceivable consequences of oil operations such that there is no potential Impact that does not also have a solution (Li 2009, 2015). The question of *whether* the project should proceed at all becomes unthinkable.

The practices of making an EIA render the material, historical, social, and aesthetic aspects of the place as Impacts in the document. Impacts are discrete, value-free descriptors, that allow for neutral evaluation of a potential project. In an era of risk assessment, many assume that the process of creating and approving an EIA enables better governance of industry. Increased documentation is expected to lead to greater accountability between companies and the places they work and, ultimately, to reduce negative environmental effects. Given the requisite legal status of the EIA in many countries, the document has become the principal means of assessing, documenting, and preventing environmental harm produced by industry. Under Ecuadorian law (Regulation for Social Participation 1040), an EIA must be presented to the affected community in order for any proposed operations to proceed. However, the Ecuadorian state also has a financial interest in developing oil reserves. Rather than being an objective mechanism of evaluation, through ethnographic example, I will demonstrate that the EIA shapes a world that it purports to only represent. By bounding the Impacts of oil production in time and space, the EIA establishes a political and dialogical space in which potential negative consequences for human and animal life are discounted while the benefits brought by oil extraction remain unquestioned.

The Cardno Entrix consulting company completed the EIA referenced here for Andes Petroleum. I was present for the public presentation (*socialización*) of the EIA document I am working from in this chapter, as well as for multiple other EIA presentations in the region. The tensions evident in the opening presentation highlight the dramatic differences in the concerns of company representatives, environmental authorities, and the community. In order to understand these contested positions on the EIA, I conducted informal and semi-structured interviews with community members in Amazonian communities, technicians from local and national offices of the Ministry of the Environment, government officials working in the Program for Environmental and Social Reparation in Quito, and private environmental consultants in Quito over the course of 24 months of fieldwork from 2011 to 2013. In order to situate this meeting and document within the broader regulatory process, I conducted participant observation of multiple EIA presentations and reviewed other EIA documents completed within the past 10 years. While the examples cited in this chapter are drawn from one particular EIA document, I am concerned with the function of the EIA in the oil industry more generally.

It is important to note that I selected this particular EIA because environmental consultants repeatedly mentioned that Cardno Entrix had a reputation for high quality studies. I am not arguing against the use of the EIA as a tool of accountability and environmental protection, nor do I aim to critique the authors of this particular document or question the caliber of the scientific practices. Many individuals with whom I spoke mentioned EIAs that were poorly executed or obviously copied from previous studies; these are other concerns entirely. Instead, I want to call attention to the ways in which the practices that result in an EIA formalize the consequences of the oil industry. Despite its narrow legal designation, the EIA has become a proxy forum for broader discussions about the consequences of oil development in Amazonian communities. The intention of this chapter is to attend to the ways in which the representative practices of making Impacts in EIAs shape how the industry proceeds in the Amazon.

## Oil Production and Environmental Regulation in Ecuador

The past half-century has marked a dramatic transformation of the northeastern Ecuadorian Amazon. Responding to land crowding in the Sierra and a drought in the southern highlands in the 1960s, government officials mistakenly equated abundant jungle flora for rich agricultural soils, imagining the vast territory east of the Andes to be the next breadbasket of the nation. Through the state-led Agrarian Reform and Colonization program, settlers set out en masse to claim 50 hectares of land each, half of which they were required to make "productive" through crops or cattle ranching in order to receive their land title. At the same moment, Ecuador was on the brink of becoming an oil-producing nation. At the government's request, the Texaco-Gulf Company built roadways in the Amazon to facilitate colonization. Notably, construction of the Sistema de Oleoducto Transecuatoriano (SOTE)—Trans-Ecuadorian Oil Pipeline System in English—in 1973 completed the route between Quito and Lago Agrio, enabling settlement of the Amazon (Figure 4.1). These processes of oil development and state-sponsored colonization resulted in the arrival of more than 200,000 settlers, with more than 4,500,000 hectares of land claimed under the Agrarian Reform program (Sawyer 2004). By the year 2000, satellite imagery showed that more than half of the *Oriente* region had been deforested (Wasserstrom and Southgate 2013).

In 1972, Ecuador began commercial oil production. The oil era began through a consortium between the newly created state company Corporación Estatal Petróleos del Ecuador (CEPE) and the Texaco and Gulf Oil Companies of the United States. For the first two decades, the industry operated with minimal oversight. It was not until 2001 that the current regulation, the *Regulation to Replace the Environmental Regulation for Hydrocarbon Operations, Decree No. 1215,* was developed in response to the deficiencies of early iterations of the 1995 Ministerial Agreement (No. 621). Borrowing heavily from the US Environmental Protection Agency's (EPA) policies, Regulation 1215 implemented the EIA, Environmental Management Plans, and Environmental Audits as the principle mechanisms of regulatory control. Parallel to these developments, the EIA, first established as part of the US National Environmental Policy Act (NEPA) in 1969, had become a "global tool of accountability" required in all World Bank projects by the 1990s (Li 2009; Sadler 1996). The EIA has since become the most common form of environmental assessment, now employed in more than 170 countries (Hochstetler 2011; Morgan 2012).

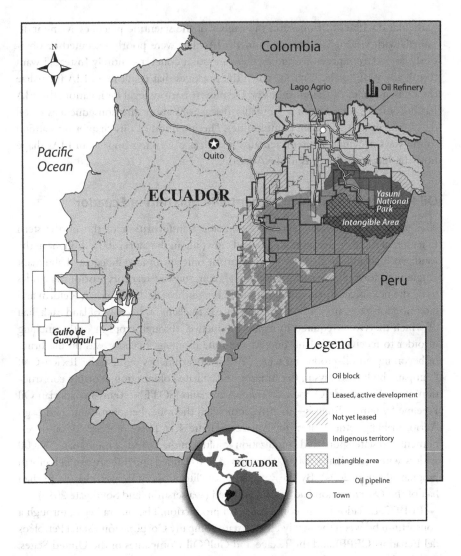

**FIGURE 4.1** The government of Ecuador has invested heavily in developing oil reserves in the Amazon region. Environmental Impact Assessments of Amazonian oil projects often serve to normalize negative impacts on local communities and fail to question alleged benefits like economic development. Map by Donna Gayer, Artasaverb.

Regulation 1215 marked the beginning of an era of unprecedented documentation for the oil industry in Ecuador. Oil companies hire an environmental consulting company from a list pre-approved by PetroEcuador, the state oil company, to complete their EIAs and Environmental Management Plans. The consulting company should be a third party, not vested in the project. Often based in Quito, the environmental services company assembles the technical team that will complete the study.

Following the field portion of the study, a draft of the EIA is then shared with the affected community, in accordance with the *Regulation for Social Participation 1040*. Passed into law in 2008, 1040 guarantees the right of communities to be informed of any activity that may affect the area in which they live, "ensuring respect for the collective right of every citizen to live in a healthy environment that is ecologically balanced and free from contamination." The authorities from the Ministry of the Environment are required to record the community's response to the EIA.

Several points deserve emphasis. First, the Ecuadorian government owns all oil reserves in the country. Presently, the government depends on oil for 44% of its revenue (Gill 2013). PetroEcuador, the state oil company, has a two-thirds venture with Andes Petroleum, the Chinese company of this example. PetroEcuador has contracted with Andes Petroleum to produce oil, for which Andes Petroleum will receive approximately one-third of the revenue and the state will take the rest. Thus, although the Ecuadorian regulatory process loosely imitates the NEPA model from the United States, there is an important distinction: the US EPA does not have a financial stake in the projects they evaluate; the Ecuadorian Ministry of the Environment does by virtue of national mineral rights. This underlines what many interlocutors expressed: the role of the EIA as a regulatory mechanism in the Ecuadorian oil industry is largely perfunctory.

Further, the EIA relies on numerical values in order to make comparisons and determine the comparative importance of Impacts. Impacts are compiled, compared, and made commensurate through numerical evaluations and turned into percentages that correspond to their overall significance in relation to the project. The work of assigning numerical values is always informed by the broader political economy of oil production. In the case of Ecuador, oil's importance to the national economy is an important part of the context in which EIAs operate: oil is the chief national export, representing 52.3% of total exports in 2014 (Comisión Económica para América Latina y el Caribe 2016) and providing a quarter of the national budget (Herrera, López, and Arias 2012). At present, 65% of the Amazon has been zoned for drilling (Finer et al. 2008). This particular project in the Tarapoa area is part of a package of oil and mining projects in which the Chinese government has lent Ecuador $7 billion at 7.5% interest to be repaid with oil and minerals (Gill 2015). The pre-determined importance of oil to the Ecuadorian state is an essential feature of the political landscape in which the EIA operates.

Second, the oil industry and processes of colonization and settlement worked in tandem to transform the region. Visitors today find cacao fields and cattle entangled with oil wells and pipelines. The state and the oil industry directly and indirectly enabled the current configuration of roads, settlement, and fields of cacao, yucca, and plantain. This is important because, as I will show, the calculation of Impacts in the EIA relies on an untouched natural ideal to which all forms of disturbance are compared. Evidence of anthropogenic disturbance serves to justify lower evaluations of natural resources in these sites. By not accounting for complex historical processes, Impact assessment justifies the continuation of industrial projects because the project sites are determined to already be degraded.

Lastly, regulation of the oil industry has inserted new forms of bureaucracy and accounting into the daily lives of those living in the region. Since the introduction of the first comprehensive hydrocarbon regulation in 2001, residents of the Amazon have become familiar with terms such as "Environmental Impact Assessment" or "Contingency Plan," in addition to learning to navigate the many administrative offices of the oil companies and environmental authorities in order to register complaints or to seek compensation for damages. Despite the narrow focus of the EIA on Impact identification, EIA presentations have become routine moments of negotiation and interaction with oil companies and state authorities in a place where the state owns all subterranean mineral rights. In short, this regulatory apparatus is a crucial dimension of living with oil in the Amazon today.

Before proceeding, I return to the presentation of the document that opened this chapter. Discussion continues about the location of the well: the Ministry of the Environment representative states that the regulation requires monitoring and follow-up of all activities. Another community member stands to clarify the question, *But there's no rule that you can't put a well right here in the middle of the community?* Mauricio from the Ministry of the Environment begins, *Not within 500 meters of homes.* But the engineer cuts him off, *Make sure this is recorded.* The engineer pauses, waiting for the man with the recorder to make his way to the front, *There is no set limit. What does exist is the "Area of Influence." For example, we could put the well 250 meters from the school as long as we can guarantee the noise won't reach "x" decibels during the day. Anything below "x" decibels is permitted.*

Audible dissent is heard from the audience. Another community member stands: *What about the families affected by the widening of the road? Some of us live less than three meters from the road.* The only presenter not outfitted in the all-denim uniform of the oil industry steps up. He is Andes Petroleum's superintendent of Community Relations, and will be this community's primary contact through drilling and operations: *Well, obviously this is a process. Once the project is approved, then we'll talk about these concerns—such as widening the road. We are getting ahead of ourselves with these sorts of adjustments. We'll deal with them when the time comes. Once, of course, we have your permission to start.*

Impacts like roads or noise are never experienced in isolation, but rather as part of a broader historical process of extraction. As the legally recognized evaluation of places scheduled for oil extraction, the EIA sets the terms through which the Ministry of Environment will evaluate extractive projects and their consequences. What might seem like concerns about minutiae—"x" decibels, or the official boundaries of influence of the project—have a profound effect for those living alongside industry. This example is illustrative of how the EIA proceeds: the concerns of the community are minimized as Impacts are made into calculated, individualized measures that are managed by state regulation, while broader concerns associated with the oil industry operating in the middle of the community are eclipsed. When Impacts or the "Area of Influence" are extracted from an EIA and invoked as uncomplicated natural objects, the power of the EIA to shape public debate and understanding about how oil acts on environments is evident.

## The Baseline Study and Area of Influence

Consulting teams that work on EIAs mobilize a range of scientific practices in order to transform a place (a home, a forest, a cacao field) into facts (numbers, graphs, categories, and narrative) necessary for evaluating a project's anticipated Impacts. There is nothing easy or intuitive about this shift from place to facts to Impact. The document opens with the baseline study, which establishes the state of the area prior to the initiation of the proposed project. The authors evaluate the project in light of the information assembled in the baseline study in order to anticipate how the environment will be affected. The authors then determine the project's "Area of Influence," analyze potential risks, and identify and evaluate the anticipatable environmental impacts. The EIA's conclusion consists of the Environmental Management Plan, which addresses how to prevent or deal with the Impacts the study has identified, along with a monitoring plan that environmental authorities will use to register company compliance with the Management Plan's guidelines.

A central organizing intention of the baseline study is to isolate a moment in time against which all subsequent changes ("potential Impacts") can be compared. The baseline study relies on the fiction of being able to stop time in order to make future predictions about harm, thus divorcing historical processes from their outcomes. By dividing the terrain being studied into two distinct parts—Direct and Indirect "Areas of Influence"—the affected region emerges as a circumscribed time and space. It includes the physical spaces in which infrastructure like well platforms and access roads will be constructed, as well as political spaces such as the company's administrative offices. The authors describe the baseline study as a "prior vision" against which all future monitoring will be compared. The establishment of "prior" and "post" visions is a critical intervention: only by establishing an image of a particular point in time of the "original state" of the place is it possible to anticipate the future Impacts that could result from the project's execution (Cardno Entrix 2012, 41). It bears asserting that these boundaries the baseline establishes are not given, but are artifacts of the study.

Characterization is never "just" characterization; the compilation of information is not a disinterested activity (Latour 1986). These devices work in conjunction to produce the material and political space of oil's influence. Such boundaries are informed by a particular scientific vision and do not represent a natural means of demarcating a project's influence, yet they are often invoked as mirrors of reality rather than instrumentalized ideals produced to answer a particular objective (Lampland 2010, 386). Yet, in the process of translation from field to document, the contingencies of the EIA disappear. The EIA shapes places that it claims to only represent.

## Impacts and Disturbance

The proposed project will be located in an area that has already experienced significant human intervention, by both oil companies and colonist farmers (Figure 4.2).

**FIGURE 4.2** Residents of many Amazonian communities live alongside the proliferating infrastructure of the oil industry, including wells, pipelines, gas flares and waste pits. Photograph taken by Amelia Fiske, January 2012.

The recent history of simultaneous processes of oil development and settlement has created a region in which distinctions between residential and industrial land use are blurred. The study describes the lowland areas as presenting "strong anthropogenic intervention due to human settlements that exert pressure on the periphery of the landscape" (Cardno Entrix 2012, 78). Rivers in the study area were found to be contaminated with high levels of fecal coliforms, which, when combined with large cultivated areas and significant habitat fragmentation, resulted in a rating of "medium" for the "natural state" of the study area. Part of the EIA's task in establishing the "prior vision" of the baseline study is to document all anthropogenic alterations to a putatively "pure" nature that precedes the particular project. In other words, the evaluation of Impacts also serves the purpose of specifying environmental degradation for which the oil company *cannot* be held accountable, including that of prior industrial activity and the varied effects of colonization. Doing so limits a company's responsibility to the precise window in which they operate.

In the EIA, great concern is given to the "quality" of the natural resources that exist at the time of the study; these resources are evaluated by the degree to which they have been altered by human activity such that "more significant impacts may occur in less disturbed environments and vice versa" (Cardno Entrix 2012, 41). One environmental consultant described how company administrators often complain that the environmental impact that the well platform would produce is minor compared to the deforestation caused by the farming and ranching of colonists. He emphasized the importance of completing the baseline study, in part to establish that oil operations are not responsible for the existing alterations to the natural environment:

> That's why you do the baseline, and you see how the environment is previous to the project. So you compare the baseline to the project and see how the project is going to affect the baseline, and the impact is going to be less because [the place] is already damaged. The comparison between the possible impacts and the baseline gives you the Environmental Management Plan (April 25, 2013).

When the baseline is already degraded by previous settlement or oil activity, as is often the case, the anticipated Impact of the project will be small in comparison, producing what conservation biologists have referred to as "shifting baseline syndrome" (Papworth et al. 2009). When the Impacts anticipated in the EIA are small, environmental authorities are much more likely to approve the project being proposed. The EIA's "vision," its predictive capacity that rests on construction of comparisons between before and after, is closely attuned to assessment of micro level, discrete Impacts while ignoring broader processes such as the history of oil and settlement that are obfuscated by the baseline study. This vision intersects with assumptions about anthropogenic disturbance such that evidence of human intervention serves to numerically justify the continuation of industry.

The assessment of an environment's quality in the baseline study affects the degree of exigency of the Management Plan. In the Environmental Management Plan, the consulting group describes how the company will address and mitigate potential impacts. The EIA makes it possible to evaluate places from offices hundreds of miles away in an abstract form. When officials from the Ministry of the Environment in Quito (who will not visit the site) review the regulatory precautions of the Management Plan, they will consider the numerical value given for the natural resources in the baseline study. As the same consultant went on to explain, "In a pristine area, in the baseline you will have a very sensitive area and of course the Management Plan will include many more activities to protect flora, fauna, water resources, and the arrival of colonists." A low value in the baseline study will mean fewer provisions necessary in the Management Plan. Once approved by the Ministry of the Environment, the Management Plan establishes the standards of operations and environmental protection practices specific to that particular project.

The result is that in areas the EIA describes as "more disturbed," that is, less natural or already showing evidence of human presence in the landscape, the impact of future oil activities is judged less important. Differentiating among degrees of environmental disturbance presumes the existence of an Amazonian wilderness without culture; this natural ideal in the EIA depends on the absence of humans. The historical conjunctures that have shaped places that the EIA evaluates as "monotonous" or as demonstrating "anthropogenic intervention" disappear in these evaluations.

No note is made of the existence of oil operations in the area for the past several decades, nor of the relations between oil development and settlement in shaping the region. In this framework, it is precisely in those locations where human health and wellbeing would likely be of greatest concern—places where there are high degrees of disturbance because communities live and farm in them, or use the surrounding rivers for drinking, bathing, or washing clothes—that the Impacts from oil development would potentially be evaluated as less important in the EIA.

## Governance and Alternatives

While the EIA channels "Impact" into delimited effects with corresponding management plans, usually what residents, environmentalists, and observers mean when they speak of the impacts of fossil fuel industries is much broader. One of the effects of the EIA is to keep these broader meanings out of view. In this final section, I illustrate the political consequences of Impacts as they are employed in the document. In particular, I consider how oil's status as a "strategic resource" can foreclose meaningful contemplation of impacts, broadly conceived.

Since the mid-1960s, politicians have heralded oil as a promise of modernity for the nation. Politicians continue to promote oil in such terms, despite widespread environmental contamination and growing critiques of the uneven forms of prosperity and inequality oil extraction generates, as well as concerns about the unsustainability of the industry. Under President Correa, the promise of oil has been rearticulated as critical and necessary to combatting poverty. In 2011, the Correa administration founded the Coordinating Ministry of Strategic Sectors with the stated goal of making rational, efficient, and sustainable use of strategic resources such as copper, hydrocarbons, and water. The Ministry promotes the sovereignty and productivity of Ecuador's natural resources in order to overcome the socio-economic challenges facing the country (see also Renfrew and Santos, Chapter 2). Making intelligent use of these resources promises to reduce poverty and improve every citizen's quality of life, as well as improving income distribution, job opportunities, investment, and economic growth. The EIA is one document in a longer process of oil development; revenue and investment calculations have already been done by the state and operating companies prior to beginning the EIA. In defining oil as a strategic resource of the state, the benefits exploitation will bring are naturalized: the EIA is completed in a place where oil's importance to the nation exists *a priori*. Unlike the spatially and temporally circumscribed Impacts in an EIA, benefits can subsequently be invoked in the document and in political discourse as unbounded and timeless.

Every EIA must contemplate several alternative ways to implement a project, in order to produce the least negative impact possible. This involves weighing the relative importance of the Impacts in the Area of Influence against the project's contribution to the country in terms of investment, foreign exchange earnings, and employment (Cardno Entrix 2012, 187–188). In this instance, the primary concern raised by residents was the location of the well. The "geologically optimal" site is on the farms of several community members. Residents had stressed that the well was too close to their homes and schools and asked for it to be moved.

In light of these concerns, the study considers three alternative sites. Only one proposed option involved not proceeding with the project. I quote the entire explanation in the document for why the option of not drilling was deemed not viable:

> Another alternative to consider is to not execute the project, in which case there will be no impacts caused by the partial and reversible loss of habitats, movement of soil, entrance of machinery, additional staff, generation of noise, emissions, wastes, and discharges. However, this alternative is not viable, considering that, on the one hand, Andes Petroleum Ecuador Ltd. needs to comply with the contract it has with the Ecuadorian State and other commitments, and on the other hand, the project will be a source of income for the Ecuadorian State, both in production quotas as well as taxes.
>
> If the project is not executed, consequently this will eliminate the generation of financial resources, which on the national level, revenues from hydrocarbon activities represent the largest share of revenue to the State; further, and although of a marginal manner, the project represents income for the community given that it will be necessary to hire local labor during the construction phase and, although in lesser number and for less time, also in the drilling and operation stage.
>
> *(Cardno Entrix 2012, 188)*

Following this, two alternative locations for the well are discussed and compared in a table based on the relative influence they would have on biotic, abiotic, socioeconomic, and technical-economic concerns. Regardless of the Impacts the study identified, the possibility of abandoning the project altogether was dismissed as unviable because of the company's pre-existing contractual obligations with the state.

The Impacts identified in the study are used as part of the analysis in the document to make recommendations about how best to execute and manage the operations. Yet, despite the authors' caution that Impacts can be both positive and negative, positive and negative Impacts are not treated symmetrically. In the entirety of the 357-page document, only a handful of sentences address the project's benefits, with vague references to the "beneficial impact that the increase in hydrocarbon production represents for an increase in income for the country" (Cardno Entrix 2012, 249). While negative Impacts are detailed to a degree of technical exhaustion over hundreds of pages, charts, and analyses, the benefits the extracted oil will bring are taken for granted. Revenue and production quotas are not calculated in the EIA, nor are the jobs that the project would generate; such calculations are left for internal investment plans in which the decision to proceed with the project was already taken. This asymmetry in the EIA contributes to the idea that extracting oil is unequivocally beneficial, allowing for the brevity of the above statement to suffice for an explanation of why it was not necessary to consider not proceeding with the new wells. In the EIA's analysis of alternatives, not executing the project is not an option.

While the EIA articulates Impacts as proximal effects in a highly circumscribed time and space, it invokes benefits in terms of the nation at large and "the future." Because the EIA constructs Impacts in relation to their control, by definition there can be no negative Impact that cannot be managed and therefore cannot be justified by the assumed benefit that a project will bring (Li 2009). This asymmetric accounting is further compounded by the way harm to environments and human health unfolds, often over lengthy time scales that exceed the predictive scope of an EIA. In contrast, benefits are lofty potentials such as the end of poverty or the key to development, all of which are routinely cited in presidential speeches, radio programs, and state-sponsored billboards announcing the investment of profits from oil extraction. The result is twofold: the calculation of Impacts minimizes the total effect of the project by making such discrete effects manageable, while the benefits of expanding drilling can be invoked as boundless promise.

## Conclusion

The Impacts produced in the EIA do not remain confined to the document, but are taken up and travel as part of discourses, legal claims, and presidential speeches; Impacts are the means through which regulation is operationalized. As they travel, the reality of what they present becomes increasingly solid. That Impacts are contingent elements of a model shaped by particular rhetorics, practices, and assumptions becomes difficult to recognize. As the EIA has become the most common form of environmental assessment around the world, it is increasingly accepted as the most legitimate means of assessing or anticipating the impacts of future operations. This is particularly significant given the Ecuadorian state's ownership of national mineral rights: if the EIA is to function as a scientifically and socially meaningful evaluation of places designated for development, the state cannot have vested interest in the document's making or outcome.

The complexity of oil's consequences as they unfold over decades of production, settlement, and daily life fall outside official bounds of Impacts. This chapter has juxtaposed the ways that discrete, local effects are made manageable through their calculation as Impacts in the EIA, while the benefits of drilling are expansively invoked through future, national promise in the document and in political discourse. The EIA presentation has increasingly become a forum for negotiation between communities and companies that it was not intended to be. In order for genuine consideration and debate of the benefits and consequences of oil production to take place, impacts and benefits must be evaluated symmetrically in official, public forums. And alternatives—such as not proceeding with drilling—must be viable possibilities rather than perfunctory checkmarks in the EIA.

Oil extraction raises many persistent problems, one of which is that its effects are difficult to anticipate or control. Recent scholarship points to the spatially unbounded and multi-temporal dimensions of ecological harm, underlining the insufficiency of conceptualizing harm in the form it appears in EIA Impacts. This chapter has sought to call attention to the violence produced by categorization that determines what counts as environmental harm and the knowledge practices such categories imply and exclude (Haraway 2006). One way to denaturalize the official Impacts of the EIA is to insist on recognizing the multitude of impacts from oil extraction that overflow the circumscribed boundaries drawn by regulatory practice. This raises a practical question: what would be a fair environmental evaluation prior to extractive development? Where does company and state responsibility begin (and end) for degraded environments, historical processes of colonization, or inequality? In this chapter I argue that such boundaries need to be more inclusive than their present delimitation in order to accommodate the complex of changes brought by oil extraction.

## Notes

1 I am grateful for the generous support of this project from the Social Science Research Council, Wenner-Gren Foundation, National Science Foundation, and University of Chapel Hill Institute for Latin American Studies, as well as to Kirk Jalbert and David Casagrande for their editorial guidance.
2 Italics without quotation marks in this chapter indicate conversation reconstructed from fieldnotes. I have done my best to accurately re-create what was said; however statements should not be taken as direct quotes unless indicated. All names have been changed.
3 I capitalize the word Impact to denote the specific object produced by the EIA. Politicians, environmental consultants, oil company workers, farmers, and activists used the word impact frequently throughout my research. At times, they were making specific reference to the Impacts as defined by the EIA, while at other times they used impact to refer to the consequences of oil production more generally. By capitalizing Impact, as the specific object and unit of assessment in the EIA, I aim to denaturalize it, and to call attention to the slippage when Impact comes to stand in for a confluence of impacts.

## References

Cardno Entrix. 2012. *Fase de desarrollo y producción sector sur del campo Mariann, construcción de la plataforma Mariann 30 y de su vía de acceso, perforación de 8 pozos de desarrollo y construcción y pperación de líneas de flujo para pruebas y producción*. Environmental Impact Statement elaborated for Andes Petroleum Ecuador Ltd, May. Quito, Ecuador.

Comisión Económica para América Latina y el Caribe. 2016. *Base de datos y publicaciones estadísticas*. Ecuador: Perfil Nacional Económico. http://interwp.cepal.org/cepalstat/Perfil_Nacional_Economico.html?pais=ECU&idioma=spanish (accessed January 20, 2016).

Finer, Matt, Clinton N. Jenkins, Stuart L. Pimm, Brian Keane, and Carl Ross. 2008. Oil and gas projects in the western Amazon: Threats to wilderness, biodiversity, and indigenous peoples. *PLoS ONE* 3, 8:e2932.

Gill, Nathan. 2013. Ecuador economic growth stagnates as oil drop cuts spending. *Bloomberg.com*, January 9. www.bloomberg.com/news/articles/2013-01-09/ecuador-economic-growth-stagnates-as-oil-drop-cuts-spending-1- (accessed January 20, 2016).

Gill, Nathan. 2015. China rescues Ecuador budget from deeper cuts as crude drops. *Bloomberg.com*, January 13. www.bloomberg.com/news/articles/2015-01-13/china-rescues-ecuador-budget-from-deeper-cuts-as-crude-drops-1- (accessed January 20, 2016).

Haraway, Donna. 2006. A cyborg manifesto: Science, technology, and socialist-feminism in the late 20th century. In *The International Handbook of Virtual Learning Environments*, edited by Joel Weiss, Jason Nolan, Jeremy Hunsinger, and Peter Trifonas, 117–158. Dordrecht: Springer.

Herrera, Juan Jose, Julio López, and Karla Arias. 2012. El liderazgo de la gestión petrolera regresa al Estado, monitoreo 2011. *Lupa Fiscal*, Informe 4.

Hochstetler, Kathryn. 2011. The politics of environmental licensing: Energy projects of the past and future in Brazil. *Studies in Comparative International Development* 46, 4:349–371.

Lampland, Martha. 2010. False numbers as formalizing practices. *Social Studies of Science* 40, 3:377–404.

Latour, Bruno. 1986. Visualization and cognition: Drawing things together. *Knowledge and Society* 6, 1:1–40.

Li, Fabiana. 2009. Documenting accountability: Environmental impact assessment in a Peruvian mining project. *PoLAR: Political and Legal Anthropology Review* 32, 2:218–236.

Li, Fabiana. 2015. *Unearthing conflict: Corporate mining, activism, and expertise in Peru*. Durham, NC: Duke University Press.

Morgan, Richard K. 2012. Environmental impact assessment: The state of the art. *Impact Assessment and Project Appraisal* 30, 1:5–14.

Papworth, S.K., J. Rist, L. Coad, and E.J. Milner-Gulland. 2009. Evidence for shifting baseline syndrome in conservation. *Conservation Letters* 2, 2:93–100.

Sadler, Barry. 1996. *Environmental assessment in a changing world: Evaluating practice to improve performance*. Ottawa, Ontario: Canadian Environmental Assessment Agency: International Association for Impact Assessment.

Sawyer, Suzana. 2004. *Crude chronicles: Indigenous politics, multinational oil, and neoliberalism in Ecuador*. Durham, NC: Duke University Press.

Wasserstrom, Robert, and Douglas Southgate. 2013. Deforestation, agrarian reform and oil development in Ecuador, 1964–1994. *Natural Resources* 4, 1:31–44.

# 5

# THE POWER AND POLITICS OF HEALTH IMPACT ASSESSMENT IN THE PACIFIC NORTHWEST COAL EXPORT DEBATE

*Moriah McSharry McGrath*[1]

A wave of proposals to export coal from US Pacific Northwest ports presents new opportunities for both economic growth and health harms in the region. These possibilities exist in high tension due to two sometimes-divergent aspects of the region's culture: a declining natural-resource-based economy and libertarian politics that coexist with a strong environmental consciousness and its companion emerging "green" business sector. Consequently, the coal export proposals leave urban and rural communities, tribal nations, corporations, and environmental activists jockeying for power and opportunity in the face of local and global ramifications of shipping millions of tons of coal through the region.

This policy process sets the stage for this chapter, which discusses efforts to use the emerging practice of health impact assessment (HIA) to foster health equity in policy decisions related to the export proposals. The chapter explores efforts to evaluate the potential human health impacts of the export proposals and questions the emphasis on technical procedures that purport to definitively and/or quantitatively measure impacts of these large projects. I argue that the shortcomings of legally mandated impact assessment procedures, coupled with stakeholders' efforts to compensate for gaps in these procedures, create an environment where it is difficult to realize HIA's potential for promoting health equity in all policy decisions. As a consequence, advocacy for HIAs of coal export proposals may actually create a barrier to achieving its desired goal of elevating health and social equity concerns into the decision-making process.

I propose an unveiling of the use of science in the decision-making process, shining a light on the relationship between values and assessment techniques. I argue that demanding additional assessment procedures—such as HIA—can have the unintended side effect of reifying the purported neutrality of science, thus preventing a frank accounting of the values driving public policy decisions. Ultimately, overtly value-laden knowledge production may foster better policy than maintaining the false dichotomy between advocacy and science that animates the debate over assessing health impacts of coal export.

## A New Energy Geography

While the Pacific Northwest historically depended on "dirty" coal-burning power plants in the past, these facilities have largely disappeared thanks to increasingly stringent federal regulations, environmental activism, and declining natural gas costs (Profita 2015; Shearer et al. 2015). However, starting in 2010, the region suddenly faced the prospect of coal returning as a feature of everyday life due to proposals for coal export terminals. Under the new proposals, coal mined in the Powder River Basin (PRB) of Wyoming and Montana would travel 1,000 miles along rails and waterways—including through the Columbia Gorge National Scenic Area—to reach Oregon and Washington's Pacific coastline where it would then be loaded onto ocean freighters (Figure 5.1).

PRB coal has increased in popularity because the deposit's relatively low sulfur content makes it easier for power plants to meet Clean Air Act emissions standards (Malvadkar, Smith, and McGurl 2004) and because economic growth in Asia has increased demand for trans-Pacific shipment. The proposed US terminals have a capacity of handling 125 million tons per year, which would increase exports more than ten-fold. A Seattle think tank estimates that the volume of coal proposed for export from Oregon, Washington, and British Columbia facilities would emit 264 million metric tons of carbon dioxide per year when burned, dwarfing the 149 million metric tons that would be produced from the fuel that might be transported in the controversial Keystone XL natural gas pipeline (de Place 2014).

As of this writing, plans for four of six proposed terminals appear to have been abandoned, but two large projects remain under consideration (see Learn and Friesen 2012 for a helpful map and summary of the proposals). Though opponents are relieved that only two proposals remain on the table, there is a sense of Pyrrhic victory because the collapse of the other proposals was attributed to business reasons rather than based on the protection of human or environmental health.

## Values in Conflict

Energy companies that extract and sell coal clearly stand to gain from export proposals, but other stakeholders are invested as well. For example, coal is important to US railroad companies. The majority of coal (approximately 70%) is shipped by rail, comprising about a third of all rail tonnage and more than a quarter of railroads' revenue (AAR 2012). Though shipping volumes of other commodities have increased in the recovery from the 2008 economic decline, the weekly average number of US railcars carrying coal has consistently declined since 2008 (AAR 2014). Freight companies and their investors have a strong interest in maintaining rail traffic, particularly as other freight-intensive industries, such as timber, are also in decline. Furthermore, 40% of Washington State's economy is based in these sectors.

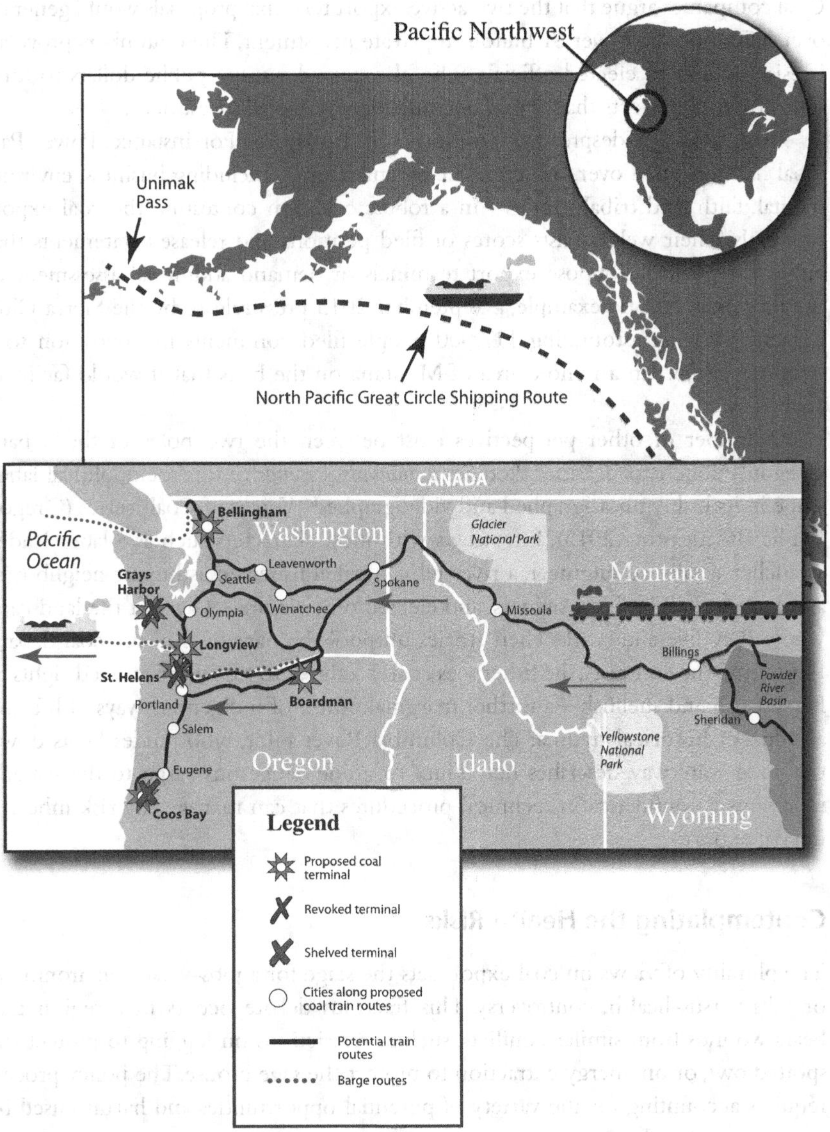

**FIGURE 5.1** Proposed coal export terminals in the Pacific Northwest would dramatically increase the volume of coal traveling by rail and barge through the region. It remains questionable whether Health Impact Assessments (HIAs) can address the many potential health impacts to communities along the shipping routes. Map by Donna Gayer, Artasaverb.

Coal companies argue that the two active export terminal proposals would generate over 8,500 jobs and over $1 billion in private investment. These numbers prove an irresistible lure to elected officials, who also consider using public dollars to fund infrastructure projects that would encourage private coal investment.

There is also widespread opposition to coal exports. For instance, Power Past Coal has convened over 100 member organizations—including business, environmental, faith, and tribal groups—in a robust coalition contesting the coal export proposals. Their website lists scores of filed petitions and released statements that either categorically oppose export terminals or demand additional assessment of the proposals. As one example, a September 2015 press release by the Sierra Club contends that an astounding 117,000 people filed comments in opposition to a small rail project in a remote area of Montana on the basis that it would facilitate coal export.

A number of other perspectives exist between the two poles of the debate. Oregon Public Broadcasting sketches a *dramatis personae* of this sociopolitical landscape in its lushly photographed and videographed "Voices of Coal" series (Oregon Public Broadcasting 2013). Interviews with local characters such as a labor leader, a rancher, a railroad engineer, a river pilot, a tribal fisher, an asthmatic neighbor of a rail yard, small business owners, and elected officials, are set against the landscape where they live and work. Their stories unspool the narratives of the coal debate. Illustrating the contrasts, the fisher sees coal as a threat to treaty-guaranteed rights to harvest fish and shellfish—a further marginalization of indigenous ways of life and a redux of historical trauma. The Columbia River pilot, who guides boats down the same waterway, describes her ability to guide dangerous cargo to the sea and represents a confidence in technical procedures that can manage the risk inherent in coal export.

## Contemplating the Health Risks

The plurality of views on coal export sets the stage for a jobs-versus-environment, or jobs-versus-health, controversy. This fractious debate occurs in a region that bears wounds from similar conflicts, such as restrictions on logging to protect the spotted owl, or on energy extraction to protect the sage grouse. The policy process requires accounting for the variety of potential opportunities and harms raised by community members.

While employment and wealth are widely understood to improve individual and community well-being, pursuing them through coal exports raises the specter of many health risks. Residents worry about inhaling the coal dust that comes off train cars as they roll past homes, or that so many very long coal trains moving through intersections will snarl traffic and delay emergency vehicles. The trains themselves also present health hazards: diesel exhaust, noise, and collisions are associated with health outcomes including heart and lung problems, cancers, stress and mental health problems, and traumatic injury. Beyond the rail routes, the global health impacts of the coal cycle include ecosystem destruction resulting from coal extraction and the climatic consequences of burning coal (Woodcock et al. 2009).

Assessing risks to human health entails understanding both exposure (how much people come into contact with a given hazard) and physiology (what happens to the body at a given level of exposure). In the case of the coal export proposals, both of these are challenging undertakings. The complexity of the projects and the potentially global scale of impacts make it difficult to predict exposure. There is also limited scientific evidence about the effects of inhaling ambient coal dust (as opposed to the higher levels experienced through occupational exposure, which is well documented). Furthermore, a health analysis of coal exports conducted by the Multnomah County Health Department in Portland, Oregon, found that coal export could exacerbate local environmental racism and health inequities because people of color are numerically overrepresented in the area surrounding train tracks (McGrath et al. 2013). Ultimately, it is difficult to quantify these impacts or extrapolate findings to a larger geographic area because of the complex interplay between social, natural, and built environments.

## Shortcomings of Statutory Assessment

While federal and state laws—the National Environmental Policy Act (NEPA) and the state-level "little NEPAs" or SEPAs—mandate environmental impact assessment (EIA) of projects such as the proposed coal export terminals, this process can fail to reconcile the diverse health concerns generated by public debates. One reason is because EIA practices have been criticized as technocratic failures, and as inadequate for addressing human health impacts. Both problems have emerged in the coal export policy process.

EIA is practiced by governments as a rationalist procedure to enable efficient decision-making. This presumes that bureaucrats can make decisions divested of personal interest and that there is one outcome that best serves the public good, as opposed to acknowledging the plurality of interests in a community (Weston 2010). It also ignores the fact that assessment itself is shaped by human values. The acts of defining the problem and determining which evidence is valid for describing it create the cultural understanding of a situation (Sangaramoorthy and Benton 2012), or as Fiske (Chapter 4) puts it, "EIA shapes a world that it purports to only represent."

Oregon's Morrow Pacific coal export proposal shows how a situation can change based on problem definition. The Army Corps of Engineers began an environmental assessment (EA) of how the project would affect the 276-mile length of the Columbia River, but later revised the scope of assessment to include only an area within a 3,000-foot radius surrounding the project. While the National Marine Fisheries Service and environmental advocates maintained that the facility would affect living and non-living elements of the environment throughout the watershed, the Corps argued, in the words of spokesperson Scott Clemans:

we need to study the effects of the action we are permitting, which is the construction of the dock. Other activities associated with this project located physically farther away are too far removed from the action for us to study in any detail. The Corps of Engineers is not going to exceed its regulatory authority.

*(Profita 2013)*

This provides an example of "narrow boundary setting, data gaps and simplified assumptions" that Wilkins (2003, 403–404) says plague EIA.

Reviewing NEPA's implementation over the years, Mandelker (2010, 294) finds that a growing "understanding that environmental systems are complex, dynamic, nonlinear, and mutually independent, making environmental prediction a much more difficult task" renders obsolete the initial premise that it is possible to conclusively determine impacts. Consequently, EIA reports have the potential to be what Clarke (1999) deems "fantasy documents"—artifacts that purport to understand and explain complex systems for the purpose of convincing the public that unknown dangers can be controlled. Despite their fantastic nature, the reports escape scrutiny about their validity and quality because EIA is viewed as a technical and rational process (Birley 2003). As Li (2009, 222–223) describes it, "[i]nformation acquired through mapping, measuring, and classifying elements of the landscape contributes to the sense of technical vigor that the EIA is intended to convey, allowing it to circulate as an 'objective' source of scientific knowledge." Fiske (Chapter 2) notes that the omission of community health concerns in the EIA process operates as a form of violence.

Segmenting a project for the purpose of assessment prevents understanding the full interactions between the project and the environment, a phenomenon that can result in health impacts being ignored over the strenuous objections of local health officials (Benusic 2014). The Morrow Pacific project demonstrates this type of segmentation. Separate reviews of air quality, water quality certification, water pollution control, and stormwater runoff were undertaken by the state Department of Environmental Quality, as well as a review of a permit application (denied) to the Oregon Department of State Lands to build pilings in the Columbia River. While NEPA directs agencies to consider human health impacts, standard EIA practices generally take a narrow view of health effects and only consider those impacts directly caused by the project. Meanwhile, many scholars contend that EIA is inadequate for addressing the cumulative and synergistic health effects of multiple projects (Fehr et al. 2014; Harris et al. 2009; Morgan 2011).

In the case of Pacific Northwest coal exports, many stakeholders have called on the agencies leading EIA to adopt a regional scope to address the interplay of the multiple coal export proposals. However, for all three projects that have undergone any federal review—the Gateway Pacific project near Bellingham, WA; the Morrow Pacific project in Boardman, OR (on pause as of this writing); and the Millennium Bulk Terminal near Longview, WA—a single-project scope was adopted. A commentator in a Bellingham environmental newspaper responded with sarcastic incredulity to the Army Corps of Engineers' assertion that it considers Gateway Pacific a standalone project not connected to any transportation corridor: "Who knew that the coal was teleported from the subsurface of Montana to [the project site], and again teleported to China after it leaves the terminal? I guess you learn something new every day" (Wells 2013). Ultimately, local non-profits filed a lawsuit accusing the Army Corps of Engineers of narrowing the assessment scope for the purpose of avoiding analysis of known health hazards. Because situations like this are not uncommon, Weston (2010, 364) argues, "decision-making procedures such as land use planning and decision-making tools, such as EIA, are little more than a smokescreen behind which decisions are legitimized."

## The Promise of HIA

Given the extensive health concerns related to coal export and the insufficiencies of EIA, activists have proposed health impact assessment (HIA) as an alternative strategy for evaluating the proposals' effects. HIA is an emerging public health technique that evaluates impacts of policy decisions in a holistic manner, incorporating multiple stakeholder perspectives with the ultimate goal of producing health-supporting recommendations for decision-makers. The stages of HIA are: screening, scoping, assessment, recommendations (policy formulation), dissemination, and evaluation.

HIA is rooted in explicitly articulated values of democracy, equity, sustainable development (considering short- and long-term issues, as well as direct and indirect impacts), and ethical consideration of evidence. This is a sharp contrast to EIA, which is conducted as an ostensibly neutral process whose objectivity would theoretically produce the same results no matter who conducted it. The HIA process, on the other hand, is understood to produce very different conclusions based on the context and stakeholders involved. In many cases, an HIA collects no new primary data, but rather sets an assessment scope that incorporates multiple types of data, including lived experience. In this way, HIA may offer a path through policy obstacles such as the narrow focus on measurement techniques and quantitative (especially monetary) estimates (Mayoux and Chambers 2005), as well as the complexity of documenting social and environmental changes (Morrice and Colagiuri 2013). HIA is also viewed as a tool for bringing health to the table, often building cross-sector relationships through collaboration and consensus rather than relying on discrete analysis. For example, through its early adoption of HIA, the San Francisco Health Department built consultative relationships with other city agencies, such as the San Francisco Planning Department. As a result, the Planning Department began considering gentrification and displacement as health issues when it evaluated development proposals (Corburn and Bhatia 2007).

By reconciling disparate perspectives, HIA has the potential to integrate information that gets segmented by the EIA process. However, effectively using HIA requires technical capacity, political focus, and decision-making power. The procedural flexibility of HIA charges the analyst with defining an assessment scope appropriate to the decision-making context, which is an inherently social or "soft" judgment. Influencing policy with HIA also requires that the practitioner have allies sympathetic to the process in government agencies.

## The Assessment Vacuum

While there is a high level of technical capacity for HIA in the Pacific Northwest, the necessary political power has not been well aligned to utilize this capacity. HIA has been highly desired by the public, yet no agency, academic institution, or community group has stepped forward to lead an HIA. Most HIA practitioners in the region are housed at local government agencies and public health non-profits, neither of which have been successful in getting state support for HIA. This assessment vacuum occurred because the political economy of natural resource decision-making spans a large geographic region involving multiple government jurisdictions, transnational shipping industries, and large resource extraction companies. While these factors may limit the effectiveness of EIA through segmentation, in the case of HIA they became barriers to adoption due to power imbalances among stakeholders.

HIA practitioners in the Pacific Northwest responded to this complex political climate by adopting advocacy-based strategies focused on local impacts rather than forcing a region-wide analysis. For instance, one study evaluated the impacts of rail traffic in Multnomah County (McGrath et al. 2013). Another was a so-called baseline study, led by Washington State University (still underway at the moment of this writing), piloting techniques for assessing specific exposures to air and noise pollution. Yet advocacy for a broader coal HIA continued, becoming a rallying cry for both the anti-coal movement and local leaders who wanted a better understanding of the merits and demerits of the coal proposals. In most cases, people advocating for the coal HIA had never previously conducted an HIA, and many likely had never even read an HIA report. HIA had become something of a totem.

### Valorizing HIA

In Oregon, the Environmental Justice Task Force, the state chapter of Physicians for Social Responsibility, and the Yakama Nation (a confederation of Native American bands and tribes) pressured the governor for an HIA. A long list of local governments, concerned about impacts yet feeling unable to address them on their own, pledged funds to produce an HIA. Small businesses jumped on the bandwagon, such as a bed-and-breakfast in the San Juan Islands that called on its website for neighbors to contribute to a fund for the HIA, listing seven cities and counties that had already pledged funds to the effort. Distrustful of the EIA process, advocates viewed the HIA as a silver bullet that would document all the problems that the EIA would not consider.

From these synergies a hero narrative began to emerge, with the San Juan County, Washington, Health Officer promoting the proposed HIA staff as a "team of the Pacific Northwest's leading public health researchers" (Tucker House Inn 2013) and the Whatcom Community Foundation lauding the fact that Washington State University was "answering the call" for an HIA (Whatcom Community Foundation 2012). The foundation cheered concerned citizens who contributed, offering people hope that they could change the course of a development trend threatening to alter the local landscape and global climate. The Mayor of Seattle promoted a coal HIA in testimony to Congress (Energy and Commerce Committee 2013) and the CEO of the Oregon-based Coalition of Community Health Clinics added a personal note exhorting the governor to "Sieze [sic] the future!" in his letter urging an HIA (Physicians for Social Responsibility 2015).

## Proliferating Assessments

The calls for HIA illustrated the public's belief that institutions (acting through the EIA process) were failing to respond to health concerns raised by coal export proposals, yet the advocacy in its own way exacerbated fragmentations of the policy landscape by focusing on the local. This HIA vacuum spawned a proliferation of assessments (Table 5.1), each with different scopes, geographies, and assessment methods depending on the interests and values of the assessors—or the people who hired them. The kaleidoscope of assessments highlights the myriad ways that health issues can be sliced and some of the downsides of HIA practice in the Pacific Northwest. Looking at one place or issue at a time, as opposed to the cumulative and synergistic impacts of the proposals, fragmented knowledge. Variations in methods also complicated findings that could conceivably be assembled, as piecing together a story from diverse sources requires considerable effort and interpretation.

None of the assessments was a true HIA, but the State of Washington agreed to incorporate a section into the SEPA assessment of the Gateway Pacific Terminal entitled "health impact assessment" (US Army Corps of Engineers, and the State of Washington Department of Ecology 2014). However, community groups and health practitioners are skeptical that this assessment will meet HIA standards (Bhatia et al. 2014) given the fact that the SEPA will be conducted by an environmental consulting firm with limited stakeholder engagement. The firm is also one of fourteen subcontractors associated with the Gateway Pacific Terminal EIA, a status that might compromise the quality of an HIA.

## Reinscribing Harm

The disorientation that results from trying to draw conclusions from the many coal-related assessments likely produces a more realistic, but less definitive, representation of potential impacts than segmented EIA analysis does. But this proliferation of HIA assessments (re)produced two harms. The first is a seemingly insurmountable burden of information generated by each successive study, where mountains of paperwork and conflicting assessments can often distance affected parties from decision-makers (Morrison-Saunders et al. 2014). The coal EIA processes alone are massive time- and resource-intensive endeavors. As an example of the effort

**TABLE 5.1** Diversity of impact assessments of Pacific Northwest coal-shipping, which have proliferated in absence of a comprehensive health impact assessment (HIA)

| Organization | Assessment type | Assessment question | Geographic scale |
|---|---|---|---|
| Western Organization of Resource Councils | Policy analysis | How would the addition of these projects affect the Western US rail network? | Western USA |
| Washington State University "baseline study," linked topic-specific studies (in progress) | Air quality monitoring and modeling | What is the air quality at a few specific sites where coal trains travel by? | A few specific sites |
| | Noise monitoring and modeling | What is the extent and type of noise at a few specific sites where coal trains travel by? | |
| | Spatial analysis | How do the demographic conditions along the export pathway in Washington state compare to the state as a whole? | Washington state, by census tract |
| | Transportation demand modeling | How would the presence of coal trains affect the road traffic network in Washington state? | Washington state |
| Army Corps of Engineers and State of WA Dept. of Ecology Gateway Pacific project EIS (environmental impact study) | NEPA SEPA "HIA" with SEPA analysis | What would be the environmental impact of developing the Gateway Pacific Terminal? How would the development of facilities disrupt existing communities? How would socially vulnerable groups be affected by the projects? | Area surrounding the proposed terminal |
| Army Corps of Engineers, State of WA Dept. of Ecology, and Cowlitz County Millennium Bulk project EIS | NEPA SEPA | What would be the environmental impact of developing the Millennium Bulk Terminal? | |

| Organization | Question | Analysis type | Geographic scope |
|---|---|---|---|
| Missoula City-County Health Department | What is in the dust shed by coal trains? | Laboratory assay | A few specific sites |
| Puget Sound Keeper | How much dust is coming off trains in the Puget Sound area? | Observational study | |
| U. Washington Bohell | What is the air quality at a couple of sites where coal trains travel by? | Air quality monitoring | |
| National Wildlife Federation | What are the cumulative environmental impacts of coal use at every stage of the life cycle? | Life-cycle analysis | Western USA |
| Climate Solutions Seattle | How will the Gateway Pacific project affect property values in Seattle? | Real estate analysis | Seattle metro area |
| City of Seattle | How will coal train travel affect traffic on roadways in Seattle? | Traffic demand modeling | City of Seattle |
| Multnomah County Health Department | How will coal train transportation through the county affect residents' health and how will these impacts affect different racial and economic groups? | Prospective health analysis | Multnomah County, Oregon |
| Puget Sound Regional Council | What would be the impact of coal export projects on the regional economy of the Gateway Pacific terminal? | Economic impact analysis | Puget Sound region (Washington state) |
| National Coal Council | How does the coal industry affect the national economy? | Economic benefit analysis | Entire USA |

involved in just one small piece of a proposal, the Oregon Department of State Lands spent two and a half years reviewing a permit proposal to build a dock for the Morrow Pacific facility. They received 20,000 public comments that took months to process, the deadline for the applicants to respond to questions from the state was extended eight times, and the review included three public review periods. The additional assessments intended to address EIA's shortcomings seemed to increase this volume exponentially. This dilemma can lead to what scholars of technology call the "consent dilemma" (Hanks 2010), where people who stand to be affected by a decision are unable to participate in decisions about their risk due to lack of expertise and resources. Not only are they burdened with the fear of potential harms, but they are also saddled with the responsibility to prove that each of these threats is real in the face of mounting counterevidence produced by more powerful stakeholders.

The second harm produced in this case is somewhat counterintuitive: advocacy for HIA may have threatened HIA as a practice. That is, pushing for HIA *as a technique* to be used in decision-making instead of advocating for the incorporation of HIA *values* (holistic view of health, multiple perspectives, deliberative policy recommendations) into the decision-making process has put HIA at risk of becoming yet another formulaic assessment procedure whose primary beneficiaries are environmental consulting firms. The infiltration of technical consulting firms into HIA practice—as has been proposed by the state of Washington for the Gateway Pacific EIS—replicates patterns seen in EIA, where private interests are overrepresented through this reliance on technical procedures (Chase 1990; Li 2009). Anthropological research suggests that assessments conducted by consultants are inclined to overemphasize positive impacts and minimize harms (Fisher 2008). Furthermore, even very seasoned HIA practitioners may find HIA's values undermined when HIA falls under the control of techno-bureaucracy. This occurred when a preeminent HIA consulting firm in the USA signed a contract to lead an HIA of a massive port expansion project and found their work stifled by the strictures of their contract (Iroz-Elardo 2014).

In short, HIA's trendiness may be creating a situation where interest in HIA is outpacing the development of a professional community of practice that understands how HIAs should be implemented. For example, neither the HIA within the Gateway EIS nor the baseline study project led by Washington State University meets practice standards for HIA (such as Bhatia et al. 2014; Heller et al. 2013), yet both have been called HIAs in the media and by advocates, thereby shifting the meaning of the term.

## Conclusion: Outing Technocratic Science

Debates over how to analyze the health impacts of coal export proposals in the Pacific Northwest show how policy formulation is a potent mix of conflicting interests and values, where the purported neutrality of science is used as a tool to advance policies that support specific interests. Backdoor dealings are an open secret in politics, but how the science gets made is rarely discussed even though it seems to be a part of the policy process that occurs in plain sight. Like the fictional Wizard of Oz, the science of EIA can be cloaked in mystery and ostensibly operates at a distance from everyday realities. Just as the wizard's power depends on his obscurity, the public is kept in the thrall of a science that does not necessarily serve their interests when technical information is accepted as unassailable fact.

While HIA is perceived to provide more comprehensive and community-driven analysis of health impacts, its potential to counter the hegemonic science of EIA is undercut when advocacy for HIA emphasizes the assessment technology is divorced from its core values. Both types of impact assessment can invigorate public debate through introducing new information, but acknowledging values in the public debate may be the key to unmasking power structures that purport to protect health, yet do so by coopting health as yet another metric to be quantified. As an explicitly value-laden science with one of whose values being the multiplicity of perspectives— HIA's practice standards demand that conflicting values (e.g., jobs vs. environment) take center stage instead of being reduced to the simplistic finding "no significant impact" often produced through the alchemy of environmental assessment.

However, the political challenges of applying HIA to coal exports in the Pacific Northwest also demonstrate HIA's vulnerability to appropriation. This suggests that efforts to use HIA to respond to the burgeoning resource extraction industry in the USA will require both political and scientific savvy. Politically speaking, HIA practitioners must be sensitive to power dynamics in the policy arena so that they may effectively "screen" a potential HIA project for the ability to legitimately influence a policy decision. When decision-makers will not use HIA findings, or when the HIA process may be coopted due to power imbalances, HIA should not be pursued. However, given situations like the coal export debate, where there is a strong demand for additional health information, HIA practitioners and public health scientists need to have other tools at the ready to fill the vacuum that can be created. Telling concerned members of the public that an HIA "won't work" is an unsatisfactory response to the fear and distrust engendered by EIA and other bureaucratic procedures that minimize the realities lived by potentially affected parties.

Scientifically speaking, current standards for HIA practice in the USA (Bhatia et al. 2014) can provide a useful map for innovation within these political constraints. HIA practitioners should advocate for high quality science by critiquing traditional assessment practices, evaluating purported HIAs (such as the Gateway Pacific subcontractor's forthcoming report) on the basis of the established HIA practice standards, and proposing new strategies for measuring impacts. Doing all of these things demands that HIA practitioners be fluent in a complement of applied research tools. That is, HIA practitioners themselves need to take a holistic approach to working public health information in community settings. In this way, rather than being employed as a technique, HIA should be viewed as an ideology for conceptualizing health-supporting policy and HIA practitioners should see themselves as partners in advocacy for health equity rather than experts in a particular method. Given the dynamic and enduring impacts of resource extraction, this offers a much-needed complement to well-established scientific and activist traditions.

## Note

1 I am grateful to Jessica Hardin, Dawn Salgado, and Jen Bhalla for their help in developing my ideas for this chapter, as well as to the members of the Society for Applied Anthropology, particularly Kirk Jalbert and David Casagrande, for encouraging my work and providing kind and capable editorial guidance.

## References

Association of American Railroads (AAR). 2012. *Railroads and coal.* Washington, DC: Association of American Railroads.

Association of American Railroads (AAR). 2014. *Rail time indicators: A review of key economic trends shaping demand for rail transportation (June 2014).* Washington, DC: Association of American Railroads.

Benusic, Michael A. 2014. Mandatory health impact assessments are long overdue. *British Columbia Medical Journal* 56, 5:238–239.

Bhatia, Rajiv, Lili Farhang, Jonathan C. Heller, Murray Lee, Marla Orenstein, Maxwell Richardson, and Aaron Wernham. 2014. *Minimum elements and practice standards for health impact assessment.* Oakland, CA: North American HIA Practice Standards Working Group.

Birley, Martin. 2003. Health impact assessment, integration and critical appraisal. *Impact Assessment and Project Appraisal* 21, 4:313–321.

Chase, Athol. 1990. Anthropology and impact assessment: Development pressures and indigenous interests in Australia. *Environmental Impact Assessment Review* 10, 1:11–23.

Clarke, Lee Ben. 1999. *Mission improbable: Using fantasy documents to tame disaster.* Chicago, IL: University of Chicago Press.

Corburn, Jason and Rajiv Bhatia. 2007. Health impact assessment in San Francisco: Incorporating the social determinants of health into environmental planning. *Journal of Environmental Planning and Management* 50, 3:323–341.

de Place, Eric. 2014. *Northwest fossil fuel exports.* Seattle, WA: Sightline Institute.

Energy and Commerce Committee. 2013. U.S. energy abundance: Regulatory, market, and legal barriers to export. *Testimony before the Subcommittee on Energy and Power of the House Energy and Commerce Committee,* June 18. Washington, DC: US House of Representatives. https://energycommerce.house.gov/hearings-and-votes/hearings/us-energy-abundance-regulatory-market-and-legal-barriers-export (accessed March 22, 2016).

Fehr, Rainer, Francesca Viliani, Julia Nowacki, and Marco Martuzzi, eds. 2014. *Health in impact assessments: Opportunities not to be missed.* Copenhagen: WHO Regional Office for Europe.

Fisher, Robert. 2008. Anthropologists and social impact assessment: Negotiating the ethical minefield. *The Asia Pacific Journal of Anthropology* 9, 3:231–242.

Hanks, Craig. 2010. *Technology and values: Essential readings.* Malden, MA: Wiley-Blackwell.

Harris, Patrick J., Elizabeth Harris, Susan Thompson, Ben Harris-Roxas, and Lynn Kemp. 2009. Human health and wellbeing in environmental impact assessment in New South Wales, Australia: Auditing health impacts within environmental assessments of major projects. *Environmental Impact Assessment Review* 29, 5:310–318.

Heller, Jonathan C., Shireen Malekafzali, Lynn C. Todman, and Megan Wier. 2013. *Promoting equity through the practice of health impact assessment.* Oakland, CA: PolicyLink.

Iroz-Elardo, Nicole. 2014. *Participation, information, values, and community interests within health impact assessments.* PhD Dissertation, Urban Studies and Planning, Portland State University.

Learn, Scott, and Marc Friesen. 2012. Map: Possible coal train routes. *The Oregonian*. http://projects.oregonlive.com/coal/map.php (accessed March 22, 2016).

Li, Fabiana. 2009. Documenting accountability: Environmental impact assessment in a Peruvian mining project. *PoLAR: Political and Legal Anthropology Review* 32, 2:218–236.

Malvadkar, Shreekant B., Dennis Smith, and Gilbert V. McGurl. 2004. Supply curves for using Powder River Basin coal to reduce sulfur emissions. *Journal of the Air & Waste Management Association* 54, 6:741–749.

Mandelker, Daniel R. 2010. The National Environmental Policy Act: A review of its experience and problems. *Washington University Journal of Law & Policy* 32:293–312.

Mayoux, Linda, and Robert Chambers. 2005. Reversing the paradigm: Quantification, participatory methods and pro-poor impact assessment. *Journal of International Development* 17, 2:271–298.

McGrath, Moriah McSharry, Elizabeth J. Clapp, Julie E. Maher, Gary Oxman, and Sonia Manhas. 2013. *The effects of coal train movement through Multnomah County, Oregon: A health analysis and recommendations for further action*. Portland, OR: Multnomah County Health Department.

Morgan, Richard K. 2011. Health and impact assessment: Are we seeing closer integration? *Environmental Impact Assessment Review* 31, 4:404–411.

Morrice, Emily, and Ruth Colagiuri. 2013. Coal mining, social injustice and health: A universal conflict of power and priorities. *Health & Place* 19:74–79.

Morrison-Saunders, Angus, Jenny Pope, Jill A.E. Gunn, Alan Bond, and Francois Retief. 2014. Strengthening impact assessment: A call for integration and focus. *Impact Assessment and Project Appraisal* 32, 1:2–8.

Oregon Public Broadcasting. 2013. *Voices of coal*. http://opb-mini-sites.s3.amazonaws.com/coalvoices/index.html (accessed March 22, 2016).

Physicians for Social Responsibility. 2015. *Proposed coal exports threaten Oregon and the northwest*. www.psr.org/chapters/oregon/environmental-health-/proposed-coal-exports.html (accessed March 22, 2016).

Profita, Cassandra. 2013. Army Corps shrinks endangered species review for Columbia River coal export project. *Earthfix*, September 5. www.opb.org/news/article/corps-shrinks-endangered-species-review-for-morrow/ (accessed March 22, 2016).

Profita, Cassandra. 2015. The Northwest struggles with coal-generated power from out of state. *Earthfix*, April 2. http://earthfix.info/news/article/the-northwest-struggles-with-coal-generated-power-from-out-of-state/ (accessed March 22, 2016).

Sangaramoorthy, Thurka, and Adia Benton. 2012. Enumeration, identity, and health. *Medical Anthropology* 31, 4:287–291.

Shearer, Christine, Nicole Ghio, Lauri Myllyvirta, and Ted Nace. 2015. *Boom and bust: Tracking the global coal plant pipeline*. San Francisco, CA: CoalSwarm and the Sierra Club. www.criticalcollective.org/?publication=boom-and-bust (accessed March 22, 2016).

Tucker House Inn. 2013. *Coal battle continues: Help needed for strategic health impact assessment*. www.tuckerhouse.com/blog/2013/05/coal-battle-continues-help-needed-for-strategic-health-impact-assessment/ (accessed March 22, 2016).

US Army Corps of Engineers, and the State of Washington Department of Ecology. 2014. *Gateway Pacific Terminal EIS, FAQ on scope of EIS studies for Gateway Pacific Terminal/Custer Spur (GPT)*, February 13 version. www.eisgatewaypacificwa.gov/sites/default/files/content/files/GPT-%20FAQ%20-7-30-13%20Final_0_1.pdf#overlay-context=resources/project-library (accessed March 22, 2016).

Wells, James. 2013. Gateway Pacific Terminal: Agencies decide to look at actual reality. *Whatcom Watch Online* 22, 9. www.whatcomwatch.org/php/WW_open.php?id=1614 (accessed January 5, 2017).

Weston, Joe. 2010. EIA theories—all Chinese whispers and no critical theory. *Journal of Environmental Assessment Policy and Management* 12, 4:357–374.

Whatcom Community Foundation. 2012. *Coal export health impact study fund.* www.what comcf.org/www/pdf/CoalExportHealthImpactStudyFundFinal.pdf (accessed March 22, 2016).

Wilkins, Hugh. 2003. The need for subjectivity in EIA: Discourse as a tool for sustainable development. *Environmental Impact Assessment Review* 23, 4:401–414.

Woodcock, James, Phil Edwards, Cathryn Tonne, Ben G. Armstrong, Olu Ashiru, David Banister, Sean Beevers, Zaid Chalabi, Zohir Chowdhury, Aaron Cohen, Oscar H. Franco, Andy Haines, Robin Hickman, Graeme Lindsay, Ishaan Mittal, Dinesh Mohan, Geetam Tiwari, Alistair Woodward, and Ian Roberts. 2009. Public health benefits of strategies to reduce greenhouse-gas emissions: Urban land transport. *The Lancet* 374, 9705:1930–1943.

# 6

# CONTINGENT LEGAL FUTURES

## Does the Ability to Exercise Aboriginal Rights and Title Turn on the Price of Gold?

*Andie Diane Palmer*[1]

### *Tsilhqot'in v. BC:*[2] A Landmark Court Decision

The year 2014 marked a banner year for Aboriginal rights in Canada, and for the Tsilhqot'in First Nations of what is now British Columbia (BC) in particular. For the first time in its history, the Supreme Court of Canada made a finding of Aboriginal title, recognizing the collective right of the Tsilhqot'in to the exclusive use and occupation of nearly 1,800 km² of land within their wider traditional hunting and gathering territory, including "the right to choose to what uses land can be put, subject to the ultimate limit that those uses cannot destroy the ability of the land to sustain future generations of aboriginal peoples,"[3] and the right to benefit from the land. Those seeking to use Aboriginal title lands must now obtain the consent of the titleholders prior to doing so. This vesting of control has opened the door for a fundamental shift in the power to shape resource development agreements between First Nations, the federal and provincial governments, and industry. Yet, ongoing resource development pressures faced by the Tsilhqot'in and by neighboring Secwepemc First Nations, particularly with respect to a vast gold-copper mine project proposed for their hunting and fishing territories immediately outside of the Aboriginal title area, are matters of continued concern to members of these First Nations and affect their potential exercise of Aboriginal rights and title.

While the finding of Aboriginal title would at first seem to protect Tsilhqot'in interests in the land, and potentially the interests of other First Nations now pressing to have their own title claims recognized, such title has limitations: where the government finds an overriding legislative objective, certain developments on the land may proceed without titleholders' consent. The legal scholar Kent McNeil has argued that the Court has prepared the way for giving priority to private interests over those of First Nations by way of an earlier decision, *Delgamuukw v. BC* (McNeil 2004), which laid out Aboriginal title in principle and set the conditions for the exercise of title as finally brought to ground in *Tsilhqot'in*. In the *Delgamuukw* decision, then-Chief Justice Lamer wrote that:

> The development of agriculture, forestry, mining, and hydroelectric power, the general economic development of the interior of British Columbia, protection of the environment or endangered species, the building of infrastructure and the settlement of foreign populations to support those aims … in principle, can justify the infringement of [A]boriginal title. Whether a particular measure or government act can be explained by reference to one of those objectives, however, is ultimately a question of fact that will have to be examined on a case-by-case basis.
>
> *(at para. 165, original emphasis removed)*

I will therefore consider whether the meaningful exercise of Aboriginal title is, from the very outset of the court decision, effectively ruled out in some circumstances as ever-shifting prices for such commodities as gold, timber, and oil could have considerable influence on what is seen as a positive "general economic development" by governmental decision-makers. Gold prices, which soared to US $1,899.70 per ounce in 2011, create economic circumstances, however temporary, that could tip the balance toward legally permissible infringement of Aboriginal rights and title by mining concerns in BC. The *Tsilhqot'in* decision created no absolute bar to infringement, despite partial safeguards "consistent with the Crown's fiduciary duty towards Aboriginal people";[4] the balancing of the needs of "a broader social, political and economic community"[5] achieved by legislative objective remains open to interpretation. As I will argue below, the situation has been further destabilized by the removal of some environmental protections and the modification of objectives for environmental review boards through federal legislation enacted in 2010 and 2012. Less-than-stringent provincial permitting processes for mining operations, as brought to the public's attention following a catastrophic breach of a mine tailings pond in Secwepemc territory at Mount Polley in 2014, have not been improved in spite of the findings of an independent investigation commissioned by the BC government. This chapter provides a first look at the practical unfolding of a legal precedent and changing regulatory frameworks *in situ*, and should provide early notice of implications for those facing similar extractive development pressures elsewhere in Canada, as well as in the transnational zones where the impacts of resource extraction cross into American territory via key watersheds.

The fundamental expression of the local First Nations' interests outside of a juridical framework may be found to counterbalance legislative actions that could otherwise privilege economic interests of corporations over the interests of First Nations and settler citizens. Local First Nations governments and individuals have marshalled their own expertise, political skill, and knowledge of their history to carve out a space in which to reconcile their interests with those of settler society, but on their own terms, and indeed have been doing so for over 200 years. Current positions include those articulated by First Nations Women Advocating Responsible Mining (FNWARM), a coalition with a strong base in Secwepemc and Tsilhqot'in political leadership. I also draw on the aspirations of a key figure, Chief Roger William, who, together with his Tsilhqot'in Nation of Xeni Gwet'in, fought for decades to achieve recognition of rights to land in court, culminating in the 2014 *Tsilhqot'in* decision. His words may provide us with a better understanding of fundamental principles that guide a continued life on the land, in a way that is respectful of First Nations' interests, as affirmed in the courts and constitution, and as derived from pre-existing, Indigenous legal systems.

## Historical Background: Struggles Over Resources from the 1850s to 2000

As the California gold rush of 1849–1855 played out, prospectors and the merchants who made a living "mining the miners," moved north to the next big strikes near the mouth of the Fraser River. By 1861, 27,000 of these newcomers had traveled farther upriver or crossed over land to British Columbia's interior plateau, drawn by the Cariboo Gold Rush to the home territories of the Tsilhqot'in and Secwepemc First Nations (Figure 6.1). The Tsilhqot'in were able to forcibly block a surveying party's planned road across their territory to the gold fields with some loss of life, but resistance along the more accessible river and land routes in Secwepemc territory was hampered in part by the effects of a smallpox epidemic, which accompanied the miners into these territories and resulted in the deaths of an estimated 40 to 60% of the Indigenous inhabitants in 1862–3 (Boyd 1994; Palmer 2005). In the ensuing land rush, Secwepemc traditional territories along the Fraser River were largely taken up by the staked claims of settlers, and on both sides of the Fraser the high plateau grasslands were assumed by the Crown, and licensed to cattle ranching operations. This stampede for resources took place on lands where no treaties had been brokered between the colonial government and the first inhabitants,[6] and has led to an ongoing contestation of these First Nations' rights to fish, trap, hunt, and gather and of their practices of self-governance within their traditional territories.

The Xeni Gwet'in experienced further incursions into their territory in the 1980s, when the province granted licenses to logging companies to clear-cut two timber blocks, without consultation. Wild fish and game in the area are integral to Tsilhqot'in livelihood, and the potential loss of forest in their accustomed areas was of grave concern. Court actions initiated by Xeni Gwet'in against the logging companies and the Crown were subsequently combined and amended to include a claim to advance Aboriginal title on behalf of the Tsilhqot'in. Led by then-chief Marilyn Baptiste, the Xeni Gwet'in staged a bridge blockade in 1992, barring improvements that would allow access to logging trucks. They ultimately secured an injunction and a promise from the BC premier that the area would not be logged without their consent.

The Xeni Gwet'in government also made their intentions regarding the stewardship of the area and its resources known to the wider public through their 1989 issuance of a written *Declaration* in English and Tsilhqot'in (Dinwoodie 2002, 86–87; Glavin and The People of the Nemiah Valley 1992). An accompanying map, formulated under the direction of then-chief Annie Williams, set out the boundaries

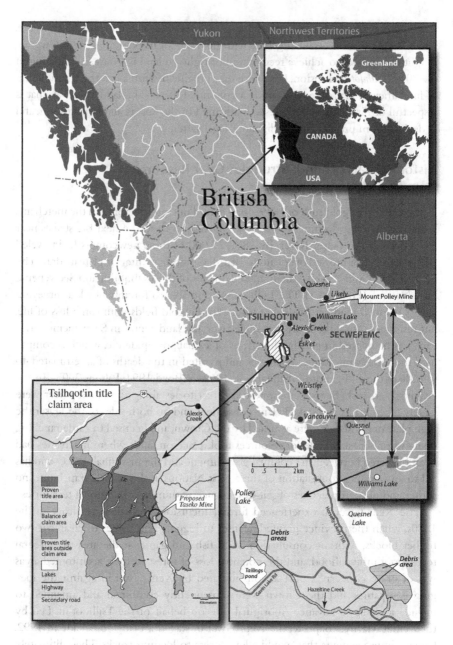

**FIGURE 6.1** Map of British Columbia with traditional territories of the Tsilhqot'in and Secwepemc First Nations indicated. Aboriginal title to lands in Tsilhqot'in territory were recently recognized by the Canadian Supreme Court, as shown in the inset, but Tsilhqot'in and Secwepemc territories would nonetheless be impacted by Taseko's proposed mine. Environmental contamination from the Mount Polley Mine tailings spill disaster in Secwepemc territory exemplifies the threat that mining poses to Indigenous uses of land. Map by Donna Gayer, Artasaverb.

of a "Nemiah Aboriginal Wilderness Preserve." The preserve is designed in part to exclude commercial logging, mining, and the damming of local lakes and rivers, while permitting non-Aboriginal people to use the land for hunting, hiking, and camping, subject to Tsilhqot'in-issued permits. While not formally recognized by the provincial or federal government, the courts would later note that the *Declaration* and map provided a clear notice of the delineation of territory and intention to regulate activities within its boundaries by a self-governing First Nation.

At the same time that the Xeni Gwet'in were taking action against clear-cutting in the early 1990s, extensive test-drilling of a gold and copper deposit in their territory was being carried out under a provincial permit issued to the parent company of Taseko Mines, Ltd. (hereafter, Taseko) in the vicinity of a highly prized alpine trout-fishing lake and spiritual site known as Fish Lake, or Teztan Biny. Whether Taseko will ultimately win approvals to mine in the area has yet to be determined; the shifting regulations, legislation, and jurisprudence with respect to this project are the subject of the next section.

## Taseko's Gold-Copper Mine Proposal and the Process of Environmental Assessment

Taseko's plans for a gold-copper mine include an open pit 525 meters deep and 1,600 meters wide, and a tailings pond sited just 500 meters from Teztan Biny, on lands where the Xeni Gwet'in have proven Aboriginal rights to hunt, fish, and trap, but outside of the area of recognized Aboriginal title. Taseko's plans include roadwork, and the clearing of a forest reserve for a right-of-way for a 125 km electric power transmission corridor stretching from the mine across the Fraser River into adjacent Secwepemc territory (Figure 6.2). The transmission corridor would cut through or encroach upon key Secwepemc hunting areas, wildlife corridors, an important salmon dip-netting site on the Fraser's east bank, which has been in continuous use since time immemorial, and archaeological sites including pithouses and graves.

On these lands, where there is a prima *facie case* for Aboriginal title, Secwepemc and Tsilhqot'in should reasonably expect the Crown to uphold its honor through meaningful consultation and accommodation with respect to their concerns, as per the *Haida* decision regarding the Crown's duty to consult.[7] The permitting and approvals process for mines in British Columbia is not yet fully coordinated to integrate consultation and review by the provincial and the federal governments; separate federal and provincial approvals are required, and the honor of the Crown is at stake in consultation at both levels. The province granted permits to Taseko without, in my view, adequate provision for consultation. The Tsilhqot'in National Government has gone so far as to call the provincially-issued permits a "rubber stamp,"[8] and a Northwest Institute for Bioregional Research Report commissioned by West Coast Environmental Law found that "some adverse effects found by the Federal Review Panel were not evaluated by the BC EAO" [British Columbia's Environmental Assessment Office] (Haddock 2011, 4).

**FIGURE 6.2**  View west across the Fraser River, above a key Secwepemc salmon dip-netting site in the proposed path of transmission lines for Taseko Mines' proposed New Prosperity gold–copper mine. Photograph by Andie Palmer, August 19, 2013.

Taseko has proposed two consecutive plans for resource extraction, gaining approval for each at the provincial level subject to a number of conditions, but achieving no success at the federal level. For each proposal, an independent three-member federal review panel appointed by the Canadian Environmental Assessment Agency (CEAA) then held a month of public hearings in the City of Williams Lake, in smaller towns in the Cariboo-Chilcotin region, and on the main reserves of directly affected Tsilhqot'in and Secwepemc communities. First Nations prepared formal written submissions and members gave testimony in opposition to the proposed mine, as did volunteer and contracted subject specialists and legal representatives. The federal panels heard near unanimity in opposition to the proposed project at the reserve hearings.

The 2010 CEAA assessment found significant adverse environmental effects to fisheries and waterways from the proposed mine could be anticipated, as well as impacts to First Nations' interests. The federal Minister of the Environment, for whom the CEAA report is advisory as opposed to binding, subsequently rejected Taseko's proposal. Taseko submitted a modified plan in 2011. A second public review, with similar stresses on the First Nations communities, was held in 2013. In February 2014, the CEAA concluded that the proposed New Prosperity mine was likely to cause:

significant adverse effects on water quality and fish and fish habitat; significant adverse effects on the current use of lands and resources for traditional
purposes by [Tsilhqot'in and Secwepemc] … on their cultural heritage and
on their archeological and historical resources; significant adverse effects on
wetland and riparian … ecosystems; and significant adverse cumulative effects
on the regional grizzly and moose populations, unless necessary mitigation
measures are effectively implemented.

*(CEAA 2014)*

Both review panels heard testimony that the environmental impact statements submitted by Taseko were remarkably deficient in their accounting for Aboriginal uses
of the land and the fishery, and the cultural heritage values of the area. The federal
Minister of the Environment rejected both plans on the basis of the review. Taseko
nonetheless received an invitation from the federal government to revise their proposal and submit a third plan.

As BC Supreme Court Justice Brauer remarked in a related oral judgment
ordering an injunction against Taseko's continued test drilling for the project:

The bands of the Tsilhqot'in Nation vigorously opposed the original
Prosperity Project, and put a great deal of blood, sweat and tears into edu-
cating the Federal Review Panel about their concerns, and how the project
would impact them. This was an exhausting exercise.[9]

The uncertainty continues, as there is presently no bar on the number of times a
company can revise and submit proposals for such projects.

If Taseko submits a third proposal to the CEAA for review, it will be evaluated
according to a new set of environmental standards. Extensive changes to federal environmental legislation were made in 2010 and 2012 through two omnibus bills (the
*Jobs and Economic Growth Act* and the *Jobs, Growth and Long-Term Prosperity Act*), which
were swiftly passed by the majority Conservative government under then-Prime
Minister Steven Harper. The new *Canadian Environmental Assessment Act*, the *Fisheries
Act*, and the *Navigation Protection Act* (formerly the *Navigable Waters Protection Act*) have
weakened longstanding federal environmental protections for fish habitat and water
quality. Under these new regulations, only proposed projects on a few key waterways trigger full environmental risk assessments; the federal government's approach
has become, in large part, to simply avoid regulatory assessment on the majority of
projects. By way of example, where the *Navigable Waters Protection Act* once applied to
all of the country's waterways deemed to be of a depth navigable by a commercial
freight canoe, less than one percent of the rivers in the country are subject to the new
version of the *Act*. Even the upper reaches of the Fraser, the source of the salmon
fishery for Tsilhqot'in and Secwepemc People, are not protected under the new Act.
Regulatory changes may make the radical alterations to the waterways and fisheries
as contemplated by Taseko Mines permissible under legislation.

Under the new regulatory framework, a CEAA review panel is instructed to take into account the economic benefits of development projects in addition to considering environmental and cultural impacts. These changes affect the way that the Prosperity gold-copper mine proposal could be assessed should Taseko decide to put forward a third plan for review. Taseko has made projections regarding the project's potential economic impact, reporting that "the company has spent $140 million trying to develop" the mine, which Taseko estimates to be worth $1.5 billion dollars (Bennett 2014). If persuaded in the future that Taseko's gold-copper mine project could substantially contribute to the economic development of BC, federal reviewers could look more favorably on the project. The monetization of resources as drivers of economic development means that an absolute valuation of Aboriginal title lands as sacrosanct cannot be relied upon.

The possible relief for local First Nations opposed to the development of the mine comes with the price of gold falling below levels at which it is profitable to run a mine. As the price per ounce sank to its then-lowest level in five years, at US $1,085 in July, 2015, James Sutton of JP Morgan Chase & Co. opined that, "the industry, on average, needs about $1,200 an ounce to break even when all costs are considered," (Riseborough and Biesheuvel 2015; also widely quoted in the national press). Each mine has a different mix of operating costs and opportunities, however. As of this writing, on January 22, 2016, the price of gold stands at US $1095.65 per ounce.

It is a costly proposition to move and treat an extraordinary amount of rock and water to extract the minerals given the low-percentage assays associated with Taseko's Prosperity gold-copper porphyry deposit. While the costs of bringing gold from the ground to market vary widely, the mine could nonetheless be made highly profitable if the real costs of lost enjoyment of the land were largely borne by others; in this case, the First Nations who would be deprived of the use of their accustomed fishing and hunting areas by the development of the mine. Recourse to the law has no certain outcome, as the courts currently view mining interests' attachment to land as merely temporary, and not as attachments that would result in alienation of the land from its owners. The expectation of land restoration, even if many decades in the future, is written into mining proposals and commented on in mining application approvals. Yet, during a project's span of resource extraction and potential restoration over 20 to 30 years and sometimes more, First Nations are deprived to some extent of the enjoyment of the land for which they hold use rights. Their costs can be very high, as intergenerational transfer of knowledge about a given area of land is fundamental to cultural integrity. Co-optation of the area for resource extraction can interrupt specific practices associated with land use. The harm that First Nations face is to their continuation of a way of life, and a loss of some practices that are incommensurate with potential profits from the mining of gold. Anthropologist Tania Li has summed up the difficulty of considering such differential costs to communities in the path of resource extractive industries:

Harm is sometimes recognized as a sacrifice, a price that some are asked to pay so that others may prosper. More often though the sacrificial aspect is disavowed by means of the argument, or the implicit assumption, that the people who are harmed now will benefit later through mechanisms that aren't specified and seldom tracked.

*(Li 2013, 702)*

Permanent and irreparable harm caused by mining to traditional hunting, trapping, and fishing lifeways, and the intergenerational transfer of spiritual and practical knowledge of those lifeways, could result in land use practices that benefit neither the current nor succeeding generations of Tsilhqot'in and Secwepemc.

Taseko has yet to submit a third proposal, and is currently pursuing alternative or additional strategies. Taseko initiated legal proceedings against the Canadian Minister of the Environment and an environmental organization regarding the 2014 decision rejecting Taseko's application for a federal permit to mine, arguing that the project, once permitted by the provincial authorities, cannot be rejected solely on environmental grounds. The case is currently before the courts.

## After *Tsilhqot'in:* Dasiqox Tribal Park

Tsilhqot'in leaders have proactively sought to reduce the threats to their livelihood, and to further improve institutional land management arrangements while establishing inclusive relationships with settler communities, on Tsilhqot'in terms. Following on their development of the Nemiah preserve in 1989, land was set aside in 2015 to establish Dasiqox Tribal Park. The Park is also referred to as Nexwagwezʔan, meaning "it is there for us," in the Tsilhqot'in language (Friends of the Nemiah Valley n.d.). Chief Russell Myers-Ross, of the Yuniset'in (Stone) Tsilhqot'in has described three objectives guiding the Park's creation: "ecosystem stewardship; economy for a sustainable livelihood; and then a focus on cultural revitalization" (Canadian Broadcasting Corporation 2015). In public and press discussions of the Park by the leadership of the constituent Tsilhqot'in First Nations, there has been an emphasis on consultation in the formulation of a plan for use, particularly with local non-Tsilhqot'in people, some of whose families are recognized as having relationships with Tsilhqot'in that have lasted as long as four generations. Existing permits issued by the provincial government for guiding, trapping, and tourism operations prior to the Supreme Court title decision have been honored for at least one year by the First Nation on their Aboriginal title lands, as they continue to consider ways of respectfully managing relations with non-Tsilhqot'in people in their territory for the future.

## ʔEsggidam: *"jurisdiction, language, culture, laws, respect, and honour"*

ʔEsggidam, glossed simply as "ancestors," refers to those who lived from the earliest times of the Tsilhqot'in people through to the time of the current leaders' great-grandparents.[10] ʔEsggidam include those who encountered the first Europeans in the area. It would seem that the ancestors are also marked as ʔesggidam by their ways of *being* on the land, and by their ability to exercise their sovereignty and autonomy, including through acts of hospitality toward visitors, and by their ways of being accountable to themselves rather than observing an external source of governance. In a recent conference address, Chief William reflected on the significance of the term:

> I always, always think about this word, ʔesggidam. And this, this word to Tsilhqot'in, ʔesggidam, is very important to us. ʔesggidam was an individual Tsilhqot'in person, at 1862, prior to smallpox, an individual who had jurisdiction, language, culture, laws, respect and honour. When this person took you in their home, it was like your home … And since, I always think of that Tsilhqot'in war of 1864, and then, then later in the 1800s, where reservations, reserves, residential school, this ʔesggidam has been impacted.
>
> *(William 2005)*

Chief William stressed the impact on ʔesggidam of Canadian incursions, but in his turn of phrase here and elsewhere in his speech, is an indication that these important qualities of the ancestors as ʔesggidam, as self-governing, might yet be achieved by those now living:

> We always say, in the Tsilhqot'in, we're never concerned about what the government is doing—we are concerned about us. We're concerned about me, because ʔesggidam is being impacted. Title is with me. Title is with my community. Title is with my nation. That is first and foremost, important, because if we can't do that, if we can't say that, this is where the government has control.
>
> *(William 2005)*

Thus, the conception of ʔesggidam may be seen as a component of Tsilhqot'in traditional law, and as aspirational for future relations governing the land and its use by all in Tsilhqot'in territory. In an interview with *Vancouver Sun* reporter Tracy Sherlock (2015), Chief William stated, "A lot of us have got to the point where we don't respect other people or the land, and we need to fix that, to get back to ʔesggidam, to get back to being that person."

Chief Roger William offers insights about what all of this is for: the struggle against the siting of a gold-copper mine is not only a struggle against the loss of use of cherished fishing, hunting, and berrying grounds, it is also the loss of potential to share those lands with the next generations and the loss of the ability to extend to others the hospitality associated with the fruits of those harvests. Chief William is linking his way of being in the world with the way the ancestors lived, as beings exercising their autonomy, with the capacity to help others, to extend hospitality, from one's own position of strength, or, to turn away and be left alone. What is therefore so deeply troubling about the current efforts to build the New Prosperity gold mine on Tsilhqot'in and Secwepemc territories is that the lack of consultation with First Nations is not merely an abrogation of the Crown's "duty to consult" but also of a fundamental duty to acknowledge, to listen, to count the needs and indeed the aspirations of Secwepemc and Tsilhqot'in Peoples as those who will continue to dwell on what is left of the land, no matter what price the gold underneath it will fetch.

The Tsilhqot'in government has exercised a sense of ʔesggidam in drawing up a 19-page draft document, in English and Tsilhqot'in, outlining the terms under which they might consider mining opportunities in parts of their territory, including exploration permits and shared benefit agreements. Former Xeni Gwet'in Chief Marilyn Baptiste, a member of FNWARM as well as a 2015 recipient of the Goldman Environmental Prize, has stated that Xeni Gwet'in are not opposed to mining *per se*, but rather to Taseko and its tactics. Taseko has been criticized for its defamation lawsuit against an environmental group critical of its mining plan.[11] Furthermore, Taseko has become known for disrespectful acts and disparaging remarks with regard to First Nations ceremonial practices, inadequate reporting of First Nations' interest in land in the Prosperity EIS, as well as for forwarding two proposals that would destroy or render unrecognizable the lake called Teztan Biny. Repeated public statements by Baptiste, and by the FNWARM Chair, Chief Bev Sellars of the Xatsull First Nation (the Secwepemc of Soda Creek), encouraging responsible mining practices developed in full consultation with resident First Nations, raise the possibility of new gold mining ventures being welcomed into the territories of Tsilhqot'in and Secwepemc in the coming years—with the free, prior, and informed consent of those First Nations.

## Recommendations for Responsible Mining: The Mount Polley Disaster

On August 4, 2014, a catastrophic breach of a tailings pond occurred at the Mount Polley open pit copper-gold mine facility near Likely, BC. The spill most directly affected the Secwepemc territories of the T'exelc First Nation (Williams Lake Indian Band) and Xat'sull First Nation (the constituency of FNWARM member Chief Sellars). The spill has been documented by a government-commissioned Independent Expert Engineering Investigation and Review Panel (IEEIRP 2015) and an expert group hired by Imperial Metals' Mt. Polley Mining Corporation (Mount Polley Mining Corporation 2015). According to their reports, the collapse sent approximately 25 million cubic meters of tailings and interstitial water coursing downstream, thoroughly scouring the bed of Hazeltine Creek, as well as sending 18.6 million cubic meters of tailings and scours to the western arm of Quesnel Lake and the adjoining Edney Creek. Metals released into the waters via the mine tailings include copper, as copper sulfide, and selenium. An at-risk subspecies of coho salmon, shore-spawning kokanee, and rainbow trout that would typically migrate up Hazeltine Creek to Mt. Polley Lake were all affected, along with the Aboriginal and sports fishers who rely on them for harvest. Cleanup and restoration efforts are underway and are expected to take five years. Despite the continued discharge of tailings water into Quesnel Lake in 2016, and concerns over the health of anadromous fish in the lake, the mine has been authorized by the province to partially restart their operation in just the second year of cleanup.

The mining reforms recommended by the IEEIRP in the wake of the disaster include: monitoring and review of tailings ponds by a truly independent board; and adoption of best available practices for all new tailings generated, including the production and placement of filtered, or "dry stack" tailings, despite increased costs over the use of tailings ponds (IEEIRP 2015, 123). Both the proposed New Prosperity tailings pond and the failed tailings containment systems at the Mt. Polley facility are designed with earthen dam structures to hold back the tailings, meet the same standard of reliability, and are subject to the same level of oversight and reporting. A cumulative effects analysis prepared by the BC First Nations Energy and Mining Council, based in part on the IEEIRP report, concludes that, "without significant changes to the current mining practices, in British Columbia alone we can expect two tailings dam failures every ten years" (IEEIRP 2015, 3).

The provincial government has not, however, withdrawn the permit it has awarded to Taseko Mines to develop a third set of plans for a gold mine in the Cariboo. Instead, in January 2015, the BC Minister of the Environment granted Taseko Mines a five-year extension of their Environmental Assessment Certificate for development of the Prosperity gold-copper project. Though greater oversight with respect to operating mines is now recognized by the BC government as necessary, no curbs on exploration permits issued to mining companies have been entertained.

## The Source of Aboriginal Title

As no orders for the institution of best practices such as dry stack tailings in the place of tailings ponds have been brought into effect by the BC government, and salmon- and trout-bearing waterways continue to be polluted with mine waste in the Fraser watershed in 2016, the only clear relief, however temporary, for First Nations and other communities dependent on healthy water and fish would seem to come with the falling price of gold. If the price of gold rebounds within the next few years, however, the stage is set for continued and wearying campaigns against unwanted, and potentially unstable, mining operations in BC.

Once again, we are reminded that Aboriginal rights and title may be trumped by prevailing economic interests, as perceived by the government of the day. The system of values that spawned this, in my view, unjust weighting of interests in Aboriginal title, may be found in the additional instructions from then-Chief Justice Lamer:

> First, from a theoretical standpoint, [A]boriginal title arises out of prior occupation of the land by [A]boriginal peoples and out of the relationship between the common law and pre-existing systems of [A]boriginal law. Aboriginal title is a burden on the Crown's underlying title. The Crown, however, did

not gain this title until it asserted sovereignty and it makes no sense to speak of a burden on the underlying title before that title existed. Aboriginal title crystallized at the time sovereignty was asserted.

(*Preamble to* Delgamuukw v. BC)

Aboriginal title, as Lamer's discussion of title above would confirm, is a judge-made construct, forged not from the need to reconcile Peoples with each other, but in the case at hand, from people ostensibly but imperfectly relying on English Common Law, not taking into account other systems of law, such as those of the Tsilhqot'in and Secwepemc at the time of contact, and having to reconcile their own system to account for these, post hoc. "Aboriginal title" as a theory of land tenure, is constrained by the precedents of Common Law in an attempt to reconcile pre-existing legal systems while still holding economic development to the benefit of corporations as a greater societal good than the sovereign exercise of a relationship with the land by Canada's First Nations. In this way, the nature of Aboriginal title does, indeed, turn on the price of gold; when gold prices rise sufficiently, the destruction of ways of life on the land can legally follow. In a system to which we might aspire, however, such as the system in which First Nations' interests are held to be fundamentally important, and environmental degradation is not held to a floating and often arbitrary value of a commodity, we might find the principle of ʔesggidam, and the associated principles of the leaders of FNWARM, afford us a way to responsibly and equitably share in the benefits and the costs of managing the land.

## Notes

1 The author thanks David Dinwoodie, Carly Dokis, Bruce Barry, Patu and Erena Hohepa, Makere Stewart-Harawira, and as ever, Carl Urion for thoughtful suggestions. Kirk Jalbert and David Casagrande provided helpful edits and kind encouragement to bring this work to its final form. I owe deep thanks to Esk'etemc First Nation, the late Angela George and her extended family, Betty Belanger and Dorothy Johnson, Chief Frank Robbins and Councillors, Shirley Robbins, and all who lent their support and expertise through testimony during the CEAA hearings at Esk'et in 2010 and 2014, including Chief Roger William and Chief Marilyn Baptiste and Councillors and community members of Xeni Gwet'in.

2 *Tsilhqot'in Nation v. British Columbia,* 2014 SCC 44, [2014] 2 S.C.R. 256 [*Tsilhqot'in*].

3 *Delgamuukw v. British Columbia,* [1997] 3 S.C.R. 101, at para. 166 (emphasis in original) [*Delgamuukw*]; see *Tsilhqot'in, ibid.* at para. 67 for McLachlin's rephrasing.

4 *Tsilhqot'in, supra* note 2 at para. 84.

5 *Delgamuukw, supra* note 3 at para. 161, citing *R. v. Gladstone,* [1996] 2 S.C.R. 723 at para. 73.

6 Historic treaties signed between the Crown and First Nations in what was to become British Columbia included the Douglas Treaties of Vancouver Island in the 1850s (Tennant 1990). No further treaties were entered into following the opening of the province to settlement, with the exception of the 1899 adhesion to Treaty 8 (Ray 1999).

7 *Haida Nation v. British Columbia (Minister of Forests),* [2004] 3 S.C.R. 511, 2004 SCC 73, at paras. 27 and 47 [*Haida*].

8 Tsilhqot'in National Government. 2010. Press Release to the Vancouver Media Co-op, January 18. http://vancouver.mediacoop.ca/newsrelease/2478 (accessed February 24, 2017).

9 *Taseko Mines Limited v. Phillips,* 2011 BCSC 1675 at para. 16.

10 The term ʔesggidam appears in the testimony of a number of Tsilhqot'in lay witnesses giving evidence in the BC Supreme Court, and as subsequently used by Justice Vickers in his *Opinion, Tsilhqot'in Nation v. British Columbia*, 2007 BCSC 1700 at para. 22.
11 Justice Funt recently dismissed Taseko's defamation case against the Western Canada Wilderness Committee (WCWC), awarding costs to the defendant, and stating that Taseko's seeking of punitive damages "was an economic threat [to the WCWC]. In the context of a defamation action, seeking punitive damages may serve to silence critics" (*Taseko Mines Limited v. Western Canada Wilderness Committee*, 2016 BCSC 109 at para. 200).

# References

Bennett, Nelson. 2014. Taseko seeks damages over Prosperity decision. *Business Vancouver*, October 13. www.biv.com/article/2014/10/taseko-seeks-damages-over-prosperity-decision/ (accessed December 15, 2016).

Boyd, Robert. 1994. Smallpox in the Pacific Northwest: The first epidemics. *BC Studies* 101:5–40.

Canadian Broadcasting Corporation. 2015. *Tsilhqot'in celebrate BC's first ever tribal park*. Interview of Chief Russell Myers-Ross, July 21. www.cbc.ca/news/canada/kamloops/tsilhqot-in-celebrate-bc-s-first-ever-tribal-park-1.3161818 (accessed March 11, 2016).

Canadian Environmental Assessment Agency (CEAA). 2014. *New prosperity gold-copper mine project*. Reference number: 63928. www.ceaa-acee.gc.ca/050/details-eng.cfm?evaluation=63928 (accessed March 11, 2016).

Dinwoodie, David. 2002. *Reserve memories: The power of the past in a Chilcotin community*. Lincoln: University of Nebraska Press.

Friends of the Nemiah Valley. n.d. *Dasiqox Tribal Park: Nexwagwez?an*. www.dasiqox.org (accessed March 11, 2016).

Glavin, Terry, and The People of the Nemiah Valley. 1992. *Nemiah: The unconquered country*. Vancouver: New Star Press.

Haddock, Mark. 2011. *Comparison of the British Columbia and federal environmental assessments for the Prosperity mine*. Northwest Institute for Bioregional Research. http://northwestinstitute.ca/images/uploads/NWI_EAreport_July2011.pdf (accessed February 27, 2017).

Independent Expert Engineering Investigation and Review Panel (IEEIRP). 2015. *Report on Mount Polley tailings storage facility breach*. Province of British Columbia, Victoria, BC. www.mountpolleyreviewpanel.ca/final-report (accessed December 15, 2016).

Li, Tania Murray. 2013. Review of *Economies of abandonment: Social belonging and endurance in late liberalism*, by Elizabeth A. Povinelli. *American Anthropologist* 115, 4:702.

McNeil, Kent. 2004. The vulnerability of indigenous land rights in Australia and Canada. *Osgoode Hall Law Journal* 42, 2:271–301.

Mount Polley Mining Corporation. 2015. *Mount Polley mining corporation post event environmental impact assessment report—key findings report*. Submitted June 5, 2015. Vancouver: Golder and Associates. www.imperialmetals.com/assets/docs/mt-polley/2015-06-18-MPMC-KFR.pdf (accessed January 9, 2017).

Palmer, Andie Diane. 2005. Chapter 2: A brief history of responses to colonialism. In *Maps of Experience: The anchoring of land to story in Secwepemc discourse*. Toronto: UBC Press.

Ray, Arthur J. 1999. Treaty 8: A British Columbian anomaly. *BC Studies* 123:5–58.

Riseborough, Jesse and Thomas Biesheuvel. 2015. Price plunge puts gold miners on a knife-edge. *Edmonton Journal*, July 23. www.pressreader.com/canada/edmonton-journal/20150723/282570196802735 (accessed March 23, 2017).

Sherlock, Tracy. 2015. Tsilhqot'in chief looks to a powerful future. *Vancouver Sun*, January 2. www.vancouversun.com/health/Tsilhqot+chief+looks+powerful+future/10697684/ story.html (accessed March 23, 2017).

Tennant, Paul. 1990. *Aboriginal peoples and politics: The Indian land question in British Columbia, 1849–1989*. Vancouver: UBC Press.

William, Roger. 2005. *Panel two: Existing indigenous protocols and models of exercising FPIC*. Chief Roger William, Speaker. William David, Moderator. (Minutes 22:00–45:00.), May 20. Isuma TV. www.isuma.tv/fpicforum/panel-two-existing-indigenous-protocols-and-models-of-exercising-fpic (accessed December 15, 2016).

## Cases Cited

*Delgamuukw v. British Columbia*, [1997], 3 S.C.R. 1010 *R. v. Gladstone*, [1996] 2 S.C.R. 723

*Haida Nation v. British Columbia (Minister of Forests)*, [2004], 3 S.C.R. 511, 2004 SCC 73

*Taseko Mines Limited v. Phillips*, 2011 BCSC 1675

*Taseko Mines Limited v. Western Canada Wilderness Committee*, 2016 BCSC 109

*Tsilhqot'in Nation v. British Columbia*, 2007 BCSC 1700

*Tsilhqot'in Nation v. British Columbia*, 2014 SCC 44, [2014] 2 S.C.R. 256

## Legislation Cited

*Canadian Environmental Assessment Act*, RSO 1990, c. E-18

*Canadian Environmental Assessment Act*, 2012. S.C. 2012, c.19. s.52

*Fisheries Act*, RSC 1985, c. F-14

*Jobs and Economic Growth Act*, SC 2010, c. 12

*Jobs, Growth and Long-Term Prosperity Act*, SC 2012, c. 19

*Navigation Protection Act*, RSC 1985, c. N-22

*Navigable Waters Protection Act RSC*, 1985, c. N-22 (in force between March 1, 1999 and May 10, 2004)

# 7

# COREXIT TO FORGET IT

## Transforming Coastal Louisiana into an Energy Sacrifice Zone

*Julie K. Maldonado*

Driving south down the bayous of coastal Louisiana for the first time in September 2009, I saw a sweeping landscape of grey, dotted with the bare skeletal remains of trees with limbs pointing to areas that once were land but now are water. I passed scattered houses and trailers: some empty, some occupied, some elevated nineteen feet to prevent flooding, and some on the ground and in danger. At the time, I could not imagine the web of family, tribal, and colonial relationships that intertwines with the water and the vanishing land to shape coastal lives. When I moved to the region two years later and residents allowed me into their homes and communities, this intricate web—punctuated by individual inhabitants and stories of life on the bayous—became visible. Among the most striking stories was that of the relationship between the government, the oil and gas industry, and the consequential decimation of coastal land, culture, and lifeways.

Fueled by government–corporate partnerships, the oil and gas industry has transformed coastal Louisiana into an energy sacrifice zone and manufactured communities' vulnerabilities to land loss, disasters, climate change, and displacement. Loopholes in environmental regulations and the privatization of lands and waters have enabled environmental destruction and put communities in harm's way. With the capitalist drive for power and economic gain taking the lands, waters, and minerals of the Earth as commodities to be controlled, owned, exploited, and sold to the highest bidder, places like coastal Louisiana embody what Reid and Taylor (2010, 11) call "new geographies of domination." In the United States and elsewhere, this power structure is exemplified by the relationship between state and federal governments and the oil and gas industry and by the governments' protection of industry interests over community wellbeing (Houck 2015; Silverstein 2013).

This chapter illustrates how the capitalist-driven political-economic structure manufactures the vulnerability of coastal Louisiana's communities, transforming the region—once a place of refuge for displaced Native peoples and ethnic minorities

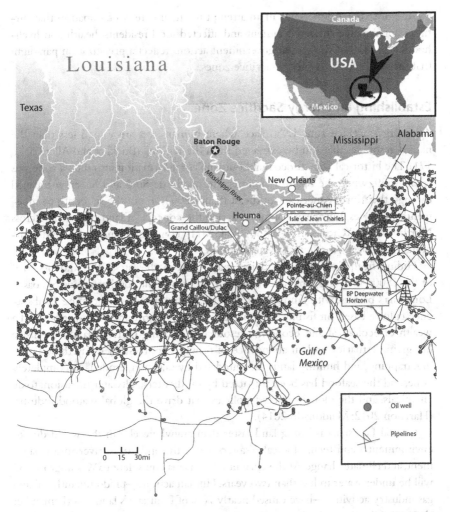

**FIGURE 7.1** There are approximately 25,000 miles of pipelines and 3,500 offshore production facilities in the central and western Gulf of Mexico's federal waters, three-quarters of which are off the coast of Louisiana. The three tribal communities discussed in this chapter are located amidst this sacrifice zone. Map by Donna Gayer, Artasaverb.

(e.g., Acadians)—into what I will argue is an energy sacrifice zone that risks setting the stage for future disasters (Figure 7.1). Based on ethnographic research conducted primarily between October 2011 and September 2012 with three tribes in coastal Louisiana (the Isle de Jean Charles Band, the Grand Caillou/Dulac Band of Biloxi-Chitimacha Choctaw, and the Pointe-au-Chien Indian Tribe), it highlights the 2010 British Petroleum (henceforth, BP) *Deepwater Horizon* oil spill disaster—the most recent infamous event in a century-long story of smaller-scale environmental and social disruptions. More critically and specifically, it examines the use of Corexit dispersants in an attempt to ameliorate contamination that further contaminated the environment and affected local residents' health and livelihoods. My analysis shows that government actions reflect a privatization paradigm that inevitably leads to energy sacrifice zones.

## Establishing an Energy Sacrifice Zone

An energy sacrifice zone is "a place where human lives are valued less than the natural resources that can be extracted from the region" (Buckley and Allen 2011, 171). The historical stage for coastal Louisiana's transformation into such a zone was set in 1539, when the Spanish explorer Hernando de Soto and his crew traveled through the North American southeast (Saunt 2004). From the sixteenth to nineteenth centuries, European colonists carried the concept of land ownership across North America (Cronon 1983; Kain et al. 2011), converting lands once held communally by local tribes into private holdings.

Hiding from government-ordered relocations in the late 1700s and first half of the 1800s, Native people established settlements at the southern ends of coastal Louisiana's bayous, with families living in small clusters and maintaining a subsistence culture based on fishing, trapping, hunting, and farming. Coastal tribes had a wealth of ecological and economic resources, including barrier islands, extensive life-giving estuaries, and an abundance of fishing resources. Yet today these farming, trapping, and hunting lands are inundated by saltwater, eroded, or completely gone, and the seafood has been impacted by oil disasters, saltwater intrusion, toxic chemicals, and the global capitalist policies that drive the global seafood industry (Harrison 2012; Maldonado 2014).

Coastal Louisiana is losing land faster than anywhere else in the world due to environmental and technological disasters, extractive industries, river mismanagement, and climate change. At the current rate, an area equivalent to Washington, DC will be under water in less than two years. Human actions—predominantly oil and gas industry activities—have caused nearly 70% of Louisiana's land loss (Penland et al. 2000). Like the region's river management system—initiated by settler colonists who drained the land for agricultural production and built levee systems to control flooding—the oil and gas industry dredged passageways through the marsh for pipelines and navigation, once again extending human control over the environment. Starting with the first coastal zone oil lease in 1921, the dredged passageways enabled water to rush in from the Gulf of Mexico during storms and high tides, causing severe land loss, erosion, and saltwater intrusion (Austin 2006; Turner 1997). In the 1950s, oil company representatives coerced local citizens into signing agreements to lease or sell their land, land which they privately owned (the bayou tribes are not currently federally recognized and therefore lack reservation lands). As one Pointe-au-Chien tribal member explained to me in April of 2012, because people could not read the English forms, they would "just put a cross. So someone wants to forge a cross, they can. Was told someone signed a form after he was dead for his property." Instead of property being passed down from one generation to the next as had occurred in the past, residents needed official papers and documents to prove property ownership after land and oil developers arrived in the area.

Also in the 1950s, the national demand for energy led to the creation of a vast petrochemical industrial complex along the Mississippi River between Baton Rouge and New Orleans—now known as "cancer alley"—and the construction of hundreds of oil and gas platforms to pump crude oil and natural gas from the earth along the coast. With coastal Louisiana's economic activities already dominated by extractive industries like logging, the timber industry set the precedent for industry/government cooperation (Freudenburg and Gramling 2011). The colonial settler process continued into modern times; by the 1980s, five private corporations owned one-quarter of the entire Louisiana coast (Houck 2015). There are now approximately 25,000 miles of pipelines and 3,500 offshore production facilities in the central and western Gulf of Mexico's federal waters, three-quarters of which are off the coast of Louisiana (Freudenburg and Gramling 2011, 171).

As the oil industry became further embedded in the physical topography, and economic diversification declined, the oil industry "not only molded the politics and economics of Louisiana, it molded the mind" (Houck 2015, 192). The state's reliance on one type of resource production and global market integration created a fixed economy that hinders economic expansion and new job creation, a situation reminiscent of an Appalachian coal industry that systematically prevents residents "from developing community resources in ways outside the state's agenda—an agenda that systematically protects coal" (McNeil 2011, 65).

## The Extractive Industry–Government Relationship

The industry–government relationship that produces the destruction of coastal Louisiana is reflected in several decades of policy and regulation. The US Department of Interior has historically adopted practices and standards developed by the American Petroleum Institute (API)—the largest US trade association for the oil and natural gas industry and the industry's principal lobbyist—as formal regulations (National Commission on the BP *Deepwater Horizon* Oil Spill and Offshore Drilling 2011). Every major oil company CEO is on the American Petroleum Institute board (Juhasz 2011), raising questions regarding whether these practices and standards actually make operations safer or, alternatively, encourage industry sovereignty and profitability by eliminating government oversight. The oil and gas industry is exempt from major provisions of seven major federal environmental laws including the Safe Drinking Water Act and Clean Air Act (Environmental Defense Center 2011). Furthermore, the Deep Water Royalty Relief Act of 1995 cut the already low fees the USA was charging oil companies to drill on the Outer Continental Shelf.

Specific to Louisiana and the Gulf Coast, the 1978 Amendment to the Outer Continental Shelf Lands Act of 1953 singled out the Gulf of Mexico for milder environmental oversight, exempting oil and gas lease-holders on the Shelf from submitting development and production plans for agency approval (National Commission

2011). The state of Louisiana currently provides corporations with over $1.79 billion per year in subsidies, incentives, and tax breaks, with a large portion of this money benefiting the oil and gas industry (Silverstein 2013, 48–49). Many Louisiana government officials and environmental agencies are directly connected to the oil and gas industry and oil interests control state-promoted restoration efforts.

The relationship between the oil industry and the state was recently highlighted when the Southeast Louisiana Flood Protection Authority-East (SLFPA-E) filed a lawsuit in July 2013 against 97 oil, gas, and pipeline companies for "ravag[ing] Louisiana's coastal landscape," demanding that the companies restore the damaged wetlands or pay for irreparable damages (Jones, Swanson, Huddell, & Garrison 2013, 3). Only three SLFPA-E board members voted against the resolution supporting the lawsuit, all of them appointed by Louisiana Governor Bobby Jindal (Schleifstein 2013a). Claiming it was not in line with Louisiana's coastal restoration policy, Jindal subsequently signed legislation blocking the lawsuit and preventing Louisiana government agencies from accepting litigation challenging the oil and gas industry. Local environmental groups claimed that Jindal's opposition is tied to the over $1 million he received in political contributions from the oil and gas industry (Schleifstein 2013b). Seventeen additional parishes have since joined together to file a lawsuit against the oil and gas companies. While these lawsuits are currently languishing in the court system, their outcomes could have subsequent effects on other lawsuits against oil and gas corporations, including claims against BP for compensation following the 2010 BP *Deepwater Horizon* disaster (Neuhauser 2014).

## The BP Deepwater Horizon Oil Disaster

On April 20, 2010, eleven men were killed when BP's *Deepwater Horizon* oil rig exploded. Nearly five million barrels of oil spilled into the Gulf of Mexico, affecting approximately 1,100 miles of coastal wetlands. BP initially estimated that between 1,063 to 14,226 barrels of oil spilled into the Gulf per day (Markey 2010), but because the 1972 Clean Water Act applies penalties for each spilled barrel, it behooved BP to underestimate the spill's size (Juhasz 2011). In early 2010, BP was the largest oil and gas producer in the Gulf of Mexico and the USA as well as the fourth largest corporation in the world by revenue (Juhasz 2011).

The BP *Deepwater Horizon* oil disaster further exposed the role of government and industry in manufacturing the energy sacrifice zone. Part of the problem with the haphazard cleanup was BP's Oil Spill Response Plan for the Gulf of Mexico. Portions of the response plan were copied from material on US National Oceanic and Atmospheric Administration (NOAA) websites and failed to consider the applicability of the information it contained to the Gulf of Mexico context (National Commission 2011). In the plan, BP named a wildlife expert on whom it would rely for expertise, yet this person had passed away several years before the Plan was submitted (National Commission 2011). The US Minerals Management Service approved the plan without adequate attention to detail, as evidenced by the clear errors in the plan. The approval of oil spill response plans without close attention to detail are systemic throughout the oil and gas industry; ExxonMobil, Chevron, ConocoPhillips, Shell and others drilling in the Gulf of Mexico submitted nearly identical response plans prepared by the same contractor, all approved by the Minerals Management Service (National Commission 2011).

In 2014, a US District Court of Eastern Louisiana judge issued an historic ruling stating that BP exhibited "gross negligence" and "willful misconduct" leading up to the BP disaster. However, with governments continuing to permit extractive corporations to explore and drill in increasingly precarious environments (e.g., the Arctic), hydraulic fracture for natural gas around sacred sites (e.g., Chaco Canyon), extract toxic unconventional hydrocarbons (e.g., Alberta tar sands), and violate the human rights of local communities (e.g., the Niger Delta), it is yet to be seen if the 2014 ruling of "gross negligence" indicates any real and lasting change.

The 1990 Oil Pollution Act deemed that a private company responsible for a spill would be required to plug the well, clean up pollution resulting from the spill and its aftermath, and compensate the people affected. BP established a $20 billion fund to compensate individuals and businesses for environmental and economic damages, subsistence losses, property damage, and compensated state and local agencies for response costs (Landrieu 2011; Weber 2011). The lack of transparency in the claims process, high rate of denial and inadequacy of compensation, and the perception that the compensation fund administrator was heavily influenced by BP left those affected by the disaster frustrated and confused (Weber 2011).

## Local and Subsistence Effects

The essence of a sacrifice zone is that subsistence livelihoods are often destroyed in pursuit of national or global energy. Nearly three years after the spill, I watched Isle de Jean Charles' tribal members fill out claims forms, which asked for paperwork and past fishing licenses that most people did not have. To be eligible for compensation, BP required three years' paystubs, paychecks, tax returns, and documents created prior to the 2010 spill (Juhasz 2011). However, many people had lost these items due to flooding during Hurricanes Gustav and Ike in 2008. On top of this, sediment erosion was increased by oil-related damage to vegetation and root systems, exacerbating coastal communities' vulnerability to storms (NAS 2013; National Commission 2011). Many activities related to subsistence claims were conducted informally and had no written record. Local people were frustrated that no one seemed to know the status of the claims process. With layers of disasters and events occurring in the region, it was exceptionally challenging to document a direct link between livelihood impacts and the BP disaster, especially when effects could occur in any number of places along the aquatic food chain.

Some coastal residents and fishing families took action to counter BP's media campaign, which cost nearly $93.5 million in advertising between April and July 2010 (more than three times the amount spent during the same period in 2009) (Waxman and Stupak 2010). For example, a life-long fisher from Pointe-au-Chien drove around in his boat taking pictures "in case they tried to say it didn't happen over here. Know they'd try to get out of paying people, so I have pictures." Others spoke out publically, refuting the assertations made by the media campaign. As a tribal resident from Grand Caillou/Dulac explained, "BP is telling everyone that the people from the bayous are fine. They are lying. It has taken away our livelihood. Our seafood that feeds our families is no longer safe."

While impacts on fish reproduction, development, and populations might take years to determine, the BP disaster raised public concerns about the safety of Gulf of Mexico seafood (NAS 2013); residents were no longer certain what they were putting into their bodies. Locally observed deformities in seafood species matched research studies documenting fish with lesions and deformed shrimp (Jamail 2012). Human health concerns were vindicated when high levels of compounds present in crude oil released during the BP disaster were found in shrimp and oysters in the northern Gulf of Mexico (Sammarco et al. 2013). Crude oil contains high levels of volatile organic compounds like benzene, a known human carcinogen and the cause of other serious health effects (Juhasz 2011; Solomon and Janssen 2010).

Government officials made statements confirming the safety of seafood harvested from the portion of the Gulf that had been reopened after being closed immediately following the spill (NOAA 2010). However, what the government and BP were saying about the seafood was distinctly different from what local fishers and residents were finding. While locals could not always pinpoint exactly what was happening, they did know that what they were seeing and experiencing was different from anything they had seen before. For instance, at a 2012 community forum in Houma, Louisiana held by the Gulf Organized Fisheries in Solidarity and Hope Coalition (GO FISH), someone brought up their recent sighting of shrimp caught without eyeballs. Like a wave around the room, people murmured, "we have some too", and "we all have some." An elderly shrimper observed that the 2012 season was the worst catch he had ever seen. Another resident noted that before the spill he would always see oyster shells filled with baby oysters, but now the shells were turning black and once that happened the shell was dead. And a young crabber stood up at the community forum to say that the compensation he was receiving was "like a slap in the face ... our livelihood is priceless." The greatest uncertainty was not knowing what they would see the following year. As it turned out, it was not only the oil that people were concerned about, but also the Corexit dispersant used to sink the oil after the spill.

## Corexit to Forget It

Substantiating my argument that government/industry involvement has created a sacrifice zone, the US Environmental Protection Agency (EPA) approved using dispersants—Corexit 9527A and then Corexit 9500A—below the surface of the water for the first time following the *Deepwater Horizon* explosion (Center for Biological Diversity 2014), applying approximately 1.84 million gallons of dispersant to the Gulf waters by boats and airplanes (United States Coast Guard 2011). Dispersants do not entirely remove oil from the water, but rather work in conjunction with the wind and waves to accelerate dispersal by allowing the oil to mix with water. The use of dispersants, one local fisher remarked to me in May of 2012 during a conversation on his porch, made a four-mile by six-mile wide spill sink and disappear. The cleanup approach could be seen as matching the way local communities are made invisible by the role of government/industry—out of sight, out of mind.

Subsequent to the decision to use Corexit, EPA studies found that of the eighteen approved dispersants, twelve are more effective on southern Louisiana crude oil than Corexit, and the toxicity of these twelve was either comparable to Corexit or, in some cases, significantly lower (Quinlan 2010). And, although Corexit was on the EPA's National Contingency Plan Product Schedule, the testing it had undergone did not consider the product's long-term impacts.

Corexit 9527 and 9500 contain propylene glycol and Corexit 9527 contains 2-butoxyethanol (2-BE). Both are toxic and both bioaccumulate up the food chain (Center for Biological Diversity 2014; Subra 2010). 2-BE was identified as a cause of chronic health problems and even several deaths among cleanup workers after the 1989 Exxon Valdez oil disaster (Center for Biological Diversity 2014; Juhasz 2011). The health effects on Gulf residents have also proven problematic. An Isle de Jean Charles' tribal member recalled to me in July of 2012:

> We was working out there when they sprayed that dispersant … My memory since that oil spill, that stuff I tested positive, I got a loss of memory … they're gonna pay you for your health … but the money's not gonna do much good … I never had much money in my life and what's it gonna do now? I'll be sick and I won't be able to enjoy it when I'll be going down the road and forget what I'm doing.

The full potential health effects of Corexit are unknown because the dispersant's manufacturer has refused to reveal all of its ingredients, citing their proprietary nature (Center for Biological Diversity 2014). A University of South Florida study found that Corexit broke the oil droplets into smaller drops and created a plume that caused the die-off of foraminifera—amoeba-like creatures that are the basis of the Gulf's aquatic food chain (Pittman 2013). One recent study found that adding Corexit 9500A to the oil spill in the Gulf made the mixture up to fifty-two times more toxic than the oil itself (Rico-Martínez, Snell, and Shearer 2013).

Nalco Company, which manufactures and sells Corexit, included in its portfolio "technologies that increase production, reduce operational costs and protect assets in challenging environments like Deepwater & Ultra-Deepwater, Oil Sands, and High Temperature High Pressure Corrosion. We also have chemistries designed to treat the heaviest crudes and oil spills" (Nalco 2014). Thus, Nalco is encouraging drilling under more precarious circumstances, while also selling products supposedly designed to clean up the spills caused by such drilling, further perpetuating the idea that it is okay to sacrifice some areas.

With chemicals from dispersants still infusing the Gulf's waters, fishers are experiencing bacterial infections years after the spill, but finding it increasingly difficult

**FIGURE 7.2** Cleanup workers place booms around Isle de Jean Charles to try to prevent oil from the BP spill coming ashore. Photograph by Julie Maldonado, 2010.

to attribute them to a particular source. For example, standing on the deck of a docked shrimp boat at the southern end of Pointe-au-Chien in late 2014—four and a half years after the spill—a friend told me why he had not been shrimping much this season. A couple months prior he was cleaning his boat with the same chemicals he had used for years, but something in the water had mixed with the chemicals, went through his boot, and made him sick for weeks. He told me another fisher friend had recently passed away due to a similar incident.

Considering the layers of disasters affecting the region, many coastal residents worry about what will happen when the next storm hits and brings more oil and chemicals onshore (see Figure 7.2). How much more will be sacrificed? As one local resident voiced to me in May of 2012, "what will happen when the next hurricane comes and brings all that oil into our homes? What are we supposed to do then? With each storm that passes we never know what we will come back to."

## Conclusion: Colonial Legacies and the Sacrifice of Coastal Louisiana

Embedded in historically and economically driven processes that have decimated coastal Louisiana's lands and waters—taking along with them local people's health, livelihoods, and cultures—the US federal and Louisiana state governments backed the interests of private oil corporations and developers over the rights of local bayou residents. As an Isle de Jean Charles' tribal member described:

> [White men] have cut through our marshes, our ancestral mounds, and left our once fertile lands barren from saltwater intrusion. They have poisoned our bounty from the waters with their quest for monetary gain from oil, not only with the oil itself but from the chemicals they used to cover up their mistakes. They have killed our trees, which were once plentiful and marked our lands and left in their place a shadow of what once was (January 17, 2013).

Subsistence-based livelihoods, cultural practices, traditional skills and knowledge, as well as community and social networks are today jeopardized by the same loss of land and livelihood—coupled with increased impacts from storms, as well as more intense hurricanes due to climate change (Carter et al. 2014)—that have forced many residents to relocate. The 2010 BP disaster accelerated the trajectory of a shrimping industry already in decline due to industrial restructuring and aquaculture imports of farm-raised shrimp from low-wage producers in other countries (Harrison 2012). When I shrimped with locals, their disappointment was palpable as they compared the thousands-of-pound catches of the past to the now typical couple-hundred-pound catch that barely allowed them to break even.

The effects of contamination, dispossession, and land loss are cumulative and mutually reinforcing. In Louisiana, once land disappears under water, the state takes possession and the submerged area can then be leased to oil and gas corporations. Advocating for land restoration efforts, a Pointe-au-Chien tribal resident explained to me in June of 2012, "The most important thing to me is trying to get the parishes to save what is left of our land, the land they want to see wash away so the oil companies can take over." The legacy of privatization of the Earth's waters, lands, and minerals for corporate profit have continued to subjugate and marginalize tribes like Isle de Jean Charles, Point-au-Chien, and Grand Caillou/Dulac, as well as many other coastal communities. As the resources of the Gulf and its life-giving estuaries continue to be commodified, the prevailing development regime has rendered it acceptable to ravage the environment for corporate profit. With corporations exercising the rights of citizens, one is left to question which citizens our governance system serves and protects. These processes indicate that by destroying the environment—and the possibility of physical and cultural reproduction within that environment—we are also destroying select populations to make way for profit. Talking about Louisiana's land loss problem, one coastal resident said to me in July of 2012, "it's just going to be sacrificed. It always makes you figure you're just being sacrificed for bigger benefits."

Indigenous and non-Indigenous communities in coastal Louisiana have accrued layers of multiple, chronic, and recurrent disasters and injustices (Laska et al. 2015), yet many residents take action to resist and/or adapt to challenging circumstances. They elevate their houses, document impacts, lease waters back from the oil companies so their families can continue to access the water for fishing, and pursue proactive community-led relocation to a safer area still close enough to their culturally significant resources (Maldonado et al. 2015).

As drilling is once again initiated at the site of the 2010 BP *Deepwater Horizon* disaster, the problem will clearly not be solved by environmental policies alone. Government officials who back the interests of private corporations over the rights of local communities must be held accountable and the fossil fuel companies need to pay a fair share of the costs accrued to communities. Subsistence livelihoods need to be supported, instead of destroyed. People need access to a wealth of economic alternatives rather than being forced into an economic, capitalist-based marketplace built on the platform of ever-increasing consumption and extraction. Our way forward must integrate a transformed social perspective that sees Mother Earth not as an object to be controlled and ravaged in the name of profit (Warren 2000), but as a shared home to be cherished. We can start on a new, sustainable path by looking to those most affected by such injustices—communities who have dwelled in place for centuries—and respectfully ask how their knowledge, strategies, and actions can guide us all. This new path calls for a shift from a privatization paradigm to one of shared common resources that values and respects the human–environment relationship.

# References

Austin, Diane. 2006. Cultural exploitation, land loss and hurricanes: A recipe for disaster. *American Anthropologist* 108, 4:671–691.

Buckley, Geoffrey L., and Laura Allen. 2011. Stories about mountaintop removal in the Appalachian coalfields. In *Mountains of injustice: Social and environmental justice in Appalachia*, edited by Michele Morrone, Geoffrey L. Buckley, and Jedidiah Purdy, 161–180. Athens: Ohio University Press.

Carter, Lynne M., James W. Jones, Leonard Berry, Virginia Burkett, James F. Murley, Jayantha Obeysekera, Paul J. Schramm, and David Wear. 2014. Southeast and the Caribbean. In *Climate change impacts in the United States: The third national climate assessment*, edited by Jerry M. Melillo, Terese Richmond, and Gary W. Yohe, 396–417. Washington, DC: US Global Change Research Program.

Center for Biological Diversity. 2014. *Dispersants*. www.biologicaldiversity.org/programs/public_lands/energy/dirty_energy_development/oil_and_gas/gulf_oil_spill/dispersants.html (accessed June 27, 2014).

Cronon, William. 1983. *Changes in the land: Indians, colonists, and the ecology of New England*. New York: Hill and Wang.

Environmental Defense Center. 2011. *Fracking–federal law: Loopholes and exemptions*. Santa Barbara, CA: Environmental Defense Center. www.edcnet.org/learn/current_cases/fracking/federal_law_loopholes.html (accessed June 17, 2014).

Freudenburg, William R., and Robert Gramling. 2011. *Blowout in the Gulf: The BP oil spill disaster and the future of energy in America*. Cambridge, MA: The MIT Press.

Harrison, Jill Ann. 2012. *Buoyancy on the bayou: Shrimpers face the rising tide of globalization*. Ithaca, NY: Cornell University Press.

Houck, Oliver A. 2015. The reckoning: Oil and gas development in the Louisiana coastal zone. *Tulane Environmental Law Journal* 28, 2:185–296.

Jamail, Dahr. 2012. Gulf seafood deformities alarm scientists. *Al Jazeera*, April 20. www. aljazeera.com/indepth/features/2012/04/201241682318260912.html (accessed March 16, 2016).

Jones, Swanson, Huddell & Garrison, LLC. 2013. Petition for damages and injunctive relief. Filed July 24, 2013, Civil District Court for the Parish of Orleans, State of Louisiana. http://jonesswanson.com/wp-content/uploads/2015/02/SLFPAE-Petition_Exhibits. pdf (accessed March 16, 2016).

Juhasz, Antonia. 2011. *Black tide: The devastating impact of the Gulf oil spill.* Hoboken, NJ: John Wiley and Sons.

Kain, Roger P., John Chapman, and Richard R. Oliver. 2011. *The enclosure maps of England and Wales 1595–1918: A cartographic analysis and electronic catalogue.* Cambridge, UK: Cambridge University Press.

Landrieu, Mary. 2011. *Gulf coast recovery: An examination of claims and social services in the aftermath of the Deepwater Horizon oil spill.* Hearing before the ad hoc subcommittee on disaster recovery of the committee on homeland security and governmental affairs, United States Senate, January 27. www.gpo.gov/fdsys/pkg/CHRG-112shrg66618/html/CHRG-112shrg66618.htm (accessed March 16, 2016).

Laska, Shirley, Kristina Peterson, Crystlyn Rodrigue, Tia Cosse, Rosina Philippe, Olivia Burchett, and Richard Krajeski. 2015. "Layering" of natural and human caused disasters in the context of anticipated climate change disasters: The coastal Louisiana experience. In *Disasters' impact on livelihood and cultural survival: Losses, opportunities, and mitigation*, edited by Michèle Companion, 225–238. Boca Raton, FL: CRC Press.

Maldonado, Julie Koppel. 2014. *Facing the rising tide: Co-occurring disasters, displacement, and adaptation in coastal Louisiana's tribal communities.* PhD Dissertation, Department of Anthropology, American University.

Maldonado, Julie Koppel, Albert P. Naquin, Theresa Dardar, Shirell Parfait-Dardar, and Kelly Bagwell. 2015. Above the rising tide: Coastal Louisiana's tribal communities apply local strategies and knowledge to adapt to rapid environmental change. In *Disasters' impact on livelihood and cultural survival: Losses, opportunities, and mitigation*, edited by Michèle Companion, 239–259. Boca Raton, FL: CRC Press.

Markey, Edward. 2010. *Letter to the national commission on the BP Deepwater Horizon oil spill and offshore drilling.* September 28. www.markey.senate.gov/GlobalWarming/files/LTTR/2010-09-28_toBPCommissionflowratetimeline.pdf (accessed March 16, 2016).

McNeil, Bryan T. 2011. *Combating mountaintop removal: New directions in the fight against big coal.* Urbana: University of Illinois Press.

Nalco. 2014. *Oil and gas production and pipelines.* www.nalco.com/eu/industries/oil-gas-production-pipelines.htm (accessed June 14, 2014).

National Academy of Sciences (NAS). 2013. Assessing impacts of the Deepwater Horizon oil spill in the Gulf of Mexico. *Science Daily*, July 10. www.sciencedaily.com/releases/2013/07/130710122004.htm (accessed March 16, 2016).

National Commission on the BP Deepwater Horizon Oil Spill and Offshore Drilling (National Commission). 2011. *Deep Water: The Gulf Oil Disaster and the Future of Offshore Drilling.* Report to the President. www.gpo.gov/fdsys/pkg/GPO-OILCOMMISSION/pdf/GPO-OILCOMMISSION.pdf (accessed December 12, 2016).

National Oceanic and Atmospheric Administration (NOAA). 2010. *NOAA and FDA announce chemical test for dispersant in Gulf seafood: All samples test within safety threshold.* October 29. www.noaanews.noaa.gov/stories2010/20101029_seafood.html (accessed June 2, 2014).

Neuhauser, Alan. 2014. Jindal signs bill blocking lawsuits against oil and gas companies. *US News and World Report*, June 6. www.usnews.com/news/articles/2014/06/06/bobby-jindal-signs-bill-to-block-lawsuits-against-oil-and-gas-companies (accessed March 16, 2016).

Penland, Shea, Lynda Wayne, L.D. Britsch, S. Jeffress Williams, Andrew D. Beall, and Victoria Caridas Butterwortk. 2000. *Process classification of coastal land loss between 1932 and 1990 in the Mississippi River delta plain, Southeastern Louisiana.* Reston, VA: US Geological Survey.

Pittman, Craig. 2013. Three years after BP oil spill, USF research finds massive die-off. *Tampa Bay Times*, April 4. www.tampabay.com/news/environment/water/gulf-oil-spill-killed-millions-of-microscopic-creatures-at-base-of-food/2113157 (accessed June 18, 2014).

Quinlan, Paul. 2010. Less toxic dispersants lose out in BP oil spill cleanup. *Environment & Energy Publishing*, May 13. www.eenews.net/stories/90953 (accessed March 16, 2016).

Reid, Herbert, and Betsy Taylor. 2010. *Recovering the commons: Democracy, place, and global justice.* Urbana: University of Illinois Press.

Rico-Martínez, Roberto, Terry W. Snell, and Tonya L. Shearer. 2013. Synergistic toxicity of macondo crude oil and dispersant corexit 9500a® to the brachionus plicatilis species complex (rotifera). *Environmental Pollution* 173:5–10.

Sammarco, Paul W., Steve R. Kolian, Richard A. F. Warby, Jennifer L. Bouldin, Wilma A. Subra, and Scott A. Porter. 2013. Distribution and concentrations of petroleum hydrocarbons associated with the BP/Deepwater Horizon oil spill, Gulf of Mexico. *Marine Pollution Bulletin* 73, 1:129–143.

Saunt, Claudio. 2004. History until 1776. In *The handbook of North American Indians. Vol. 14, Southeast*, edited by Raymond D. Fogelson, 128–138. Washington, DC: Smithsonian Institution Press.

Schleifstein, Mark. 2013a. East bank levee authority votes to reaffirm wetlands damage lawsuit against energy companies. *The Times-Picayune*, December 5. www.nola.com/environment/index.ssf/2013/12/east_bank_levee_authority_vote.html (accessed March 16, 2016).

Schleifstein, Mark. 2013b. Jindal opposes coastal erosion lawsuit due to oil industry contributions, environmental groups say. *The Times-Picayune*, August 28. www.nola.com/environment/index.ssf/2013/08/environmental_groups_say_jinda.html (accessed March 16, 2016).

Silverstein, Ken. 2013. Dirty south: The foul legacy of Louisiana oil. *Harper's Magazine*, November, 45–56. https://harpers.org/archive/2013/11/dirty-south/ (accessed March 16, 2016).

Solomon, Gina, and Sarah Janssen. 2010. Health effects of the Gulf oil spill. *Journal of the American Medical Association* 304, 10:1118–1119.

Subra, Wilma. 2010. *Testimony of Wilma Subra before the subcommittee on oversight and investigations of the House energy and commerce committee on local impact of the Deepwater Horizon oil spill human health and environmental impacts associated with the Deepwater Horizon crude oil spill disaster*, June 7. www.gpo.gov/fdsys/pkg/CHRG-111hhrg76584/pdf/CHRG-111hhrg76584.pdf (accessed March 16, 2016).

Turner, R.E. 1997. Wetland loss in the northern Gulf of Mexico: Multiple working hypotheses. *Estuaries* 20, 1:1–13.

United States Coast Guard. 2011. *BP Deepwater Horizon oil spill: Incident specific preparedness review.* www.uscg.mil/foia/docs/DWH/BPDWH.pdf (accessed July 28, 2014).

Warren, Karen. 2000. Nature is a feminist issue: Motivating ecofeminism by taking empirical data seriously. In *Ecofeminist philosophy: A western perspective on what it is and why it matters*, edited by Karen Warren, 1–20. Lanham, MD: Rowman and Littlefield.

Waxman, Henry, and Bart Stupak. 2010. *Letter to Representative Kathy Castor*, September 1. http://castor.house.gov/uploadedfiles/castor_bpadvertising_2010_9_1.pdf (accessed March 16, 2016).

Weber, Harry R. 2011. BP increases pay for claims czar Ken Feinberg's law firm to $1.25 million per month. *Huffington Post*, March 25. www.huffingtonpost.com/2011/03/25/bp-kenfeinberg-claims-salary-pay_n_840871.html (accessed June 27, 2014).

# PART III
# Struggles & Opportunities

# 8

# WITH OR WITHOUT RAILWAY?

## Post-catastrophe Perceptions of Risk and Development in Lac-Mégantic, Québec

*Geneviève Brisson and Emmanuelle Bouchard-Bastien*

## Introduction

On the night of July 6, 2013, a shale oil train from North Dakota derailed and exploded in the downtown core of Lac-Mégantic, Québec. The 72-car train was parked uphill from Lac-Mégantic when a fire broke out in the engine. Firemen cut the engine's air brakes, and hand brakes alone could not stop the train from descending toward Lac-Mégantic. The train accelerated and derailed in the town center. The ensuing blaze and explosions caused 47 deaths, destroyed 44 buildings, and contaminated the area's soil, air, and water. Facing serious environmental hazards, a disaster "red zone" was fenced off and over 2,000 people—more than one-third of the town's population—were evacuated (MDDELCC 2017; BST 2015).

While the tragic events of July, 2013, received international media attention, the impacts on Lac-Mégantic and its residents are far from over. A 5,350-square-foot area remains closed due to contamination, preventing movement between two central districts and impeding access to services. Decontamination work, the voluntary demolition of 37 buildings, and the redevelopment of a significant portion of the town are still underway. Major economic impacts are also evident, including the direct costs of emergency measures, decontamination work and reconstruction, as well as commercial losses associated with the destruction of the city center, its shops and trade network, and the railway that services this network. Nearly 165 people will never return to their homes.

In Lac-Mégantic, more than 50% of people exposed to the tragedy subsequently experienced a depressive episode and 29% have experienced fear, anger, and a sense of powerlessness (ASSS de l'Estrie 2015). These psychological impacts have received significant media attention. A team of psychosocial recovery specialists has been in place since August, 2013, and continues to accept new requests for support, mainly related to the resurgence or onset of post-traumatic symptoms. The situation in

Lac-Mégantic is reminiscent of other extraction-related disasters, such as the Exxon Valdez and BP oil spills (Gill, Picou, and Ritchie 2012; Maldonado, Chapter 7). But other impacts are also evident—the way in which the tragedy was managed has torn Lac-Mégantic's social fabric due to a lack of transparency, excessive interference by authorities, and the challenges that precipitated redevelopment work—thus exacerbating perceptions of disempowerment. In addition, the physical destruction of Lac-Mégantic's downtown has resulted in the loss of landmarks, activities, and important places, bringing changes to social and community life. As is the case wherever and whenever industrial activities disregard the links between humans and their *living environment*, their place—and sense of place—have been irremediably lost (e.g., Brisson 2004; Windsor and McVey 2005).

The individual psychological effects of such tragedies and the ensuing reconstruction have been thoroughly analyzed (Galea et al. 2007; Lee and Blanchard 2012), as have the negative effects on quality of life (e.g., traffic, dust, limited drinking water, noise) and the changes in physical landscape and accessibility (Rosales 2007; Stedman 2003). From a social perspective, effects of natural and technological disasters—as well as grassroots mobilizations in response to these events—have been documented by anthropologists studying risk and vulnerability (Beck 1992; Button 2010; Leiss 2001; Oliver-Smith 2009; Pelling 2001). Yet very little research has been conducted on reconstruction practices and their effects on debates about possible development trajectories. Academic discussions of disasters (Aldrich and Meyer 2014; Chamlee-Wright 2010; Maltais et al. 2000) suggest that recovery efforts often bring formerly latent disagreements about development trajectories and the role of the authorities involved to the surface.

This chapter highlights tensions that have arisen at the intersection of two very different visions of redevelopment. It considers how risk management by authorities has contributed to these tensions and examines the psychosocial consequences of these conflicts. We suggest that a lack of participatory decision-making creates social divisions, because the priority that the government places on the economy diverges from the symbolic and psychological needs of affected residents. This analysis is based on an ethnographic study requested by the local and regional public health authorities and conducted between January, 2014, and April, 2015, in Lac-Mégantic.

For new forms of unconventional energy resources being developed in North America, social acceptance is based on promises of controlled risk and local economic development. In light of the Lac-Mégantic tragedy, studies that address the relationship between redevelopment and risk are crucial. While this chapter provides an in-depth understanding of a situation unique to Québec, the oil industry's ongoing North American expansion—as oil from Alberta's tar sands, North Dakota's Bakken Shale, and Texas's Eagle Ford and Permian Basins is shipped across the continent—makes this study germane elsewhere. Since the accident at Lac-Mégantic, other incidents with spills and fires have taken place in the USA (examples include Casselton, North Dakota [December 2013]; Lynchburg, Virginia [April 2014]; and near Charleston, West Virginia [February 2015]) and Canada (for example, Plaster Rock, New Brunswick [November 2014]; Nipigon, Ontario [January 2015]; and twice at Gogoma, Ontario [February and March 2015]). These incidents remind us of the risks inherent in hydrocarbon transportation by rail (Frittelli et al. 2014; NTSB 2015; TSBC 2015).

## Social Sciences and Technological Disasters

This chapter draws on and contributes to the critical social science literature on disasters and the cultural construction of risk, particularly as discussions of these intertwined concepts relate to heated debate over a potential bypass railway in Lac-Mégantic. Differing perspectives, especially between authorities and citizens, are central in those debates. By analyzing various phases of the emergency and reconstruction, by examining concomitant understandings of the disaster, and by repositioning the catastrophe as a historical event, our study points to a better understanding of how communities cope with disasters and resolve claims about risks.

Areas affected by disaster often require renewed urban planning and a reorganization of services and infrastructure. Residents must also reconsider priorities, choices, and decision-making strategies. On the one hand, these changes—combined with the disaster itself—can permanently undermine the symbolic world of impacted residents, which requires communities to rebuild collective identities, reorient risk perceptions, and recompose social ties, families, and local management arrangements (Langumier 2008; Lezama 2009). On the other hand, catastrophes reveal the roles played by authorities in establishing the conditions for its occurrence in ways that are strongly influenced by the social context, the character and the scale of the disaster, the role of public authorities, as well as community development and participation processes (Benadusi, Brambilla, and Riccio 2009; Button 2010; Hoffman and Oliver-Smith 2009; Revet 2007).

Several studies of post-disaster reconstruction have reported tension and conflict between social groups within communities, or between public authorities and citizens over rebuilding plans, the local control of the community's future, and questions of how best to manage the risks the community faces (Dawson and Madsen 2011; Eastmond 2010; Scanlon 1998). In turn, these controversies affect social ties and psychological well-being (stress, anger, and social demobilization are common). This gap between the symbolic and psychological damages, on the one hand, and the institutional focus on technical and monetary issues, on the other, often results in decreasing trust in decision-makers, especially when they are perceived to place greater priority on the economy than on psychosocial impacts (Cornitius 1997). Social issues related to transparency, community engagement, access to resources and participation, and respect for individual and collective rights often arise, as does the issue of fairness, particularly regarding the uneven distribution of wealth and of negative consequences (Solnit 2009).

Our analysis of the Lac-Mégantic rail disaster and its relationship to current socio-political dynamics sheds light on the complexity of the social order in which social actors faced with technological disasters are engaged, as well as the different types of knowledge and worldviews that shape their perspectives and responses (November, D'Alessandro-Scarpari, and Rémy 2004). As risk becomes reality, new conversations about the future are made possible, but this process also brings previously hidden social tensions to the foreground.

## Context and Methodological Framework

Lac-Mégantic is a small town located in the province of Québec, Canada, on the Appalachian plateau, near the US border (Figure 8.1). Part of the Estrie administrative region, Lac-Mégantic has 6,000 residents as well as educational institutions, a hospital, shops, restaurants, and large stores that make it the regional service center for many smaller neighboring municipalities. The construction of the railway in 1878 played a central role in the development of the region (MCC 2016). The first Europeans settled in the area to work in forestry. Over time, the area became a strategic railway hub on the Canadian Pacific (CP) and Québec Central Railway (QCR) lines. Many of the region's companies and jobs continue to depend on the railway, both as a site for freight transfer between the USA and Canada and as an export route (e.g., a local industry called Tafisa makes plywood panels destined for North American markets and employs over 300 workers).

This study is based on semi-structured interviews with residents of the Lac-Mégantic region. Interviews were designed to better understand residents' concerns, opinions, knowledge, and wishes regarding risks and risk management, and to assess how people connect those themes in their views of risk and of the future.[1] The sample was chosen to accurately reflect the regional population and the different roles and experiences of individuals within the community; participants were selected based on their membership in different sub-groups and included citizens who were evacuated July 6, 2013 (n=11), citizens of other areas of Lac-Mégantic (n=10), citizens of neighboring municipalities in du Granit county (n=9), and local socio-economic stakeholders (n=27). The sample also included individuals of diverse age, sex, and length of residence in the community. Data collection took place in three stages (summer and fall of 2014, and winter 2015) and produced 57 interviews, with participants recruited through public notices and snow-ball sampling. This project was approved by the Research Ethics Committee of Laval University (no 2014–192).

## The Railway of Discord

This research revealed much about the social dimensions of the 2013 disaster and its aftermath. In this section we present key findings, emphasizing the tension between two perceived risks: the presence of railroad tracks in the downtown and the decline of economic development as a result of the disaster. The consequences of this tension and the role of the authorities in determining its outcome are also considered.

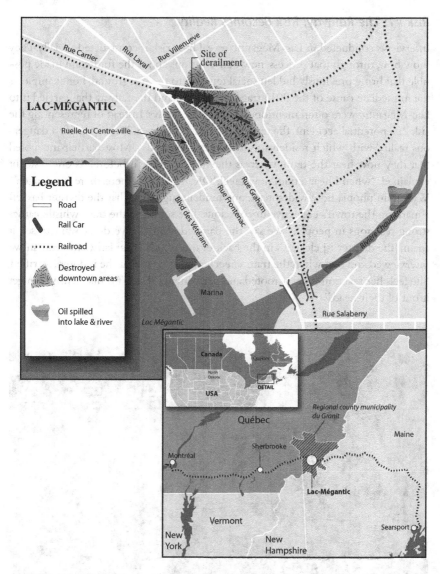

**FIGURE 8.1** Extraction and transportation processes that span broad geographies constrain potential local visions of the future. The oil transport train derailment and devastation in the town of Lac-Mégantic reveal how local psychological perceptions of risk are impacted by shale oil extraction that occurs far away. Map by Donna Gayer, Artasaverb.

### Risk #1: The Railway: Risk Becomes Reality

Interviews conducted in Lac-Mégantic reveal how risk is constructed socially. They show how, through that process, new conversations about the future are made possible that bring previously hidden social tensions to the foreground. For example, as the immediate cause of the 2013 tragedy, the train and the railway that carried it to Lac-Mégantic were often mentioned during interviews. Instead of representing the risk of a potential accident, the train and railway (Figure 8.2) now signify a dangerous reality with which residents must contend every day. Most participants noted that they now hear the train, whereas they did not hear it before. As one resident explained, "when I hear a train now I feel, 'OK, the train is there, there is a danger.'" With train phobia now widespread, one resident suggested that the disaster has left a mark on the town's collective unconscious. The sound of the train whistle causes strong reactions in people. "We say 'the damned train' … we don't want to see it again, [the disaster is] clear, it's in the back of our minds." Similarly, one woman we interviewed said that when the train screeches, she stops what she is doing, terrified. She feels her reaction is deep-rooted and permanent: "I don't think anyone can get it out of their head."

**FIGURE 8.2** The railroad was operational quickly after the train accident. The downtown is being rebuilt around the existing railroad track instead of relocating the railway to bypass the downtown. Photograph by Emmanuelle Bouchard-Bastien, June, 2014.

Lac-Mégantic residents now realize that there are many dangerous products circulating on the rails, some—hyper-concentrated fertilizers and chemicals like chlorine—even more hazardous than liquid propane and shale oil. Before the accident, most participants never saw the train as unsafe, but their perception has changed. For example, one resident told us that, in the past, the only problem was that a train crossing sometimes made her late for work. But now, she said, "We try to be as far as possible from the train. I see the DOT [the type of tank car involved in the accident] go by and say to myself, 'I have a good idea of what is in there, and it's dangerous.'" Because of these inherent risks, one resident we spoke with wants oil transport to cease: "Besides being a pollutant, it's dangerous, and for our health we may have a big problem, not only in our physical health but in our mental health."

Given their heightened sensory awareness and knowledge, many participants feel they can no longer coexist with the train due to fear (a condition psychologists associate with post-traumatic shock). Some cannot imagine a future without the construction of a bypass that prevents the train from passing through the city center. As explained by one city center resident, the fact that trains still circulate downtown is difficult to accept:

> [T]he option is to remove the rail that passes right through the city center. We are demolishing the entire city center to ensure that there are no con-taminants, and the only thing that remains unchanged is the railway: this is ridiculous … Risk management, they said: it's a risk we are no longer able to manage.

Several participants believe that moving the railway is the only way to ensure the psychological recovery of the community. Some participants believe a bypass is critical if industrial and residential functions are to coexist. Trains would be able to serve the industrial sector while ensuring that if an accident occurs, as explained by this man we interviewed, "it will not be the heart of the city that will be affected. We can't prevent trains from derailing, but we can put in place measures to reduce the risk." However, some participants added that even an increase in safety couldn't calm people's concerns. As explained by another stakeholder, "Although there are improvements in safety, there will be concerns, that's for sure."

### Risk #2: Weakened Economic Vitality

The Lac-Mégantic case reveals significant tension between risk (in the physical and psychological senses described above) and economics. The city has always been a major railway hub and residents trace its historical growth to the railway's arrival in 1878. Before the railway tragedy, however, Lac-Mégantic was recovering from a period of economic and social decline. Indeed, its prosperity still depends on sectors affected by globalization and the international economic relocations of the early 2000s, a period when garment factories, lumber operations, and plywood industries moved overseas.

Some informants we spoke with associate the destruction that occurred on July 6, 2013, with a difficult economic situation that has allowed risks (i.e., oil trains) to permeate their daily lives. Meanwhile, other participants believe Lac-Mégantic's sluggish economy needed to reinvent itself, with or without a catalyzing tragedy. As one participant put it:

> The town of Mégantic has died. There is nothing thriving in Mégantic. Lumber is no longer booming. All that traditionally kept Mégantic alive has closed. One after the other … So you had to reinvent your economy anyway.

Despite its languishing economy, urban renewal efforts of the past fifteen years had made Lac-Mégantic's downtown a place frequented for its shops, restaurants, and bars. As one informant mentioned: "You can't imagine the place the downtown held in the heart of the people of Lac-Mégantic." Compounding this decline, losing access to the downtown and the destruction of buildings meant significant losses of jobs and services. Many businesses did not survive the tragedy, because they could not find a place to relocate, the relocation took too long, or they lacked the resources and energy to start over.

Some residents of Lac-Mégantic lost their jobs due to the tragedy. In some cases, delays in the relocation of businesses lasted longer than the government unemployment support. Others managed to find jobs elsewhere, but experienced difficulty in the process. For example, one informant told us about a friend, who worked at a dollar store, who was relocated to the Montreal branch and compelled to make long and frequent trips to balance work and family life. During the closure of essential businesses, Lac-Mégantic residents had to do errands in larger neighboring cities. Although businesses have reopened, some people have retained the habit of shopping elsewhere, causing some Lac-Mégantic residents to feel that the revitalization efforts of the last fifteen years have been completely wasted. Consequently, the vast majority of interviewees are deeply worried about the future of Lac-Mégantic's downtown. Many want to leave the area, some are seriously considering doing so, and others are waiting to see how the recovery proceeds before making a final decision.

## With or Without Railway?

The issue of maintaining downtown Lac-Mégantic's railway is complicated by the fact that residents do not wish to further undermine their local economy. According to some, the bypass is not the only risk-management solution. "Would you destroy everything because of an accident?" one interviewee asked. "The railroad was there before the city," she continued, "so it is up to them to move elsewhere." Moreover, the bypass project could set a precedent for other municipalities built around railroad tracks in Québec and beyond. Such a solution would not be economically feasible, as one informant explained: "If all municipalities start asking for bypasses … The cost of relocating a track is going to be absolutely huge." Another added, "if [governments] do it for Lac-Mégantic, all the other cities are going to want to move their track too." In the same vein, a few participants said simply managing the hotspot (the accident site), or imposing stricter transport regulations, would offer logical and practical solutions because that is where the risk is greatest. Although they show empathy for their fellow mourners, or may themselves live with psychological effects, citizens with this view believe that what happened in 2013 was an accident that will not be repeated.

Permeating and underlying all of these discussions is the fact that major industries, which provide jobs in the community, depend, even today, on the railway for their activities. This reality explains—at least in part—why the railway was restored so quickly after the tragedy.

## Decision-Makers: Focused on the Economy?

After the tragedy, an array of actors needed to collectively reflect on risk and socioeconomic reconstruction. This has been a difficult exercise. People's perceptions of the accident and opinions about the railway are sometimes irreconcilable, which creates very real social dissensions. Authorities (in this case the mayor and the provincial government) play a crucial role in these processes. In this section, we consider how decision-makers have managed tensions over differing visions of the future, and, specifically, the railway.

Some Lac-Mégantic residents we spoke with feel that the authorities have put more energy into supporting the economic sector than supporting ordinary citizens, and that money is a more important driver of decisions than the well-being of the community. For example, one resident observed: "the true reality is that there are still people in Mégantic who are extremely fragile. And the decision-makers are focusing on concrete and glass." Another informant believes that "the human side has never been recognized. Despite what the mayor and her gang want us to believe, it was always just a matter of money." This point of view is echoed by other local actors, and consistent with the findings of social science researchers who have analyzed similar circumstances (Behrends, Reyna, and Schlee 2011).

Study participants offered examples that illustrate the way this dynamic operates concurrently at multiple economic scales. At a transnational scale, the railway's quick repair was interpreted to imply that the interests of the oil and railway industries take precedence over those of ordinary citizens. As one participant observed:

> One of the first things they did when they started to clean up was to restore the railway. They didn't brag about it, but they started transporting hazardous materials again. No matter what we ask for or demand, it's stronger than us.

Another resident remarked, "For sure money makes the world go round. Oil is god ... very pervasive." Some participants emphasized their helplessness in the face of oil companies, railway companies, and the federal government, which they believed lack accountability. One participant declared, "It's not a nice feeling to feel like a victim of something that you can't defend yourself against or that you can't obtain adequate justice for."

Examples highlighting the local economic scale were also offered, once again emphasizing the perception that the economy is the decision-makers' first priority. Informants spoke of new commercial developments that took precedence over the demolished downtown, including homes or workplaces offering community support services. Tourism is another part of the local economy—believed by many residents to take precedence over ordinary people, basic recovery efforts, and job creation. A number of participants noted their dissatisfaction with the expenses and choices made by the municipal council in connection with the redevelopment of the city center, citing expenses for tourists (e.g., a $CA 43,000 walking path in the city center) as a prime example. As described by one frustrated participant, "We can decide to wear rose-colored glasses and say: 'there will be a super nice memorial park with trails' ... But we must have jobs too."

### Envisioning the Future

Decision-makers' lack of a clear vision for Lac-Mégantic's future—especially in relation to the city's railway—was noted by many of our informants. According to some, authorities refuse to make decisions for fear of setting precedents. Other informants suspect that the government cannot support the bypass project because of ill-will or a lack of legal influence in the railway industry. And still others detect a lack of decision-making capacity. For example, a local socio-economic stakeholder asked: "How do you manage this? There is nobody who is trained for it. Impossible! So ... you make a decision, there are some who complain. If you don't make that decision, others complain. So there's a lot of whining and complaining." Residents also talked about how the lack of transparency and poor communication creates anxieties and frustrations. As described by one participant, "In communications, if you want to create anxiety, just be unclear. And that's exactly what they have done for a year-and-a-half."

In contrast to those who highlight indecision and lack of clarity, other informants believe the authorities already have their vision of the future. For informants who believe decision-makers have already solidified plans for the railway (specifically) and the future (more broadly), consultation strategies became suspect. A recently launched participatory process known as "Reinventing the City" is viewed with distrust. One informant described the process as "the best smoke screen I've seen in my career." Another participant added: "there was the big show 'Reinventing the City' that was all decided in advance. We went there for absolutely nothing." While less suspicious, other participants nonetheless fear that the city center will turn into a "planner's dream" rather than a reflection of residents' visions.

In response to perceived government inaction and a prioritization of economic concerns, several local citizens' groups have formed since the tragedy. These groups have advocated for the bypass, for more transparency in the municipal council, and for environmental protection. In 2015, citizen mobilization was still visible at public commemorations, municipal assemblies, and in the social media.

## Post-disaster Impacts and Citizen Voice

The tensions that surround discussions of Lac-Mégantic's future—as well as the decision-making process that will determine that future—have consequences for the community. Reflecting on the greatest impacts of the disaster, one resident said: "You might think it's the explosion, but no, it's what comes after. That's what's amazing. I would not have believed it." The social fabric in the community seems badly torn as a result of deficiencies in participatory processes, poor communication, and lack of transparency. As one resident observed, "Before, Mégantic was more serene, peaceful, now it's a bit disjointed," adding, "We had peace here, and now I do not see that anymore. People are tearing each other apart."

Somewhat unexpectedly, this tumultuous situation has empowered citizens and enabled them to voice their opinions. The majority of study participants observed that Lac-Mégantic's citizens express their views much more clearly than before. Ironically, however, many no longer dare to express these opinions publicly for fear of being associated with a faction. In spite of the polarization of opinions, citizens' groups have argued effectively for attention to environmental impacts and have called for transparency in management.

## Conclusion

In Lac-Mégantic, each person experienced the railway tragedy in his or her own unique and personal way. Out of these individual and collective experiences, however, conclusions emerge that validate our findings and confirm the relevance of previous anthropologies of disaster. The Lac-Mégantic case bears similarities to other disasters associated with extractive industries. First, the psychological impacts of the tragedy are significant and lasting (Cope et al. 2013; Lee and Blanchard 2012). Second, pre-existing social inequalities result in disproportionate vulnerability (O'Rourke and Connolly 2003; Picou et al. 2009). Third, the complicated process of disaster recovery reveals residents' loss of confidence in policy makers and risk managers (Cornitius 1997; Goodfellow and Smith 2013; Picou et al. 2009).

The social science literature tends to approach the topic of oil in terms of geopolitical conflicts related to extractive sites (Behrends, Reyna, and Schlee 2011). The story of Lac-Mégantic reminds us that oil should also be considered in terms of the human experience and local conflict it creates downstream. At Lac-Mégantic—as is often the case in the wake of oil-related disasters like the Exxon Valdez and BP *Deepwater Horizon* spills—the derailment and explosion of July, 2013, paved the way for what became a "corrosive community" (Freudenburg, in Picou et al. 2009, 284), in which already horrific initial impacts combined with new social tensions to produce "secondary disasters" (Picou et al. 2009, 284). Why did this occur? Latent disagreements about local development trajectories are crystallized, in this case, around the future of the railway in the city center. The situation following the Lac-Mégantic railway disaster brings to light underlying tensions regarding local development and local leaders. At the center of recent economic declines in the textile and lumber sectors, the community of Lac-Mégantic also now finds itself impacted by North America's unconventional oil boom.

Oil has been called "perhaps the single most controversial and influential commodity in the world" (O'Rourke and Connolly 2003, 612). In a context of accelerating development and new extractive technologies, the assessment of oil's social and psychological impacts must begin to take into account transport and other off-site risks. Passing through does not mean leaving no trace. As seen in Lac-Mégantic, distant sites may bear marks that are as strong as those experienced in extraction zones.

Lac-Mégantic offers lessons learned in the contemporary context of North America's new oil and gas industry. The Lac-Mégantic disaster reveals gaps in safety and local development as well as in public agencies and management. It highlights the inadequacy of current policies to consider communities and the environment, as well as demonstrates the need to improve governance practices and promote citizen engagement. While future research is needed to more fully comprehend the "moving risks" of oil and gas transport, it is imperative that we work to protect communities and develop public policies capable of preventing, mitigating, and effectively recovering from such disasters.

## Note

1  The interviews were conducted in French and translated in English by the authors.

## References

Agence de la Santé et des Services Sociaux de l'Estrie (ASSS de l'Estrie). 2015. Tragédie ferroviaire de Lac-Mégantic: La force d'une communauté, malgré les enjeux de taille. Communiqué de Presse, Sherbrooke, January 28, 2015.

Aldrich, Daniel P., and Michelle A. Meyer. 2014. Social capital and community resilience. *American Behavioral Scientist* 59, 2:254–269.

Beck, Ulrich. 1992. *World risk society*, Malden, MA: Polity Press.

Behrends, Andrea, Stephen P. Reyna, and Gunther Schlee. 2011. *Crude domination: An anthropology of oil*. New York: Berghahn.

Benadusi, Mara, Chiara Brambilla, and Bruno Riccio. 2009. *Disasters, development and humanitarian aid: New challenges for anthropology*. Rimini, Italy: Guaraldi.

Brisson, Geneviève. 2004. *La capture du sauvage: Les représentations sociales de la forêt québécoise: le cas d'Anticosti (1534–2001)*. Dissertation presented for the degree of PhD in anthropology. Faculté des études supérieures, Université Laval: Québec.

Bureau de la sécurité des transports du Canada (BST). 2015. *Enquête ferroviaire R13D0054*. www.bst-tsb.gc.ca/fra/enquetes-investigations/rail/2013/r13d0054/r13d0054.asp (accessed March 24, 2017).

Button, Gregory. 2010. *Disaster culture: Knowledge and uncertainty in the wake of human and environmental catastrophe*. Walnut Creek, CA: Left Coast Press.

Chamlee-Wright, Emily. 2010. *The cultural and political economy of recovery: Social learning in a post-disaster environment*. Abingdon, UK: Routledge.

Cope, Michael, Tim Slack, Troy C. Blanchard, and Matthew R. Lee. 2013. Does time heal all wounds? Community attachment, natural resource employment and health impacts in the wake of BP Deepwater Horizon disaster. *Social Science Research* 42, 3:872–881.

Cornitius, Tim. 1997. Texas city explosion: 50th anniversary marks progress. *Chemical Week* 18, 17:64.

Dawson, Susan E., and Gary E. Madsen. 2011. Psychosocial and health impacts of uranium mining and milling on Navajo lands. *Health Physics* 101, 5:618–625.

Eastmond, Marita. 2010. Reconciliation, reconstruction, and everyday life in war-torn societies. *Focaal—Journal of Global and Historical Anthropology* 57:3–16.

Frittelli, John, Anthony Andrews, Paul W. Parfomak, Robert Pirog, Jonathan L. Ramseur, and Michael Ratner. 2014. *U.S. rail transportation of crude oil: Background and issues for congress.* Washington, DC: Congressional Research Services, 7–5700.

Galea, Sandro, Chris R. Brewin, Michael Gruber, Russell T. Jones, Daniel W. King, Lynda A. King, Richard J. McNally, Robert J. Ursano, Maria Petukhova, and Ronald C. Kessler. 2007. Exposure to hurricane-related stressors and mental illness after hurricane Katrina. *Arch Gen Psychiatry* 64, 12:1427–1434.

Gill, Duane A., J. Steven Picou, and Liesel A. Ritchie. 2012. The *Exxon Valdez* and BP oil spills: A comparison of initial social and psychological impacts. *American Behavioral Scientist* 56, 1:3–23.

Goodfellow, Tom, and Alyson Smith. 2013. From urban catastrophe to "model" city? Politics, security and development in post-conflict Kigali. *Urban Studies* 50, 15:3185–3202.

Hoffman, Susanna, and Anthony Oliver-Smith. 2009. *Catastrophe and culture: The anthropology of disaster.* Santa Fe, NM: School of American Research Press.

Langumier, Julien. 2008. *Survivre à l'inondation. Pour une ethnologie de la catastrophe.* Lyon, France: ENS Éditions, coll. Sociétés, espaces, temps.

Lee, Matthew R., and Troy C. Blanchard. 2012. Community attachment and negative affective states in the context of the BP Deepwater Horizon disaster. *American Behavioral Scientist* 56, 1:24–47.

Leiss, William. 2001. *In the chamber of risks.* Montréal: McGill-Queens University Press.

Lezama, Paula Vásquez. 2009. De la tragédie collective à l'individuation du malheur: l'expérience de fin de légitimité de la condition de victime des sinistrés de la catastrophe La Tragedia (1999) au Venezuela. *Anthropologie et Sociétés* 33, 3:193–210.

Maltais, Danielle, Lise Lachance, Martin Fortin, Gilles Lalande, Suzie Robichaud, Christophe Fortin, and Anne Simard. 2000. L'état de santé psychologique et physique des sinistrés des inondations de juillet 1996: étude comparative entre sinistrés et non sinistrés. *Les Désastres Naturels* 25, 1:116–137.

Ministère de la Culture et des Communications (MCC). 2016. *Gare ferroviaire de Lac-Mégantic.* Répertoire du patrimoine culturel du Québec. www.patrimoine-culturel.gouv.qc.ca/rpcq/detail.do?methode=consulter&id=93405&type=bien#.VvE0bnp5zOA (accessed March 22, 2016).

Ministère du Développement durable, Environnement et Lutte contre les changements climatiques (MDDELCC). 2017. *Tragédie ferroviaire à Lac-Mégantic.* www.mddelcc.gouv.qc.ca/lac-megantic/lac-megantic.htm (accessed March 24, 2017).

National Transportation Safety Board (NTSB). 2015. NTSB gathering Information on CSX crude oil train derailment in West Virginia. NTSB Press Release, February 2. www.ntsb.gov/news/press-releases/Pages/PR20150217.aspx (accessed August 25, 2015).

November, Valérie, Cristina D'Alessandro-Scarpari, and Élisabeth Rémy. 2004. Un lieu en controverse: une controverse qui fait lieu(x). *Norois* 193, 4:91–102.

Oliver-Smith, Anthony. 2009. Anthropology and the political economy of disasters. In *The political economy of hazards and disasters,* edited by Eric C. Jones and Arthur D. Murphy, 11–28. Lanham, MD: AltaMira Press.

O'Rourke, Dara, and Sarah Connolly. 2003. Just oil? The distribution of environmental and social impacts of oil production and consumption. *Annual Review of Environment and Resources* 28, 1:587–617.

Pelling, Mark. 2001. Natural disasters? In *Social nature: Theory, practice, and politics*, edited by Noel Castree and Bruce Braun, 170–188. Malden, MA: Blackwell Publishers.

Picou, J. Steven, Cecelia Formichella, Brent K. Marshall, and Catalina Arata. 2009. Community impacts of the Exxon Valdez oil spill: A synthesis and elaboration of social science research. In *Synthesis: Three decades of social science research on socioeconomic effects related to offshore petroleum development in coastal Alaska*, edited by Stephen R. Braund and Jack Kruse, 279–310. Anchorage, AK: Minerals Management Service, Alaska, OCS Region.

Revet, Sandrine. 2007. *Anthropologie d'une catastrophe. Les coulées de boue de 1999 sur le Littoral central Vénézuélien.* Paris: Presses de la Sorbonne Nouvelle.

Rosales, Martin Renzo. 2007. *The Panama Canal expansion project: Transit maritime mega project development, reactions, and alternatives from affected people.* Doctoral Dissertation. Gainesville: University of Florida.

Scanlon, Joseph. 1998. Dealing with mass death after a community catastrophe: handling bodies after the 1917 Halifax explosion. *Disaster Prevention and Management* 7, 4:288–304.

Solnit, Rebecca. 2009. *A paradise built in hell: The extraordinary communities that arise in disaster.* New York: Penguin.

Stedman, Richard C. 2003. Is it really just a social construction?: The contribution of the physical environment to sense of place. *Society & Natural Resources: An International Journal* 16, 8:671–685.

Transportation Safety Board of Canada (TSBC). 2015. Derailment and fire of second Canadian National crude oil train near Gogama, Ontario. *Railway Investigation R15H0021*, www.tsb.gc.ca/eng/enquetes-investigations/rail/2015/r15h0021/r15h0021.asp (accessed August 25, 2015).

Windsor, Jim E., and J. Alistair McVey. 2005. Annihilation of both place and sense of place: The experience of the Cheslatta T'En Canadian First Nation within the context of large-scale environmental projects. *The Geographical Journal* 171, 2:146–165.

# 9

# BRINGING COUNTRY BACK?

## Indigenous Aspirations and Ecological Values in Australian Mine-Site Rehabilitation

Tamar Cohen[1]

## Introduction

In Australia, rehabilitation is defined as the process used to repair the impacts of mining on the environment (Commonwealth of Australia 2006). Under state and territory legislation, all mining operations are obligated to undertake rehabilitation. Companies are also required to meet site-specific clauses set out in formal land use agreements with Aboriginal Traditional Owners to whom the land may eventually be transferred.[2] State government regulators assess the success of rehabilitation before mining leases and associated legal responsibilities can be relinquished. The legality of mining in Australia therefore hinges on the assumption that rehabilitation *can* remediate mining-induced environmental impacts. In this context, mining companies set rehabilitation goals and objectives based on guidance provided by state government regulators.

In the Australian state of Queensland, where this research took place, regulations allow for a range of rehabilitation methods, providing that the resultant landscapes are deemed safe for humans and wildlife, non-polluting, geologically stable, and can support agreed upon post-mining land uses (DEHP 2014a). Rehabilitation is often positioned as "turning back the clock" to a set of land uses and associated values that existed prior to the commencement of mining. For instance the Queensland government outlines a rehabilitation hierarchy in which the re-creation of pre-mining native ecosystems is prioritized above other land use types (DEHP 2014a). As a result, some companies attempt to completely restore a site to its pre-mining ecosystem or establish conditions that closely resemble it. Alternatively, companies may develop landscapes that support other locally relevant land uses, such as grazing. For Aboriginal peoples affected by mining, however, rehabilitation represents a vision of the future—a future premised on greater control over their land. While mining companies have made attempts to identify and prioritize culturally significant plant and animal species for return to mined landscapes, little consideration has been given to understanding rehabilitation in relation to the lived experience and future aspirations of the Aboriginal people who may inherit these designed landscapes.

This chapter addresses this gap through an analysis of historical and current activities undertaken by the mining operation Rio Tinto Alcan Weipa (RTAW) in its attempts to rehabilitate the traditional estate of the Alngith people—one of eleven Traditional Owner groups affected by the operation's extensive bauxite mine near the township of Weipa on the western side of Cape York Peninsula, Queensland, Australia (Figure 9.1). Weipa is remote, accessible only by airplane or dirt road. Nevertheless, Alngith people's Country, as well as that of adjacent Traditional Owner groups, has been mined and successively rehabilitated or revegetated since the 1960s by RTAW (formerly Comalco). RTAW's bauxite mine is one of the largest in the world. The company's mining lease extends over more than 240,000 hectares (ha) and in recent years approximately 1,000 ha have been cleared and rehabilitated annually (DEHP 2014b; RTA 2014). The mining process involves the clearing of vegetation, scraping and stockpiling of overburden (the non-economic substrate sitting above the bauxite layer), and the excavation of a shallow layer of bauxite. The bauxite is then crushed and washed at a beneficiation plant then loaded onto ships for transport. Mine tailings consisting of fine bauxite residue and water are stored on-site in impoundments that range from 20 to 1,100 ha in surface area (DEHP 2014b). Mining activities are highly visible in and around the township of Weipa, on Alngith Country, and throughout the greater mining lease, including the traditional estates of other Traditional Owner groups. Aerial imagery reveals that more than 70% of Alngith land has been either directly mined or impacted by associated infrastructures including the town of Weipa itself.

Alngith people's relationship to RTAW's presence is complex. Although the substantive nature of mining-associated benefits in Australia has been critiqued (O'Faircheallaigh 2004), mining has provided services and economic opportunities otherwise absent in remote Aboriginal communities. Mining makes it possible for Traditional Owners in Weipa, and Aboriginal peoples in general, to remain on their lands. Whilst acknowledging this, Alngith individuals have also expressed dismay at the clearance of vast areas of bushland, reduced access to, or destruction of, culturally significant places, changes to local hydrology and ecology, and the daily activities of company personnel on Alngith land. Nevertheless, many Alngith people work—or aspire to work—for RTAW. Others have established independent businesses to service the needs of the mining operation.

In this chapter, I first analyze the company's rehabilitation practices in relation to a changing social and regulatory environment. Drawing on materials dating from the 1960s to the present, I demonstrate that rehabilitation practices are not simply technical in nature, but also socially and politically contingent. I pay special attention to recent assertions by RTAW that their current rehabilitation practices align with Traditional Owners' values relating to the Aboriginal English concept of "Country" (the territory, and system of ecological and spiritual relationships, to which an individual or group is connected) and describe how the company negotiates the

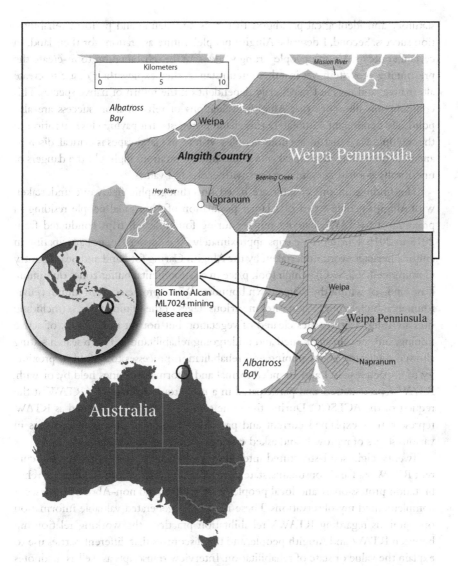

**FIGURE 9.1** Location of Weipa and Napranum townships and the approximate location of Alngith Country on the Weipa Peninsula–western Cape York Peninsula, Queensland, Australia. Alngith Country covers the western-most portion of the Weipa Peninsula between the Mission River to the North and Beening Creek to the East. Alngith Country is almost entirely encompassed within Rio Tinto Alcan's Weipa mining lease which extends north, east and south impacting the traditional estates of eleven Traditional Owner groups (including Alngith). Map by Donna Gayer, Artasaverb.

statutory and ideological paradigms that it uses to define and perform rehabilitation success. Second, I describe Alngith people's future aspirations for their land. In certain contexts, Alngith people strongly advocate for rehabilitation to re-create the pre-mining ecosystem, yet in other circumstances they express their desire to create alternative land uses not necessarily dependent on the return of native species. This contradiction illustrates that Alngith evaluations of rehabilitation success are also politically contingent. Ultimately, this chapter suggests that paying close attention to the multiple ways that Indigenous peoples wish to use landscapes is critical; discrepancies in how Indigenous speakers vocalize their aspirations highlight the dangers of uncritically conflating cultural values with ecological values.

The findings in this chapter are based on ethnographic fieldwork undertaken with Alngith people—part of a larger population of Aboriginal people residing in proximity to RTAW's bauxite mine—during four research trips conducted from 2013 to 2015. During these trips approximately 30 days were spent participating in cultural heritage work undertaken by the Alngith Caring for Land and Sea Country Committee (ACLSCC), which took place in environmental buffer zones on mining lease lands, or within the Weipa town boundary. While protected from mining, environmental buffer zones adjoin sites in various stages of the mining process (including sites awaiting clearing, sites cleared of vegetation but not yet mined, sites of active mining, and sites already mined and undergoing rehabilitation). This research setting allowed discussion about mining and rehabilitation processes to unfold in proximity to impacted sites. I also attended formal and informal meetings held by, or with, RTAW representatives and participated in a mine tour facilitated by RTAW at the request of the ACLSCC. During the mine tour, Alngith people listened as RTAW representatives explained current and past rehabilitation practices, viewed sites in various stages of regrowth, and asked questions about rehabilitation.

Twenty-eight semi-structured interviews with Alngith people, former and current RTAW staff and consultants, state government regulators, other mine-site rehabilitation professionals, and local people of Aboriginal and non-Aboriginal descent complemented my observations. These interviews generated valuable information on opinions regarding RTAW's rehabilitation practices, the working relationship between RTAW and Alngith people, and the discourses that different parties use to explain the value or state of rehabilitation. Interview transcripts as well as fieldnotes from participant-observation and informal discussions were analyzed to elucidate how different parties frame rehabilitation practices. I also compared how Alngith people talk about their land-based aspirations while engaged in formal research activities (e.g., during interviews or meetings with RTAW staff) with how they express or demonstrate these aspirations during their daily activities (e.g., fishing, traveling to visit family, carrying out errands in Weipa).

## Mining and Rehabilitating Country

The Aboriginal English term "Country" is used frequently by Australian Aboriginal people to describe the territory (including land, sea, and sky) to which an individual or group is connected. It can be considered a proper noun (Rose 1996) and is often capitalized. Country encompasses the myriad interrelationships among humans, wildlife, plants, spirits, places, and pasts that coalesce to inform Aboriginal identity, culture, and knowledge (Rose 1996). Aboriginal individuals retain strong symbolic and material connections to the species, landscape features, spiritual entities (human and non-human), songs, stories, and memories that comprise Country and sustain its inhabitants. Especially in remote regions of Australia, access to, and management of, Country is considered key for realizing many Indigenous livelihood aspirations (Scambary 2009).

Mining on Aboriginal land impacts relationships with Country, both directly (by physically destroying or polluting cultural landscapes) and indirectly (by spurring social processes that change how people use, perceive, and describe Country) (see Strang 2004). Drawing on ethnographic work with Yoggom people in Papua New Guinea, Kirsch (2004) describes the loss and alienation experienced by Indigenous peoples when familiar landscapes are rendered unfamiliar. He suggests that landscapes transformed by mining become "empty"—devoid of the physical markers that tie people to place (Kirsch 2004, 188). While complicated by similar feelings of loss, Aboriginal peoples' responses to mining and development in Australia have been characterized as relatively dynamic and accommodating, with groups negotiating the impacts, promises, and bureaucratic structures of mining alongside their own cultural politics and material aspirations (Trigger and Robinson 2004). Despite their contemporary and diverse engagements with extractive industries, bureaucratic structures, including land use agreements made with mining companies, often require Aboriginal people to express their connections to Country in reference to a traditionalist Aboriginal past. This traditionalism can then become reflected in Aboriginal articulations of cultural identity (Martin 2015). Social relationships and relationships with Country often become reified in the process, as Aboriginal groups struggle to assert their concerns in ways that are recognizable within cultural as well as bureaucratic frameworks (Merlan 2004; Povinelli 2002). That mining processes contribute to the social production of meaning suggests that mining landscapes are not truly "empty places," but are places that have been physically and ideologically altered by—and are therefore "full of"—the experiences and promises of mining. Erasing the impacts of mining during the rehabilitation period is likely to prove difficult given that people's imagined futures are informed by the physical, social, and ideological landscapes that mining processes have engendered (Halvaksz 2008).

Recent anthropological studies conducted in Papua New Guinea (Golub 2014) and Indonesia (Welker 2014) demonstrate that far from existing as coherent independent actors, "the mine" and "the community" are continually and recursively refashioned, both in relation to each other and in relation to broader expectations of what constitutes a mine or a mine-affected community. Corporate identities are produced and performed alongside, and in relation to, local identities, with Indigenous peoples and mining companies both participating actively in the process (Welker 2014). In these dynamic contexts, mining companies may co-opt objectified cultural sentiments or practices to engender local support for their operations, further reifying and legitimizing particular cultural expressions while simultaneously delegitimizing others (Horowitz 2015). As will be seen, in Weipa an essentialized understanding of the concept "Country" has been vocalized by both the community and the company to describe and legitimize different rehabilitation goals—once again demonstrating that rehabilitation is not a purely technical act but a biophysical expression of socially and politically defined values and goals (Edgar 2007).

Mining rehabilitation that occurs on Aboriginal lands must be considered in relation to such processes of mutual identity construction. Environmental legacy is a critical component of contemporary corporate identity, which encourages an alignment of rehabilitation practices and powerful discourses of environmentalism, ecological restoration, and community development—discourses designed to appeal to acknowledged societal demands for ecologically and socially responsible extraction (ICMM 2006). Influenced by activists' calls for responsible regulation and corporate citizenship, these alignments are premised on the notion that both ecological and social systems should be restored to a pre-mining condition.

Those wishing to incorporate Indigenous peoples' concerns into mine-site rehabilitation in Australia (Smith 2008), and elsewhere (Butler, Toh, and Wagambie 2012; Garibaldi 2009), argue that because native ecosystems are important to Indigenous cultural identities and livelihoods, companies must work with them to prioritize and return culturally significant species to post-mining landscapes. In relation to ecological restoration more generally, Higgs (2003) likewise claims that the restoration of native species can over time engender a revitalization of "traditional" practices (ranging from hunting to ritual activities) that depend on those species. As these examples illustrate, attempts to incorporate Indigenous values into rehabilitation and restoration often implicitly adhere to a "traditionalist" version of Indigenous identity, thus perpetuating a problematic standard of authenticity against which Indigenous aspirations and rehabilitated landscapes are judged. As the case study that follows confirms, Alngith people are compelled to articulate post-mining aspirations that reproduce expected "traditionalist" forms even when their actual aspirations—while retaining cultural distinctiveness—arise in relation to current material aspirations that include acquiring control over their traditional estate once mining has ceased.

## Changing Rehabilitation Objectives and Contexts at Weipa

Rehabilitation activities commenced at Weipa in 1966, only a few years after commercial mining started. The extensive yet shallow nature of bauxite mining at Weipa allows rehabilitation practices to be carried out concurrent with active mining on other areas of the lease. Rehabilitation objectives and practices have changed considerably since the 1960s, evolving from an original objective of creating economically productive post-mining land uses (such as grazing and forestry) to more recent aspirations of producing self-sustaining environments dominated by tree and shrub species that match the pre-mining ecosystem. These shifts parallel both changing attitudes and regulations concerning the value of landscapes at the regional and national scale and changes in corporate approaches to Aboriginal engagement. The result is a mosaic of regenerating landscapes of varying size, age, structure, and composition (Gould 2012).

The early period of rehabilitation (the 1970s and 1980s) in Weipa focused heavily on assessing the feasibility of producing economically valuable forest (stocked with non-native species like Cypress pine and African mahogany) and pasture on previously mined land. Driven by collaborations between the company (Comalco at that time) and state government departments, these experiments corresponded with a broader national agenda of converting Australia's remote north into a productive agricultural and grazing region (Holmes 2012). In public documents produced at the time, Comalco describe rehabilitation as an opportunity to create economically viable landscapes and contribute to regional development (Roberts 1985). Rehabilitation of the pre-mining ecosystem, although also attempted in this time period, was seen as having no economic value and was, therefore, described as a "waste" (Stewart 1978, 53). Stands of now unmanaged plantation trees and established weed infestations remain as the biophysical legacies of this era. Tellingly, the two weed species of most concern on RTAW's mining lease, *Leucaena leucocephala* (leucaena) and *Andropogon gayanus* (Gamba grass), were intentionally planted as pasture species in this period. Today, they are viewed as weeds to be managed and threats to current rehabilitation efforts.

In interviews, RTAW employees reflecting on the rehabilitation efforts of the 1970s and 1980s described the forestry projects (and, to a lesser extent, the pasture projects) as misconceived. They identified these earlier actions as future rehabilitation liabilities and worried that government regulators may be reluctant to "sign off" on areas damaged by earlier intervention. One staff member described the economic experiments as paternalistic attempts to engender economic development for Aboriginal people without their consultation. This charge of paternalism is consistent with broader critiques of community development initiatives instigated by Comalco as part of its "good neighbor" approach to Aboriginal relations during the 1970s and 1980s (Howitt, Callope, and Savo 1996).

During the 1990s, RTAW's rehabilitation focus shifted from creating productive landscapes to creating post-mining landscapes that were valued ecologically. The 1990s also saw a shift toward greater engagement with Aboriginal people (Howitt, Callope, and Savo 1996). The majority of rehabilitation conducted in this period aimed to establish a stable flora resembling the pre-mining ecosystem. The seed mix was composed of "native" species, although not necessarily native to the local area. Species were selected for their vigor and role in successional processes rather than for their presence in the pre-mining ecosystem. This led to the dominance of quick-growing Acacia, Eucalyptus, and Grevillea species over vast areas of Alngith Country. The result is a much denser forest than that present before mining, which has prevented the successful establishment of other native species (Murray and Mulligan 2003). Assessments of ecologically oriented rehabilitation at Weipa demonstrate that plant composition remains substantially different from the pre-mining landscape. These sites are more susceptible to fire damage and are unlikely to be recolonized by all native wildlife (see Gould 2012 for a summary of literature).

RTAW's rehabilitation objectives changed once again in 2008. Several research participants described the combined factors that triggered a shift in focus. Several negative ecological assessments of RTAW's rehabilitation efforts emerged in the early years of the new millennium (see Erskine, Vickers, and Mulligan 2008). RTAW staff told me that around the same time, RTAW's management decided to curtail practices not directly linked to its core business of extracting and selling bauxite. This managerial decision eliminated the company's interest in pursuing alternative land use options. New guidelines for rehabilitation in Queensland, released by the Queensland Government in 2006, prioritized the re-creation of pre-mining ecologies over alternative land use options (EPA 2007). In response to these factors RTAW modified the seed mix to contain only *locally* native species and the species ratio was made more consistent with the composition of the prior eco-system. During my time in Weipa, staff expressed genuine pride in RTAW's post-2008 rehabilitation efforts, although one interviewee warned that it would take at least five to ten years before these ecosystems could be deemed self-sustaining and able to withstand "unfettered access" from Traditional Owners.

## Alngith People and Rehabilitation at Weipa

In 2001, the Western Cape Communities Co-Existence Agreement (WCCCA) was signed and registered as an Indigenous Land Use Agreement. Since the agreement, RTAW has been required to consider rehabilitation in direct relation to Traditional Owners' concerns. In Weipa, the WCCCA is a formal vehicle that Traditional Owners can use to hold RTAW accountable to its social and environmental commitments. Commitments to consult with Traditional Owners on rehabilitation are legally enshrined in the WCCCA. The agreement also describes mechanisms for the transfer of rehabilitated land to Traditional Owners once mining has ceased. In the years immediately preceding and following the WCCCA signing, RTAW consulted with Traditional Owners regarding post-mining land uses and relinquishment, but reports from these processes remain confidential. In 2009, the company began a consultation process that sought to incorporate Traditional Owners' concerns into rehabilitation through the identification and prioritization of culturally significant plant species. Local Aboriginal people are also included in rehabilitation practices through the collection and sale of native seed. The company has recently started publicizing mine-site rehabilitation as an ecological framework that supports Traditional Owners' cultural aspirations (RTA 2013).

During my research, Alngith people expressed concerns about the composition of rehabilitated areas based on their knowledge of the pre-mining environment and its ecosystems, especially concerning roles of and responses to fire. Their evaluations point out the presence or absence of certain species (both native and non-native) in rehabilitated areas and highlight the occurrence of species in ecological zones where they did not previously occur (e.g., species from coastal ridges that are now present on bauxite ridges). Such descriptions are finely scaled, in some cases involving recollections of individual trees. They demonstrate that Alngith people are concerned about the return of species to their specific pre-mining locations rather than content to have species planted indiscriminately across the mining lease. Although not explored in detail here, Alngith people also worry about how post-mining landscapes affect the "old people"—deceased ancestors who are still active constituents of the landscape today. A major concern is that the spirits of the "old people" feel disoriented and that their movements through Country are hindered by the density of regrowth in areas dominated by Acacia and Grevillea species.

In response to my direct questions about how RTAW should rehabilitate Country, Alngith people often stated that the company should "bring Country back." The following statement shared by a Senior Alngith woman during an interview is representative of how Alngith people have expressed such concerns to RTAW:

> We went out to one of the mine areas … and [name removed] asked them are youse gunna put back the plants what youse took out of here? Put it back there? And they said yes. And we said to them, now we don't want no other plants from no other countries, no other places.

In addition to overt statements about rehabilitation resembling prior ecosystems, Alngith people I spoke with described multiple livelihood aspirations dependent on regaining control of mined land, but not necessarily dependent on the re-establishment of a pre-mining state. These aspirations ranged from economic ventures (e.g., establishing cattle operations) to fine-scaled enhancements of specific locations for recreational or other economic purposes (e.g., fishing or swimming sites). In some instances, these enhancements are intended to increase populations of *introduced* plant and animal species like mango and wild pig that serve as local food sources, or to increase the local density of native bush foods. In other instances, proposed enhancements would require clearing rehabilitated land. For instance the Alngith Corporation desires to sublet areas of the mining lease to Weipa residents for business development once these areas have been transferred to their control.[3] Development of Aboriginal owned businesses, and housing for Alngith Corporation members are also strategic aims of the Alngith Corporation. As one Alngith woman stated:

> We acknowledge and recognize that there is [sic] completion criteria [for rehabilitation] … but we'd like to utilize it [land] for this purpose … so we don't need it to be really rehabilitated because we are going to clear it anyway.

While Alngith people do not wish to inherit management problems associated with poorly rehabilitated land, they would like to gain immediate control over some areas so they can establish ventures that will set them in good stead once mining ceases. The most pressing concern, then, is that rehabilitated land be handed over to Alngith control in a timely fashion. When I asked one woman what she hoped to gain from the impending mining tour we were about to experience, she said, "Land back that's already been rehabilitated! That's my aim."

In summary, Alngith people approach rehabilitation in ways that are as diverse as the visions they hold for the future of their land. This complex reality implies that Indigenous aspirations may—but also may not—be consistent with the goal of rehabilitating mine sites for native species and ecological value.

## "Country" as a Rehabilitation Framework

Given the flexibility of regulatory guidelines for rehabilitation, criticism of the poor ecological outcomes of rehabilitation at Weipa, and enhanced global scrutiny of mining in general, RTAW has sought to play a leading role in shaping the future of rehabilitation discourse. RTAW now actively employs the Aboriginal concept "Country" to describe the landscapes that current rehabilitation practices will produce. In its 2013 Sustainable Development Report (RTA 2013, 28), the company states:

> Traditional Owners made clear that "Country" is very important and the legacy of "strong Country" after mining, which includes regenerating the bush for future generations, was paramount.

Rehabilitation practices at Weipa are now described as "fostering connection to Country" (RTA 2014, 38), alluding to the importance of Aboriginal peoples' active participation in the rehabilitation process and their subsequent reconnection with mined places and native species.

From interviews and informal discussions, it is evident that RTAW staff view the Country framework as countering some of the ecological and sociological failures that troubled past rehabilitation efforts. They are optimistic that the new seeding regime will produce bushland ecosystems that are better aligned to the concerns of Traditional Owners, the Queensland Government regulator, and the broader Australian society. Powerfully embodying pride in the new system, I observed one RTAW staff member get goose bumps while describing how the seed collection project has encouraged the transfer of cultural knowledge from senior Traditional Owners to younger people. Significantly, this also demonstrates that mining company staff can be personally and emotionally invested in rehabilitation processes and in the relationships they develop with Traditional Owners.

In reality, recent species prioritization work has done little to change the post-2008 seeding regime. Species prioritized by Traditional Owners, while indeed present in the seed mix, are still indiscriminately spread across the mining lease rather than returned to specific areas where they once occurred. One RTAW staff member described the results of the species prioritization work as "not surprising," since the company was already aware which species were considered culturally significant to Traditional Owners. This raises questions about the value of the work and what it intended to achieve. Moreover, the diversity of Alngith interests described above challenges assertions made by the company that "strong Country" necessarily requires re-creation of the pre-mining ecosystem over the entire mining lease. Many Alngith aspirations are, in fact, at odds with ecological indicators of rehabilitation success.

Whereas in the past, the company explored options for economically beneficial alternative land uses, current communications with Traditional Owners focus *only* on the re-creation of native bushland. Alternatives are considered too risky in a context of regulatory guidelines that prioritize re-creating pre-mining ecosystems. Logistical considerations and cost—as well as disputes over Traditional Owner boundaries and the potential that the government might lease the land to another mining operation in the future—also hinder RTAW's ability to incorporate Aboriginal aspirations into rehabilitation at the finer scale desired by Alngith people.

## Conclusion: "Country" and Rehabilitation as Politically Contingent

Alngith people at times assert a desire for rehabilitation to be commensurate with the pre-mining ecosystem, while at other times they express aspirations for rehabilitation capable of accommodating other land uses. This demonstrates that Alngith statements regarding rehabilitation are not disembodied, objective evaluations, but are instead politically situated and inseparable from the experiences of disempowerment that mining has produced. The political nature of these statements becomes clear when their context is considered. Assertions made by Alngith people that RTAW needs to "bring Country back" were most often made in response to direct questions regarding rehabilitation. In contrast, discussions surrounding alternative land uses generally arose while speakers were participating in other activities in and around the mining lease. This suggests that consultation activities that ask Alngith people to evaluate or comment on rehabilitation are politically charged engagements, in which Aboriginal speakers have an opportunity to perform their dissatisfaction and assert their right to be involved in decision-making processes.

Although formal avenues exist through which Alngith people can challenge RTAW's rehabilitation practices and corporate performance, the majority of Alngith people are unaware of how to utilize them or reluctant to do so. Instead, Alngith people draw on language that has acquired a shared meaning in the mining context to assert their rights and express their concerns. The "Country" concept allows Alngith people to describe their aspirations in reference to both a culturally distinct set of criteria (such as the impact of rehabilitation on the "old people") and to the regulatory and ideological discourse of contemporary mine-site rehabilitation. Interestingly, Alngith people's daily activities critique and challenge a static conceptualization of Country, indicating that Alngith identities and aspirations are not easily reducible to essentialist categories (Povinelli 1993).

Despite their similar rhetoric, it is evident in Weipa that Traditional Owners and company representatives view the outcomes of rehabilitation very differently. For Traditional Owners, rehabilitation is aspirational, signaling a return of their land to their control. For the company, rehabilitation is based on identifying an endpoint when their liability can be handed over to the Queensland Government who are then responsible for transferring it to a third party (such as to the Alngith people). RTAW's focus, then, is on making that endpoint acceptable to the broadest possible range of interested parties while still adhering to Queensland's regulatory guidelines and appearing to legitimately address the company's WCCCA commitments. "Country" discursively appeals to popularized notions of Aboriginal culture, in which Indigenous and ecological values are conflated and linked to a cultural and ecological past untainted by the destructive forces of mining. By co-opting the culturally legitimate discourse of Country, the company conflates Indigenous and ecological values as the morally responsible endpoint. In doing so, it increases the probability that regulators will approve their rehabilitation. Likewise, Alngith people employ the same rhetoric to describe their dissatisfaction in a way that is mutually commensurable within their own cultural paradigm and with the engagement strategies of RTAW. As demonstrated above, however, this conflation undermines Aboriginal peoples' capacity to determine—or at least influence—decisions beyond the composition of the seed mix.

The moral authority vested in the practice of rehabilitating native bushland in Weipa, drawn as it is from the notion of ecological value and the interdependence of Aboriginal peoples and native ecosystems, therefore erodes Alngith people's power to engage with RTAW regarding alternative types of rehabilitation. At best, the emphasis on creating an ecosystem that replicates the pre-mining era will delay the transferal of land to Traditional Owners, since time must be taken to assess whether regeneration is progressing along the desired ecological trajectory. Until the land is proven able to withstand local burning practices and uncontrolled vehicle access, Alngith people will be denied access to their land. Alngith people's ultimate aspirations for post-mining landscapes arise in relation to their current material aspirations—the most significant being control over their land. Despite this, Alngith people are themselves compelled to articulate their desires according to traditionalist forms.

That people employ powerful concepts, such as Country, in political ways highlights the need for mining companies, researchers, and activists to look beyond overt statements to uncover the complex ways that people feel and act in relation to extraction processes. To truly contribute to the design of socially and environmentally responsible post-mining landscapes, environmental scientists, policy analysts, and others helping to define its goals should approach post-mining rehabilitation as both a social *and* an environmental problem, not simply a technical one amenable to ecological or engineering solutions.

## Notes

1 This research was supported by a Berndt Foundation Post-Graduate Award and a Sustainable Minerals Institute Student Research Support Scholarship as well as funding from the University of Queensland's Centre for Mined Land Rehabilitation. Special thanks must be given to two senior Alngith people, Robert "Rocky" Madua Senior and Matilda John, and to staff of the Alngith Corporation.

2  Traditional Owner in the Australian context refers to local descent groups who share common affiliations to an estate. In the Weipa context, a Traditional Owner is considered a member of one of the native title claim groups that are signatories to the Western Cape Communities Co-Existence Agreement.

3  The Alngith Corporation's Board of Directors represents the full range of Alngith families. The Corporation was established as a charitable trust that manages monies acquired via the Weipa Township Agreement on behalf of Alngith people. The Weipa Township Agreement is another Indigenous Land Use Agreement between Rio Tinto Alcan Weipa and the Alngith people.

# References

Butler, Andrew, Ing Toh, and Dexter Wagambie. 2012. The integration of Indigenous knowledge into mine site rehabilitation and closure planning at Ok Tedi, Papua New Guinea. In *Proceedings of the Seventh International Seminar on Mine Closure*, edited by Andy Fourie and Mark Tibbet, 623–638. Brisbane: Australian Centre for Geomechanics.

Commonwealth of Australia. 2006. Mine rehabilitation. In *Leading practice sustainable development program for the mining industry*. Canberra: Australian Government Department of Industry Tourism and Resources. www.industry.gov.au/resource/Programs/LPSD (accessed June 6, 2016).

Department of Environment and Heritage Protection (DEHP). 2014a. *Rehabilitation requirements for mining resource activities (EM1122)*. Brisbane: Queensland Government Department of Environment and Heritage Protection.

Department of Environment and Heritage Protection (DEHP). 2014b. *Environmental authority. Permit number EPML00725113*. Brisbane: Queensland Government Department of Environment and Heritage Protection.

Edgar, Tricia. 2007. Restoration in mind: Placing ecological restoration in a cultural context. *Environments: A Journal of Interdisciplinary Studies* 35, 1:25–43.

Environmental Protection Agency (EPA). 2007. *Guideline 18: Rehabilitation requirements for mining projects*. Brisbane: Queensland Government Environmental Protection Agency.

Erskine, Peter, Helen Vickers, and David Mulligan. 2008. *Completion criteria for native ecosystem rehabilitation at RTA Weipa*. Report to Rio Tinto Alcan—Weipa Operations, 1–117. Brisbane: Centre for Mined Land Rehabilitation.

Garibaldi, Ann. 2009. Moving from model to application: Cultural keystone species and reclamation in Fort McKay, Alberta. *Journal of Ethnobiology* 29, 2:323–338.

Golub, Alex. 2014. *Leviathans at the goldmine: Creating Indigenous and corporate actors in Papua New Guinea*. Durham, NC: Duke University Press.

Gould, Susan F. 2012. Comparison of post-mining rehabilitation with reference ecosystems in monsoonal eucalypt woodlands, northern Australia. *Restoration Ecology* 20, 2:250–259.

Halvaksz, Jamon A. 2008. Whose closure? Appearances, temporality, and mineral extraction in Papua New Guinea. *The Journal of the Royal Anthropological Institute* 14, 1:21–37.

Higgs, Eric. 2003. *Nature by design: People, natural process, and ecological restoration*. Cambridge, MA: MIT Press.

Holmes, John. 2012. Cape York Peninsula, Australia: A frontier region undergoing a multi-functional transition with Indigenous engagement. *Journal of Rural Studies* 28, 3:252–265.

Horowitz, Leah. 2015. Culturally articulated neoliberalisation: Corporate social responsibility and the capture of Indigenous legitimacy in New Caledonia. *Transactions of the Institute of British Geographers* 40, 1:88–101.

Howitt, Richie, Sandy Callope, and Bella Savo. 1996. *Part of the Healing? The struggle to change mining company views of Indigenous rights at Weipa*. Report prepared for Napranum Aboriginal Council. Weipa, Queensland.

International Council on Mining and Metals (ICMM). 2006. *Good practice guidance for mining and biodiversity.* www.icmm.com/document/13 (accessed June 6, 2016).

Kirsch, Stuart. 2004. Changing views of place and time along the Ok Tedi. In *Mining and Indigenous lifeworlds in Australia and Papua New Guinea,* edited by Alan Rumsey and James Weiner, 182–207. Wantage, UK: Sean Kingston Publishing.

Martin, David F. 2015. Does native title merely provide an entitlement to be native? Indigenes, identities, and applied anthropological practice. *The Australian Journal of Anthropology* 26, 1:112–127.

Merlan, Francesca. 2004. Development, rationalisation and sacred sites: Comparative perspectives on Papua New Guinea and Australia. In *Mining and Indigenous lifeworlds in Australia and Papua New Guinea,* edited by Alan Rumsey and James Weiner, 244–269. Wantage, UK: Sean Kingston Publishing.

Murray, Mary-Anne, and David Mulligan. 2003. *Predicting long term vegetation development at the Weipa bauxite mine.* Report prepared for Comalco. Brisbane, Queensland.

O'Faircheallaigh, Ciaran. 2004. Evaluating agreements between Indigenous peoples and resource developers. In *Honour among nations? Treaties and agreements with Indigenous people,* edited by Marcia Langton, Maureen Tehan, Lisa Palmer, and Kathryn Shain, 303–328. Carlton, Australia: Melbourne University Press.

Povinelli, Elizabeth A. 1993. *Labor's lot. The power, history, and culture of Aboriginal action.* Chicago, IL: University of Chicago Press.

Povinelli, Elizabeth A. 2002. *The cunning of recognition: Indigenous alterities and the making of Australian multiculturalism.* Durham, NC: Duke University Press.

Rio Tinto Alcan (RTA). 2013. *Rio Tinto Alcan Weipa 2013 sustainable development report.* www.riotinto. com/documents/_Aluminium/RT_Weipa_SD_Report_2013.pdf (accessed June 6, 2016).

Rio Tinto Alcan (RTA). 2014. *Rio Tinto Alcan Weipa 2014 sustainable development report.* www. riotinto.com/documents/RT_Weipa_SD_Report_2014.pdf (accessed June 6, 2016).

Roberts, Brian. 1985. Workshop overview and future directions. In *Proceedings of the North Australian Mine Rehabilitation Workshop No. 9.* Edited by John Lawrie. Weipa: Comalco.

Rose, Deborah Bird. 1996. *Nourishing terrains: Australian Aboriginal views of landscape and wilderness.* Canberra: Australian Heritage Commission.

Scambary, Benedict. 2009. Mining agreements, development, aspirations, and livelihoods. In *Power, culture, economy: Indigenous Australians and mining,* edited by Jon Altman and David Martin, 171–201. Canberra: Australian National University Press.

Smith, Howard D. 2008. Using traditional ecological knowledge to develop closure criteria in tropical Australia. In *Proceedings of the Third International Seminar on Mine Closure,* 47–56. Johannesburg, South Africa.

Stewart, Karl. 1978. Regeneration experience in Weipa 1966–1977. In *Northern Engineering Conference 1978: Engineering in a Tropical Environment; Proceedings,* 45. Barton, Australia.

Strang, Veronica. 2004. Poisoning the rainbow: Mining, pollution and Indigenous cosmology in Far North Queensland. In *Mining and Indigenous lifeworlds in Australia and Papua New Guinea,* edited by Alan Rumsey and James Weiner, 208–225. Wantage, UK: Sean Kingston Publishing.

Trigger, David, and Michael Robinson. 2004. Mining, land claims and the negotiation of Indigenous interests: Research from the Queensland Gulf Country and the Pilbara Region of Western Australia. In *Mining and Indigenous lifeworlds in Australia and Papua New Guinea,* edited by Alan Rumsey and James Weiner, 226–243. Wantage, UK: Sean Kingston Publishing.

Welker, Marina. 2014. *Enacting the corporation: An American mining firm in post-authoritarian Indonesia.* Berkeley: University of California Press.

# 10

# HARMONIZING GRASSROOTS ORGANIZING AND LEGAL ADVOCACY TO ADDRESS COAL MINING AND SHALE GAS DRILLING ISSUES IN SOUTHWESTERN PENNSYLVANIA

*Caitlin McCoy, Veronica Coptis, and Patrick Grenter*

In the rolling hills of northern Appalachia, the southwestern corner of Pennsylvania unfolds into stretches of pastures, forests, and farms, as small towns momentarily rise and fall along the country roads. Washington and Greene counties are nestled there, with Ohio and West Virginia to the west and south. Running below the picturesque landscapes, historic Mail Pouch Tobacco barns, general stores, and generations-old family farms is the black vein of the Pittsburgh coal seam. Averaging between five and eight feet thick, it extends over 11,000 miles through 53 counties, making it the thickest and most extensive coal bed in the Appalachian Basin (Ruppert, Tewalt, and Bragg 1997; Tewalt et al. 2000).

People have mined coal in southwestern Pennsylvania since the 1760s (Geological Survey of Pennsylvania 1887). Mineral rights to almost all of the coal in the region were bought and sold generations ago.[1] Volumes have been written on these early years: dangerous conditions in the mines, child labor, mine disasters, the rise and fall of company towns, and clashes between unions and mining companies. Over the years, mining changed. The most dramatic change arguably arrived in the 1980s, when a new, more mechanized mining method, called longwall mining, transformed underground coal mining operations and communities in southwestern Pennsylvania.

This chapter will explore how a grassroots movement started in response to the social and environmental impacts of longwall coal mining, and evolved into a struggle for justice employing legal strategies alongside community-driven organizing work. An important response included the creation of the Center for Coalfield Justice (CCJ), a non-profit organization, which has developed over the years to meet the needs of local communities in their struggle for environmental justice. The approach CCJ has developed for working with area residents values their knowledge about the land, waterways, and communities. It seeks to provide community members with detailed information about proposed projects and potential impacts so they can make informed decisions on individual or collective actions.

CCJ's recognition of local expertise is grounded in the belief that people who live with the daily impacts of fossil fuel extraction should be treated with the utmost respect. Our work is informed and directed by how local people think these industries should be held accountable for impacts. By blending organizing and legal work, CCJ seeks to create a wider set of options for achieving justice than might be produced by following solely a legal or organizing approach.

This chapter was written by CCJ's Legal Director Caitlin McCoy with assistance from Executive Director Patrick Grenter and Deputy Director Veronica Coptis. In the text that follows, we first provide background on longwall coal mining and its environmental, social, and economic impacts in the region. We then describe the grassroots organizing efforts that developed in response to these impacts, tracing how they gave rise to CCJ in its current form, with a particular philosophy of collaboration and justice that guides its support to affected communities. We discuss selected projects that exemplify our philosophy and strategies at work in the context of CCJ's region of focus. Finally, we reflect on the continuing struggle for environmental justice in southwestern Pennsylvania.

## Longwall Coal Mining in Pennsylvania

Longwall mining is a deep mining technique capable of fully extracting huge panels of coal, frequently up to 1,500 feet wide and two miles long. Coal shearing machines known as "continuous miners" remove a "long wall" of coal in a single slice, while hydraulic jacks hold up the roof above and to the front. Once the coal has been extracted, the continuous miner and hydraulic jacks advance, leaving overlying rock to collapse into the void behind. This occurs 400–800 feet below the earth's surface, causing subsidence to both natural features and manmade structures above. Longwall mining has occurred in five counties in Pennsylvania, but Washington and Greene (Figure 10.1) are the only two counties with pending and active longwall mining permits today (Hoch and CCJ 2013).

These operations are large in scale; land extensions currently being mined or sought by companies often span 3,000 acres. Overall, a significant amount of acreage has already been mined.[2] Mining has caused extensive damage to streams, aquatic life, wetlands, domestic water supplies, homes, and other buildings. For example, about 77% of the miles of streams undermined by longwall techniques between 2008 and 2013 experienced flow loss, pooling (formation of pools instead of consistently flowing water), or both (Tonsor et al. 2015, VII–20).

Longwall mine operators are legally permitted to damage buildings and water supplies, but are required to repair homes and replace water supplies when liable for the damage. However, residents often become embroiled in lengthy battles for basic necessities, like a temporary water supply, which deters them from pursuing property damage claims. Companies regularly offer to buy homes and properties before mining, if the risk of damage is high, or after mining, if significant damage

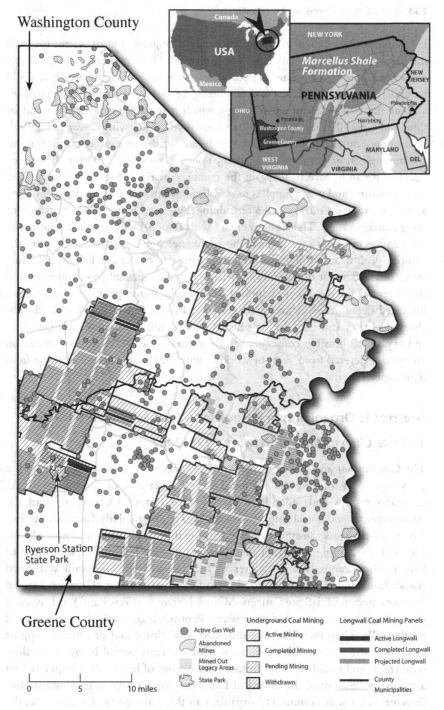

**FIGURE 10.1** Coal, gas, and oil extraction have often overlapped spatially in Greene and Washington counties in southwestern Pennsylvania, which intensifies local impacts. In addition to homes and businesses, public resources like Ryerson Station State Park have been sacrificed. Map by Donna Gayer, Artasaverb.

has occurred. This practice has systematically depopulated areas where longwall mining occurs; entire towns now sit abandoned. Homeowners wishing to stay in the area have two options: (1) purchase another home in the area that could be undermined in the future, and potentially be displaced again; or (2) purchase a home that was undermined years ago, which may have lingering issues and/or future problems (because subsidence can occur years later without warning). Both options are complicated by the fact that houses in the area rarely go up for sale, and mining companies already own many houses, removing them from the market. People constantly have to navigate the complex world of pre-mining surveys of their structures and water supplies to establish baselines for mining damage claims, as well as problems during and after mining, like negotiating with companies or filing damage claims. Their only contact with the coal company is a land agent, whose objective is usually to have the landowner sign an agreement costing the company as little as possible and eliminating the landowner as a liability. Learning from CCJ staff about the surveys and claims processes, possible consequences, and the potential for success in achieving their goals, allows people to make more informed decisions with greater confidence. In our experience, people do not always feel they can trust land agents to provide full answers to their questions and explain all possible consequences. By contrast, CCJ offers support based on knowledge derived from years of working with area residents, and learning from their experiences.

## Grassroots Organizing in Response to Coal Mining 1994–2012

### Tri-State Citizens Mining Network 1994–2007

The Citizens Mining Network formed in October 1994, in recognition of the growing impacts of longwall mining. This was a network of community-based, grassroots groups and individuals that organized around concerns about the environmental and social impacts of coal mining, particularly longwall mining. The main grassroots groups that banded together were Citizens Against Water Loss due to Mining, Nottingham Network of Neighbors, People United to Save Homes, Pennsylvania Chapter of the Sierra Club, Mountain Watershed Association, and Trout Unlimited. Shortly after forming, Citizens Mining Network became Tri-State Citizens Mining Network ("Tri-State"), as it opened up to the tri-state area of southwestern Pennsylvania, southeastern Ohio and northern West Virginia. Tri-State provided educational and organizing support to communities affected by mining, so that residents would be aware of their legal rights and could work to protect their quality of life. Tri-State operated on a volunteer basis, until the Board of Directors hired a part-time administrative director and a staff community organizer in the early 2000s. By this time, the groups that initially founded Tri-State had dissolved, and Tri-State's members were predominantly individuals living in southwestern Pennsylvania who supported Tri-State's work.

## *The Center for Coalfield Justice 2007–2012*

In 2007, Tri-State re-organized itself, changing its name to Center for Coalfield Justice, adopting new bylaws, and adding full time staff. CCJ hired a full time, paid Executive Director to carry out the organization's purpose, articulated as follows:

> The Center will provide a forum for common information and action, community and individual education, technical assistance, publicity and advocacy. It will serve as a major link among members and between members and other groups, regionally and nationally, who share a common vision.[3]

CCJ evolved over the next few years, though organizing and education work remained its core activities. CCJ produced Watchdog Workbooks;[4] attended public hearings for proposed projects; gave tours of the coalfields; pushed for changes to mining laws and enforcement; and responded to local people's questions. Legal initiatives involved occasionally hiring an attorney to write legal comments on proposed regulations or permit applications. Organizing work involved building public awareness and pressure around regional issues, and providing community groups with expertise to achieve their goals around specific projects or issues. CCJ's mission expanded "to improve policy and regulations for the oversight of fossil fuel extraction and use; to educate, empower and organize coalfield citizens; and to protect public and environmental health."[5] In January 2012, Patrick Grenter became the Executive Director of CCJ and the first attorney ever hired on staff.

During this time and into the present, more individuals have become members of CCJ by paying membership dues and donating to the organization. Members and others support CCJ's work by receiving our emails, attending events, and volunteering. Today, we have over 2,000 members and supporters, most of whom live in Greene and Washington counties in the midst of the coal mining and natural gas drilling industries.

## Adding Legal Work Alongside Grassroots Organizing

### *"Client-centered Legal Counseling"*

Grenter had a vision to expand CCJ's legal work. He saw the need for competent legal representation of residents' interests in coalfield areas, where most private practice attorneys have represented the coal industry during their careers or specialize in unrelated areas. Thus, almost all local attorneys either have conflicts of interest, or lack the necessary expertise to represent a client in an environmental matter. People often find their only choice is to work directly with the company's land agents, trying to make a deal. Meanwhile, trust in the Pennsylvania Department of Environmental Protection (DEP) has evaporated, as DEP often fails to respond to citizen complaints and to enforce laws as written.

Grenter started working on ways to assist people with legal issues without forming an attorney–client relationship. To represent individual clients would have required potential organizational re-structuring and navigating issues with CCJ's federal 501(c)(3) status. Instead, Grenter drew on his experience in the Environmental Law Clinic at the University of Pittsburgh School of Law and with founding the Three Rivers Waterkeeper in Pittsburgh. He began adapting "client-centered counseling" ideals to create a model of legal education, organizing assistance, and referral to teach individuals about regulatory processes and their legal rights, allowing them to make informed decisions on issues.

Client-centered counseling is described as:

> striv[ing] to build a "helping relationship," one in which the lawyer is demon-
> strably sincere, empathic, nonjudgmental, and honest. It focuses on the cli-
> ent—on his problem, his goals, and his feelings. The lawyer and client work
> together as partners. The lawyer supplies his expertise and skills—legal, prac-
> tical, and interpersonal—and the client sets the priorities and decides the
> major issues.
>
> *(Bastress 1985, 99)*

An attorney works to build trust and open communication, so a client feels comfortable discussing their issues to facilitate collaborative work to address the client's concerns. Overall, this model emphasizes a client's autonomy, growth, and understanding of their own legal issues, as well as the landscape of potential benefits and consequences of legal strategies and actions (Bastress 1985).

In Spring 2013, Grenter hired attorney Joanne Kilgour to serve as CCJ's first Legal Director. They established a model of consultations with community members which begin by explaining why an attorney–client relationship could not be formed with either Grenter or Kilgour. Then, the attorney explains what she can offer the community member: explanations of legal concepts, permitting processes, and enforcement procedures; information gleaned from reviewing DEP files; and stories from other people for comparison—but not legal advice. Community organizers, who also participate in such meetings, describe what they can offer: mobilizing neighbors, taking their story to the media, strategic planning, and pressuring the company or DEP with other tactics. The attorney and organizer then ask the person to explain the situation that brought them to CCJ. Staff then find out whether the impacts have been documented; hear how they hoped CCJ could help; and find out if they have shared this story with an agency or company, and with what result. This first half of the consultation is critical to the trust-building process of client-centered counseling.

The second half of the consultation is usually an educational discussion, answering questions, and providing information. It can also be a brainstorming session where staff present possible actions to achieve the community member's goals, with varying levels of escalation, publicity, and costs. The nature of this discussion depends on the issues at hand. One constant, however, is the attitude toward the community member: the central assumption underlying our model is that regardless of formal educational level, people in this region have expertise based on their lived experiences and can be trusted to make reasoned decisions. Following client-centered counseling's emphasis on the client's understanding of issues, we work to help people understand their legal rights, options, and the costs and benefits of potential actions, to support their decision-making.

This model is not without challenges. It is difficult to walk the line between explaining concepts and giving legal advice, especially when many people ask point-blank whether they should sign the gas lease, accept the offer for damages, or push for different terms. The attorney will remind them that CCJ can only inform them of their rights and options, whereas telling them what to do would constitute legal advice; Recounting contractual terms they can request in a potential agreement with a company, clarifying their rights, and sharing others' stories—these reinforce that it is their decision alone, but now they have more information and our support. Such discussions are at the center of CCJ's blended legal/organizing model and are grounded in respectfully assisting people with their issues.

## Policy Work and Litigation

Around the same time the legal/organizing consultation model was implemented, CCJ also began to engage in litigation on behalf of its members. CCJ joined a group of Pennsylvania environmental organizations challenging deficiencies in the state's mine "bonding" program for guaranteeing the reclamation of coalmines. Grenter hoped to expand that sector of CCJ's work as opportunities arose for impactful litigation that could produce meaningful changes to mining laws and enforcement. This aspect of CCJ's legal work presents unique challenges for its community organizers. Litigation is slow moving; the aforementioned mine bonding case has been ongoing for 15 years. While a case is progressing in the legal system, there is little community members can do to help the process. Many organizing activities undertaken by CCJ, such as encouraging people to write comment letters, or holding rallies or meetings, may not be appropriate during litigation. Also, we can only share limited information with the public in order to uphold confidentiality and preserve attorney–client privilege. Organizers emphasize other aspects of campaigns that are not directly implicated in the litigation to keep people engaged and connected.

## Cultural and Historical Context

Before discussing some key campaigns exemplifying our methodology, it is illustrative to describe the social and cultural nuances of the areas CCJ serves.

In Greene County, many small towns, roads, and other geographic features have multiple names known only by locals and inspired by local lore. There is a significant difference between the eastern and western sides of the county, because mining on the eastern side slowed down or ended years ago, while it is still very active on the western side. Despite the incredible amount of valuable natural resources being extracted from the area, Greene County has historically had one of the highest poverty rates in the state. Today, 16.5% of the county's population lives below the poverty line (US Census Bureau 2014).

Washington County is north of Greene County, and stretches to the edge of Pittsburgh. The differences in the atmosphere and culture of Washington County track the level of development. The northern portion of the county contains outer suburbs of Pittsburgh, more densely populated and complete with strip malls, housing developments, and park & ride lots next to the interstate highway. The southern portion is sparsely populated and rural.

In both counties, there is a regional identity with similarities to other rural areas in Appalachia and a deep connection to the land. CCJ conducted a Coalfield Listening Project from Fall 2014 to Summer 2015, asking local people about their experiences living in the region and hopes for the future. Over 30 people participated in the project, and we agreed not to share their names because of some participants' ties to the coal and gas industries.

When asked what they valued about this area, one person said:

> Everybody loves the land. They can't leave it … I notice it even in the simple comments that people make about the birds that they've seen. These are gruff old farmers, you know. One gentlemen a couple ridges over … was commenting one time about the trees, and I said, you can tell what kinds of trees these are even when they're not in leaf? And he says, well sure these are locusts, that's red oak, that's tulip poplar. He just went around the whole field and named the varieties of trees. That kind of connection to the land is really nice. That to me, that is my community.
>
> *(Center for Coalfield Justice 2015a, 6)*

We perceive a distrust of outsiders, people who are not from the region. CCJ staff understand that this distrust can be traced to years of outsiders coming into the area to exploit local natural resources. Our experience is that trust is hard-earned here, but once an individual, group, or even company earns people's trust, their word goes a long way often with fierce loyalty. People also generally trust the status quo more than new ideas. There is nostalgia for the past, the days of their grandparents. When times get tough, we think people are more likely to turn to what was done in the past rather than trying something new.

During the Coalfield Listening Project, many people spoke about the future through a lens of nostalgia, for example: "The future of this area should be what it used to be before it got run over by industry." Some people were stunned by being asked about their hopes for the future and said they did not know. One woman said that she did not feel like she had the luxury of time to think about the future, "This area's all working class people, we're all so busy with our lives, it's hard to give the attention to this that we need." Perhaps the most revealing answer came from another woman, who said:

I don't know. I don't know how to answer that question. That's sad when you can't think of anything beyond the destruction. I'll be honest with you I don't know how to answer that question. So what's that tell you? That's how bad it is. I don't. I don't see a future. I don't see what it could be that would actually change things. I have no clue. Sorry I don't know how to answer it. I can't. That's the harshness of it.

*(Center for Coalfield Justice 2015a, 15)*

CCJ's long history and good track record in the region have allowed us to overcome some of the general distrust of people from outside the area. Deputy Director Veronica Coptis grew up in Greene County and still lives there today. She opens a lot of doors through her knowledge of local geography and values. People are receptive to staff members originally from outside the region upon learning they have experience with coal issues; this demonstrated commitment seems to provide a measure of goodwill.

Douglas Reichert Powell, in creating and defining "critical regionalism," describes construction of a region through stories of specific incidents and posits that "knowledge of the incident, manifested in the ability to recount it, helps constitute one's identity as a member of that place ... telling the story is the practice that sustains the identity of the place it comes out of" (Powell 2007, 12). Mine fires, mining accidents, and the progress of the industry are often the subjects of stories that constitute this region's narrative ties. More recently, the loss of Duke Lake in Ryerson Station State Park, Greene County has become one of these incidents, dividing younger residents of the county into two groups: those who remember the lake and those who do not. We turn now to some specific examples of CCJ's collaboration with area residents to examine how our legal/organizing model works in different scenarios.

## CCJ Litigates on Behalf of the Community: The Restoration of Duke Lake

Ryerson Station State Park is one of the few public parks in Greene County and the only state park in the area. For years, the jewel of the park was Duke Lake, a 62-acre lake that was a major attraction for people across the county and region. The recreational opportunities at the lake, such as fishing, boating, and swimming, were one of the few economic drivers in the county unrelated to fossil fuel extraction. Free to the public, the lake was also one of the few places that people could go in Greene County to enjoy the area's natural beauty with family and friends.

On July 28, 2005, Duke Lake was drained by the Pennsylvania Department of Conservation and Natural Resources (DCNR) because of safety issues due to cracks in the dam (Figure 10.2) that sustained the picturesque lake. In 2010, DCNR and the Department of Environmental Protection (DEP) initiated proceedings against Consol Energy after a DEP investigation determined that the cracks resulted from subsidence caused by Consol's longwall mining at its nearby Bailey Mine.

**FIGURE 10.2** The dam, which formed Duke Lake at Ryerson Station State Park in Greene County, Pennsylvania, was compromised by land subsidence caused by longwall mining and remains partially deconstructed. Loss of the lake as a public resource serves as a symbol for activism. Photograph by Veronica Coptis, March 2016.

In April 2011, CCJ intervened in the case on behalf of our membership and the community. We did this to ensure our members' interests were represented and to move the proceedings along at a reasonable pace so that this generation of southwestern Pennsylvanians could experience the beauty of Duke Lake. We made this decision based on what we heard from community members over the years since the lake was drawn down. There was a strong desire to see the lake restored at Consol's expense, since the company had damaged this treasured place with its mining. There was also concern that DEP would not take a strong stance against Consol in the litigation, due to the close relationships area residents witnessed between DEP and the companies it regulates.

In Spring 2013, Consol settled the case with DCNR and DEP. We were pleased that there seemed to be a path toward restoration of Duke Lake. We were quite disappointed, however, that Consol admitted no responsibility for the damage they inflicted on the dam. The company agreed to pay for restoration of the lake through a $36 million settlement payment, which was neither a fine nor a penalty. DCNR agreed to convey coal and mining rights for 548,000 tons of coal inside the park's boundary to Consol, and leased the state's Marcellus Shale gas interests within the park to Consol's natural gas branch, CNX. In return, Consol agreed to convey eight surface properties adjacent to the park to DCNR, to be added to Ryerson as parkland (Commonwealth of Pennsylvania 2013). Following this resolution, we explained the nature of the settlement agreement to our members, and we have continued to hold our annual DRYerson Festival, marking each year the community has spent without Duke Lake. The year of this chapter's writing, 2015, marks ten years without the lake.[6] At the time of the settlement, it was projected that the dam would be restored in 2017; in the Fall of 2014, DCNR began dredging out the old lakebed.

On July 24, 2015, DCNR announced that the ground under the dam was still moving due to ongoing subsidence from the mining near the park ten years ago. DCNR stated it could not predict if and when it would stop and whether mining in the new Bailey Mine expansion, discussed below, would cause additional subsidence. Accordingly, the ground was not stable enough for DEP to issue DCNR a dam safety permit for reconstruction of the dam.[7] DCNR has re-directed the millions of dollars allocated for rebuilding the dam to projects that improve Ryerson Station State Park.

## Community Listening plus Litigation: Bailey Mine Expansion Appeal

After damaging Duke Lake at Ryerson Station Park, Consol is expanding the Bailey Mine to extract coal from underneath the park, per the rights granted to them in the settlement agreement with DCNR and DEP. The Bailey Mine complex is already the largest underground coal mine complex in the world. Their 3,175-acre mine expansion threatens to destroy streams that flow through Ryerson Park and the surrounding area. In total, 14 streams will be affected by this expansion. The permit application predicted several years of stream disruption and damage, so severe that "flow loss would most likely reduce, if not eliminate fishing opportunities" in Ryerson Station State Park.[8] Since the loss of the lake, the only fishing opportunities in the park today are in the streams.

This level of disruption and damage meets the definition of "pollution" under the Pennsylvania Clean Streams Law, which includes stream flow loss and impairment of uses, like fishing (25 Pa. Code § 91.1). When the DEP issues a permit for an underground mine, the Department must find that the company applying for the permit "has demonstrated that there is no presumptive evidence of potential pollution of waters of the Commonwealth" (25 Pa. Code § 86.37(a)(3)). Thus, issuing a permit with knowledge of these predicted changes in flow and flow loss is a violation of the law, yet DEP issued the permit. In May 2014, CCJ filed an appeal of the Bailey Mine expansion permit within and around Ryerson.[9] In February 2015, DEP issued a permit to undermine sections of one of the streams, Polen Run, which was subject to separate consideration due to the complexity of mining underneath it. We immediately appealed this permit and it was consolidated into our previously filed appeal of the mine expansion.

In making the decision to file the appeal, we repeated the process that led to intervention in the Duke Lake litigation, by checking in with community leaders and reflecting on the opinions of our members. As of the date of writing, we are moving toward a hearing before the Environmental Hearing Board.

In February 2015, Consol submitted an application to add 2,142 acres to the Bailey Mine for "development" mining, the first step in preparing an area for full extraction by longwall methods. This expansion along the southeastern part of Ryerson Station State Park will undermine the remainder of the park and its streams, as well as surrounding areas. It is unclear when Consol will submit the full extraction permit application for this southeastern expansion.

## Client-centered Counseling: Hydraulic Fracturing Water Filling Station

One day we received a phone call from Rich, a union pipeline construction worker and life-long resident of Jefferson Township in Greene County, who told us about a proposed water filling station along Highway 188. Water filling stations provide water for the hydraulic fracturing process often used in shale gas drilling. Private property owners construct the necessary infrastructure and, with approval from the local water authority, allow drilling companies to fill up their trucks there for a fee. The proposed site is within 300 yards of a high school, around a blind curve in the road, and there would be approximately 17 trucks per hour filling up at the station, running 24 hours a day.

The owner of the proposed water filling station had originally planned to build a campground for transient shale gas workers, and formed a Limited Liability Company (Bells Bridge, LLC) with two other people. One of these is the solicitor[10] for both Jefferson Township and the Southwestern Pennsylvania Water Authority; the other works at the Water Authority and is the auditor for the Township.

Under the Jefferson Morgan Multi-Municipal Zoning Ordinance, the proposed campground was to be located in a Single-Family Residential District. The zoning statement of purpose for that district is: "to promote the continuation of the rural character of the area … [and] to protect the stability of existing neighborhoods and to encourage desirable new residential developments, encompassing the many life styles and areas of the region" (Jefferson–Morgan Multi-Municipal Zoning Ordinance 2013, Section 3.6.01). In order to operate a campground there, it would have to be approved by the zoning board as a "special exception" to the zoning ordinance that would otherwise prohibit such activity in that district.

In June 2014, when the zoning board was scheduled to make a decision on the special exception, the zoning board's solicitor withdrew his representation at the last minute due to a conflict of interest (he is employed at the law firm of a member of Bells Bridge, LLC). The zoning board went forward with voting on the application and denied it. Bells Bridge, LLC appealed this decision in the local court as being decided without legal representation, and as having a conflict of interest, because a voting member of the zoning board lived across from the proposed campground. The judge remanded the decision back to the zoning board to be reconsidered with legal representation and without participation of the neighbor. Back in front of the zoning board, Bells Bridge, LLC announced that it would now seek approval for a water filling station instead.

CCJ worked with Rich, the concerned local resident, to write factual and procedural questions to ask the zoning board based on the zoning ordinance, the Pennsylvania Municipalities Planning Code, and relevant case law. Rich then rallied his neighbors and other community members to attend the zoning hearing on the proposed filling station and share their concerns. At the hearing, Rich asked the zoning board questions generated with CCJ's help, and our Deputy Director, Veronica, was present to support him and ask additional questions. The board could not answer many of the questions, and they decided to continue the hearing at a later date. Before the next hearing, rumors circulated that a company interested in an exclusive contract with the filling station was backing out after the public opposition. Finally, six out of the seven members of the zoning board voted against the special exception for the water filling station, because its operation would contradict the purpose and character of the Single-Family Residential District. Bells Bridge, LLC has appealed this decision and we are following the case in the local court system.

## Conclusion

CCJ's model of blending grassroots organizing with legal education and advocacy has grown out of our commitment to the local community guiding our work. Mining has dominated the local economy for decades and dictated the narrative of extraction; it is good for local people because it provides jobs and supports families. Thus, the environmental destruction from mining is a small price to pay for those jobs and the coal that powers the American economy. This narrative, wrapped in the American flag and fueled by the promise of the American Dream, is losing its persuasive power as the industry ruthlessly lays off workers, cuts pensions, and faces allegations of leaving extensive pollution in its wake. It is critical to give residents' voices a place in the struggle for environmental justice after being told how to feel about the industry for years and fearing that speaking out could cost them a job or repair work on their home or water supply. As people learn from each other and realize their power, they can begin to shift the power imbalance between people in extraction areas and extraction companies, and dismantle the regulatory system created in the industry's favor.

This power imbalance is a pervasive force across the country in communities where extraction occurs. Yet, we have seen that people are more willing now than ever to share their stories publicly, contact their legislators, ask questions, and openly express their opinions about the industry and their concerns. Learning from our work, we have adopted the approach that we encourage among community members. In 2012, we joined the Extreme Energy Extraction Collaborative,[11] which is composed of over 100 groups working on different aspects of the climate justice and anti-extraction movement with a wide spectrum of diversity in identities, issue focus, tactics, geographic base, and type and size of organization. We meet annually to discuss our work, successful tactics, and strategies to highlight the inter-connectedness of our struggles. Our goal is cross-sector collaboration, unifying groups that might otherwise be separated along lines of different issues, identities, and types of organizations. By sharing our knowledge and experiences, we hope to increase our power and collectively end the extreme energy extraction that irreparably damages our communities and the environment. We will be co-hosting the next annual summit in southwestern Pennsylvania in May 2016.

## Notes

1 "Railroads and coal operators had, in the later nineteenth century, acquired thousands of acres in coal rights, at rock bottom prices, in broad-form deeds signed over by desperate Appalachian farmers. The remaining eastern reserves were retained by landed families and realty speculators." (Vietor 1980, 18–19).

2 As of 2014 in Greene County, 65.50% of the county's land area (242,282 acres) has already been mined, is actively being mined, or is permitted for mining. In Washington County, that number is 56.89% of the county (313,712 acres) (Hoch and CCJ 2013, 47).

3 *Bylaws of Center for Coalfield Justice, A Pennsylvania Nonprofit Organization* 2007 (Article II).

4 http://coalfieldjustice.org/files/Watchdog-Workbook.pdf.

5 http://coalfieldjustice.org/about/.

6 CCJ's Americorps member Ben Fiorillo wrote an original song on the history of Duke Lake and resistance to further mining for our 2015 festival. See Center for Coalfield Justice 2015b, "We Won't Let You Dig," *Youtube* video, June 30, 2015, www.youtube.com/watch?v=OQQ7jvgL1Wo.

7 http://coalfieldjustice.org/blog/sad-news-about-duke-lake/2159/.

8 Appeal: http://ehb.courtapps.com/efile/documentViewer.php?documentID=21857, Exhibit D at pp. 15-17.

9 Docket: http://ehb.courtapps.com/public/document_shower_pub.php?docket Number=2014072. First Amended Notice of Appeal: http://ehb.courtapps.com/efile/documentViewer.php?documentID=21856.

10 A solicitor is an attorney appointed by a local government body to manage legal matters, such as litigation and providing legal advice on various issues.

11 www.stopextremeenergy.org/about.

## References

Bastress, Robert. 1985. Client-centered counseling and moral accountability for lawyers. *The Journal of the Legal Profession* 10:97–138.

*Bylaws of Center for Coalfield Justice, A Pennsylvania Nonprofit Organization.* 2007. http://coalfieldjustice.org/.

Center for Coalfield Justice. http://coalfieldjustice.org (accessed February 10, 2016).

Center for Coalfield Justice. 2015a. *Coalfield Listening Project Report.* www.coalfieldjustice.org/s/Full-Listening-Project-Report-FINAL.pdf.

Center for Coalfield Justice. 2015b. We won't let you dig. *Youtube* video, June 30. www.youtube.com/watch?v=OQQ7jvgL1Wo (accessed December 16, 2016).

Commonwealth of Pennsylvania, Department of Conservation and Natural Resources. 2013. Settlement agreement and release. March 8. www.dcnr.state.pa.us/cs/groups/public/documents/document/dcnr_20026958.pdf (accessed December 8, 2015).

Geological Survey of Pennsylvania. 1887. *Annual report of the Geological Survey of Pennsylvania for 1886, Part I.* Harrisburg, PA: Board of Commissioners for the Geological Survey.

Hoch, Richard and Center for Coalfield Justice (CCJ). 2013. *Community indicators of environmental justice: A baseline report focusing on Greene and Washington Counties, Pennsylvania.* www.coalfieldjustice.org/s/Community-Indicators-Environmental-Justice-2014.pdf (accessed December 12, 2016).

Jefferson-Morgan Multi-Municipal Zoning Ordinance. 2013. http://jeff-morgcog.org/Jefferson_Morgan_Multi_Municipal_Zoning_Ordinance_updated_5-08-13.pdf (accessed December 12, 2016).

Pennsylvania Code, Title 25, Chapter 86 § 86.37(a)(3). www.pacode.com/secure/data/025/chapter86/s86.37.html.

Pennsylvania Code, Title 25, Chapter 91 § 91.1. www.pacode.com/secure/data/025/chapter91/s91.1.html

Powell, Douglas Reichert. 2007. *Critical regionalism: Connecting politics and culture in the American landscape.* Chapel Hill, NC: Chapel Hill Press.

Ruppert, L., S. Tewalt and L. Bragg. 1997. *Map showing areal extent of the Pittsburgh coal bed and horizon and mines areas of the Pittsburgh coal bed, US Geological Survey.* http://pubs.usgs.gov/of/1996/of96-280/ (accessed December 16, 2016).

Tewalt, Susan J., Leslie F. Ruppert, Linda J. Bragg, Richard W. Carlton, David K. Brezinski, Rachel N. Wallack, and David T. Butler, 2000. Chapter C–A digital resource model of the Upper Pennsylvanian Pittsburgh coal bed, Monongahela Group, Northern Appalachian Basin coal region. In *U.S. Geological Survey Professional Paper 1625–C,* 106. http://pubs.usgs.gov/pp/p1625c/CHAPTER_C/CHAPTER_C.pdf (accessed December 16, 2016).

Tonsor, Stephen J., Alison N. Hale, Anthony Iannacchione, Daniel J. Bain, Michael Keener, Erin Pfeil-McCullough, and Keith Garmire. 2015. *The effects of subsidence resulting from underground bituminous coal mining, 2008–2013.* Pittsburgh, PA: University of Pittsburgh. www.dep.pa.gov/PublicParticipation/CitizensAdvisoryCouncil/Issue-Areas/Pages/Act54.aspx#.VrOmV2QrL5Y (accessed December 16, 2016).

US Census Bureau. 2014. Small area income and poverty estimates. www.census.gov/did/www/saipe/data/interactive/saipe.html?s_appName=saipe&map_yearSelector=2014&map_geoSelector=aa_c&s_state=42&s_county=42059&menu=grid_proxy (accessed December 16, 2016).

Vietor, Richard H.K. 1980. *Environmental politics and the coal coalition.* College Station: Texas A&M University Press.

# PART IV
# Alternative Futures

# 11

# IMAGES OF HARM, IMAGINING JUSTICE

## Gold Mining Contestation in Kyrgyzstan

*Amanda E. Wooden*[1]

> In all protest events it started with ecological concerns. Everywhere it is
> about the environment ... I too came to this understanding when I saw
> photos of the rock waste on the tongue of the glaciers. It is a catastrophic sit-
> uation now at the Kumtor mine. We are digging out a tree's roots, it can't live.
> We are digging out the glacier and the glacier is Kyrgyzstan.
>
> *(Journalist 2013)*[2]

Kyrgyzstan is caught between a rock, a hard place, and glaciers. In this chapter I analyze the politics of mining contestation in Kyrgyzstan from 1998 to 2015, beginning
with community and activist responses to a 1998 cyanide spill at the Kumtor gold
mine. I map protest tactics, discourses, and stakeholder responses to anti-mining
activism, exploring two characteristics of this shifting shape of mining contestation.
First is the role of images—photographs, satellite images, videos, films—in captur-
ing and creating public sentiment and as rhetorical devices. Second, anti-mining
activist notions and claims of justice have shifted over time, often in response to
images of mining and changing public imaginings of nature. Both of these contestation characteristics of gold mining politics in Kyrgyzstan—images and justice
claims—change and interact over time and space. Just in the last few years, images
of mining rock waste on glaciers in the Ak Shirak range have fundamentally shaped
the ways people in Kyrgyzstan imagine the future, talk about threats to the nation,
discuss what justice is and for whom this matters.

In Kyrgyzstan, this shift in existential imagination is inseparable from the post-
Soviet history of gold mining politics, global climate change discussions, and how
Kyrgyzstanis are experiencing climate change. As mining expanded into areas
previously not mined, the experiences of community members in developed mining locations influenced the expectations, rhetoric, and claims of residents in developing regions. This in turn shifted the politics and discourse of all actors involved.

That is, in order to understand just how mining politics became a national issue, inseparable from discussions about climate, and why nationalistic views of justice are currently so central, we must evaluate how justice claims shifted over time in separate mining localities. Local residents were actually learning how to resist by studying how previous residents in other locations did so successfully or unsuccessfully, as well as by reacting to shifts in government action/inaction and corporate rhetoric. The evidentiary and rhetorical use of images is central to this process.

For practitioners, it is important to see which ideas of justice resonate with the public, how images can mobilize and de-mobilize, and how justice claims and images can take on lives of their own in public discourse and resonate in unexpected ways, especially in accordance with emerging national or global political narratives. For instance, most people in Kyrgyzstan became aware of the connection between mining and climate change through pictures of rock waste dumped on the Davidov glacier at the Kumtor mine, shared in social media and news reports, and later photographed by members of a parliamentary commission investigating the mine's environmental impacts. Kumtor is the only open pit mine in the world operating on glaciers. In Central Asia, the water regime is glacial-melt dependent (Figure 11.1). Thus, threats to water supply from mining have particular social resonance. Gold accounts for approximately 20% of Kyrgyzstan's annual gross domestic product (GDP), the majority of which comes from Kumtor, the country's largest as well as its only western-run productive mine. Kumtor Operating Company (KOC), which manages the mine, is owned by the Canadian company Centerra Gold Inc. (before 2009 it was owned by Cameco Corp.); the state-owned mining company Kyrgyzaltyn holds shares in Centerra. To contest this mine is to challenge a key economic pillar, making widespread anti-mining protests even more fascinating.

## Listening to Shifting Discourses

While on academic leave in 2006–07, I served as Economic and Environmental field officer in Osh, Kyrgyzstan for the Organization for Security and Cooperation in Europe (OSCE). During this time, I learned about the Dutch NGO Milieu Kontakt's networking and environmental rights training for NGOs. OSCE-sponsored, locally run, Aarhus Centers also held workshops on environmental treaties, which I observed first-hand. I witnessed one part of the process by which international environmental rights language became part of the activist lexicon in Kyrgyzstan. In 2007, a Talas province resident, turned environmental activist, requested that my office monitor mining development in his area. When protestors began organizing in 2008 against Talas mines, national media coverage focused on theories that elites were manipulating local residents such as through payments to protest, thus dismissing local environmental concerns. My position as a regional representative for an international governmental organization, interacting with various people from community organizations to ministerial level officials, afforded opportunities to compare peoples' different views of the same issues beyond what was portrayed

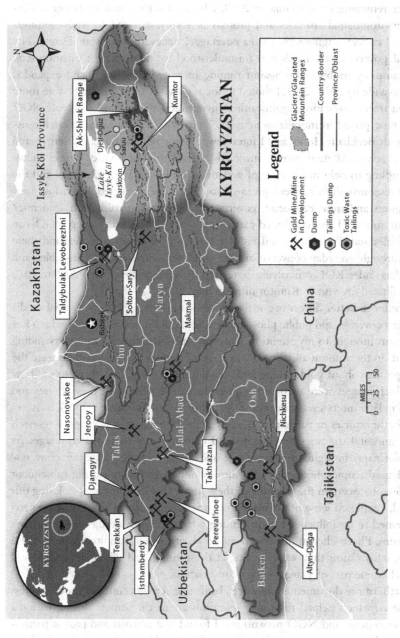

**FIGURE 11.1** Gold mines of Kyrgyzstan. The Kumtor mine has impacted four glaciers and is currently located on the Davidov glacier. The relationship between gold mining, climate change, and glaciers provides a template for activism, political change, and identity in post-Soviet Kyrgyzstan. Anti-mining activism connects local communities near mines and mine fields to cross-regional, national, and international discussions, and social networks. Map by Donna Gayer (Artasaverb) adapted from map created by Amanda Wooden and Janine Glather for Wooden (2013).

in news coverage. However, I was unsure about trusting my understanding of these political situations, given how my organizational role also shaped conversations.

After returning to academia in 2009, I began field research to better understand environmental attitudes and protests in Kyrgyzstan and to study community-level concerns ignored in media coverage. I believed these were dismissed by national government officials and misunderstood by development organizations. As community mobilization against mining increased in number and expanded country-wide by 2010–2011, I shifted to focus on why mining protests were more frequent than contestations against other environmental issues and what role NGO networking played in mobilizing activists. From 2009 to 2015, my research assistant, Sarah Beckham Hooff, and I interviewed 88 people (in Russian, Kyrgyz, and English) across different groups involved in gold mining politics. Using snowball sampling to help make sense of networks and information exchange and the mutual discourse shifts between groups, I sought to interview people in most mining regions and from corporate, government, activist, journalist, and academic/scientific spheres. I also continued participant observation by attending NGO-run roundtables and conferences and visiting mine sites. I came to understand these issues through everyday conversations on the street, at friends' kitchen-tables, and during taxi rides. KOC officials also agreed to several interviews from 2009 to 2013 and facilitated my visit to Kumtor mine in July, 2013.

In order to better dissect national discourses and images, I studied social media and news coverage and public photographs about gold mining, many of which key informants brought to my attention. My aims were, first, to gain an understanding of trends in the amount and type of coverage of mining issues; second, to trace the language used about gold mining and anti-mining protests; and, third, to see how and which images were used in the press. In turn I referenced these stories and images in later interviews, using photo elicitation methods (Bagnoli 2009), to ascertain whether stories or participation in social media exchanges influenced research participants and the ways they understood the impact of these shared images. As key informants brought glacier damage and climate change into our conversations, I used iconic photographs of Kumtor mine rock waste during subsequent interviews to ascertain the meaning of these images for different people. Using this method, I explored sense of place and discourses about identity that, for some people, seemed to be influenced by imagining what mining is doing to Kyrgyzstan's mountains. Photo elicitation allowed me to clarify when activists first used these images, what claims they were making at those times, and when these ideas and images became part of a larger public conversation.

I furthermore documented injustice claims that activists communicated in press interviews, which helped to answer questions about the impact of international treaty workshops and NGO networking. I found that activists and protest participants regularly expressed specific notions of justice. However, over time, activists expressed changing conceptualizations of justice, moving from procedural (access to information) and distributive (compensating for harm and providing social benefits for the cost of the damage, to accept that risk), to productive and ecological justice (changing industrial activity, stopping "harm industries," seeking retribution for impact on ecosystems) (Schlosberg 2007; Walker 2012). I asked gold mining executives and government officials how they perceived activist claims; through this I heard additional alternating views about justice demands; some were dismissive of local residents' understandings of justice.

## Compensation Rights and Realizing Images Matter

Prior research has shown that activists often use images to mobilize people, capture industrial impacts in the absence of independent monitoring equipment, and create public resonance and emotional responses. Organizations create "image events" (DeLuca 1999), feeding off and generating emotion (affect) to mobilize participants and gain sympathy among observers (Routledge 1997; Juris 2008). Images become rhetorical, a representation of the issue in "argumentative fragments" (Delicath and DeLuca 2003), a conversation and emotional engagement, generating new discourses and representational politics (Doyle 2007)—including the possibility of nationalistic responses and shaping popular imaginations. Images move beyond actors' tactical usage in one location to shift attitudes toward industry and government across locations, and thus shape the politics of whom or what activists choose to represent: a local community, a nation, nature.

For Kyrgyzstan, "images of threat" have led to visualizing glacier movement as a threat to Kyrgyz identity in a climate-changed world. I find that these imaginings have shifted ideas about justice from the local to the national to the natural, a shift which fits within emerging global climate justice discourses and is parallel to mining resistance elsewhere. What emerged in response were justice claims particular to this context, heralded by activists defending their locales, but wrapped up in ideas about indigeneity, patriotism, and resisting global pressures.

The origins of justice claims lie in impacted community responses to a major industrial accident, the Barskoon cyanide spill. On May 20th, 1998, a Kumtor truck spilled 1.7 tons of sodium cyanide into the Barskoon River several hundred meters from where the river enters Lake Issyk-Kul, the country's largest lake. The Barskoon Incident catalyzed a decade-and-a-half of community-scale anti-mining activism. After the spill, KOC waited five hours to inform local residents, a delay that led many to question the company's subsequent statements (see Moody 2005 for an event timeline). KOC and the international commission that investigated the accident questioned the connection between the spill, the thousands who reported to hospitals after the accident, and the four deaths community members attributed to the accident, instead ascribing the hospitalizations to panic or misdiagnosis (Hynes et al. 1998; Trilling 2013). Local residents blockaded the road from Barskoon to the capital from July 10–12th 1998, while environmentalists protested in Bishkek. The company was unresponsive to local fears, a response long-remembered by residents (Moody 2005). Trucks from this site spilled at least two other times, forming what appeared to residents as a pattern of irresponsibility. Local residents continue to argue that long-term health problems are connected to the accident, as well as noting that without monitoring, impacts cannot be proven or disproven.

In the years following the accident, residents focused on recognition and compensation rights. Erkingul Imankodjoeva founded an organization called Karek, in Barskoon, in response. Karek worked to gain compensation for fatalities and health impacts, tourism and agricultural losses from the spill. They also sought company investments in the community, access to jobs at the mine, ecological monitoring, funds for eventual reclamation, safety measures, and, at times, closure of the mine (Imankodjoeva 2009). Activists utilized economic cost arguments and framed their cause as an environmental justice and human health issue. This approach combines human rights language with socio-economic and ecological considerations. An example of this is an international human rights NGO online campaign for financial support of Karek (Urgent Action Fund for Women's Human Rights 2012).

A 2014 film about Imankodjoeva and other Karek members, entitled *Flowers of Freedom*, by anthropologist Mirjam Leuze, documents the role of women in this anti-mining movement and compares it to anti-mining contestations elsewhere (Leuze 2014). In this documentary, sisters Erkingul and Baktigul Imankodjoeva lament that they did not film or photograph the cyanide accident. According to several Barskoon residents and Karek staff whom I interviewed in 2015, officials and police kept people from photographing the day of the accident and cell phones were not yet ubiquitous. They learned thereafter the power of imagery, its usefulness legally and in mobilizing people. At one point in *Flowers of Freedom*, Erkingul is showing Mirjam (the filmmaker) photos of demonstrations in Talas against the Jerooy and Andash mines in which she took part, a demonstration of cross-national lesson sharing and solidarity among activists. During this exchange, Mirjam asks Erkingul, "Why is your film footage so important to the village?" Erkingul replies:

> I find that it's very important to document everything. Nobody filmed the demonstrations in 1998. If we had been filming back then, how the police beat people up and how they grabbed women by the hair, we would have had some real evidence!

As the protest movement grew, the activists began videotaping their protest interactions with police and officials, recording arrests. Local residents worked with environmental NGOs to block the road to Kumtor in June 2000 and regularly pressured the company to provide redress. They generated public awareness through accident victim photo exhibits and showings of a film about the accident, *Zolotaya Avariya* (Golden Accident). Karek advocated for compensation for 8 years, finally receiving US$3 million in 2005 to be distributed to residents of five villages near the spill, mostly for harvest damages. The company continues to provide community support through a local social responsibility fund, first paid to the Kyrgyz Government in 2006, and lawsuits for personal damages compensation continue. Erkingul Imankodjoeva became a Member of Parliament in 2010, elected to this office because of her sustained opposition to Kumtor.

Residents, environmentalists, and local government officials see Karek's work as successful in achieving concessions and local investment from the company, improving mining practices, and obtaining central government attention to residents' concerns. The lack of KOC transparency about the spill impacts, resistance to health claims, and the long battle to obtain compensation fundamentally shaped subsequent distrust toward gold mining companies in Kyrgyzstan (Downey 2003). Every protester and activist I interviewed talked about the Barskoon Incident as forging their concerns about risks and expected typical corporate and government response to accidents. Compensation for the Kumtor cyanide spill was gained through protests and road blockades, providing a template for using political pressure. Karek's focus on environmental issues integrated with socio-economic development considerations would serve as a motivating example for other communities opposing gold mining.

## Procedural Justice, Images as Legal Tools

In 2001, Kyrgyzstan became party to both the international Aarhus Convention on Access to Decision-Making and Access to Justice in Environmental Matters and the Espoo Convention on Environmental Impact Assessment in a Transboundary Context. Together these international conventions provided guidelines for member countries to integrate public involvement and international transparency in industrial decision-making through strengthening the public access aspects of permitting procedures (Aarhus Convention) and by ensuring member countries inform each other about potential transboundary harm (Espoo). Anti-mining activists began using these treaties—following attendance at the aforementioned Milieu Kontakt environmental activism trainings and OSCE-sponsored Aarhus workshops—to argue for procedural rights when development of new mines began after 2005. By 2008, President Bakiev's government suppressed anti-mining protests in Talas and protests against Kumtor ceased. Multiple mining executives we interviewed noted that corporate and government discourses also changed. Gold mine representatives began to use communicative approaches, recognizing the reality of local opposition they had previously dismissed as only manipulated by outsiders, and increasingly adopted social responsibility tactics to foster greater cooperation. Government officials also reacted to the heightened tensions by moving mining development discourse from combative to cooperative—distinguishing "good" mining from "bad" mining, seemingly defined by how well a company communicated with communities and supported corporate social responsibility (CSR).

These superficial changes generated frustration among those committed to opposing mining, and subsequently generated a shift in activist tactics and discourses as well. In the early Kumtor protests, photography and films were not key resources used by activists, or at least activists do not reference images in a tactical way. In Talas, however, community members started using photographs of places to be mined as a protest tactic in local meetings and presentations, according to Milieu Kontakt staff (Jakirova 2011; Volkova 2011). Anti-Kumtor activists were networking with local activists in Talas by this time—in part through Milieu Kontakt's network—and did presentations about Kumtor both in-country and at international conferences where they also learned tactics from other activists such as from Mongolia, where Centerra Gold Inc. also operates a gold mine. Karek staff learned a lesson after the cyanide spill: photograph and film everything from the beginning, as legalistic tools, as evidence, and as documentation to counter corporate assessments and claims (Duisheeva 2015; Imankodjoeva 2015).

Activists also began focusing on a procedural rights definition of justice. They utilized judicial training to question and slow down mining development. This procedural approach focused on the permit stage. If permitting agencies follow democratic decision-making procedures and conduct adequate environmental impact assessments (EIAs), theoretically only "good" mines would be allowed. Environmentalists demanded an EIA for another gold mine, called "Andash," in Kyrgyzstan's northwestern Talas province, due to Kyrgyzstan's membership in the Espoo convention requiring EIAs in (international) transboundary contexts and the mine's proximity to Kazakhstan. Conducting this EIA relieved some pressure, but public participation remained inadequate as Kyrgyz laws neglected many of the Aarhus Convention's expressed rights for public participation (Honkonen 2013). An EIA was never conducted for Kumtor or, if it was, it was not publicly shared, and EIAs have not been systematically applied to other mines in development in Kyrgyzstan.

Speaking on conditions of anonymity, mining representatives at Kumtor, Andash, and other mines talked to us about how protesters "waved these Aarhus booklets in our faces" but dismissed the protesters as ignorant, with the belief that "they didn't even understand the convention and just claimed that they have environmental rights." Also according to international NGO convention training staff, at times residents referenced the conventions to demand actions by mining companies (Jakirova 2011; Volkova 2011). However a flaw of the Aarhus Convention disclosure obligation is that it rests with public authorities not private sector actors, thus limiting information access where the operating companies conduct self-monitoring (Mason 2010). Furthermore, the Aarhus Convention information sharing responsibility onus is on governments *before* permitting. Thus, the procedural justice focus of anti-mining claimants was not a successful tactic even in gaining greater public input in the decision-making process. What it did do was highlight corruption and the absence of transparency, which became part of subsequent injustice claims, anti-government sentiment, and more forceful actions by activists. The process also revealed to community members the superficiality of many CSR approaches as a performance of public engagement—as Gilberthorpe and Banks (2012) and Benson and Kirsch (2010) have found elsewhere—even as the belief among mining companies remained that communication and community compensation distinguished "good" from "bad" miners. In 2010, the Bakiev administration, which had suppressed anti-mining activism and disregarded international treaty commitments to ecological democracy, was run out of office in a popular putsch. This marked an opening in national discourse for new ideas of justice and protest tactics.

## Populism and Distributive Justice

Although photographs were used for evidentiary and educational purposes early on, images as rhetorical instruments only became significant in anti-mining politics after 2010. Images began to shape national public conversation and activism tactics in a number of ways. Activists increasingly used images of Kumtor and other mines in development in presentations and transnational activist engagements. Discontented workers at the Kumtor mine began photographing glacier damage. Journalists and opposition politicians used these first-hand accounts, as well as satellite imagery of glacier changes, to substantiate their concerns about mining. Both anti- and pro-mining videos were circulated, demonstrating dueling rhetorical representations: Sagynbek Mombekov's 2012 YouTube music video criticizing Kumtor; a pro-mining public relations video; YouTube videos of the May 30–31st 2013 Tamga protests; a secretly filmed meeting purportedly showing protest leaders extorting Kumtor staff, and an alternative version including the film's missing moments that may reveal different intent; a January 2015 YouTube video, "Kumtor activists after detention and torture in Kyrgyz State Security prison facility" (Satke 2015a). By 2012, many public conversations about Kumtor were taking place through the medium of images.

The overthrow of the Bakiev government in April 2010 was caused in part by general public frustration with government corruption and repression while citizens suffered electricity and food scarcity (Wooden 2014). Anger about a 2009 deal with Centerra—and suspicion of bribery—became part of the backlash following the revolution. Reliance on film and video was a way of shedding light on hidden processes and part of newly populist politics by the interim government and new Jogorku Kenesh (parliament) intending to be responsive to public concern.

Thus, we see some democratizing of the decision-making process. Activists expanded their focus beyond the permitting process to demand public control of gold and nature, rather than corporate control of what are increasingly referred to as "Kyrgyz" spaces. Kyrgyz narratives about redistribution of gains and losses, at times nationalistic, emerged out of frustration with the limitations of earlier demands, socio-political instability, and public concerns about foreign businesses and corrupt officials accruing wealth rather than local communities or the nation as a whole, while residents bore the environmental costs. There was consistent and increasingly frustrated cross-national contestation at almost every mine development site in the country by 2011 (Paxton 2011) that at times became violent, with attacks on mining camps and miners. Newer activists—often young male leaders—relied on ideas of justice that were national and environmental, rather than local and economic, to contest global actors and what they often referred to as unfair distribution of harms and benefits. Activists noted how their ideas of justice shifted in frustration and awareness of environmental impacts. Karek founder, Erkingul Imankodjoeva, told me about her goals changing from wanting compensation and the Kumtor mine to work better, to frustration with KOC and the Kyrgyz government's lack of response, to hoping for closure of the mine, to banning mining in glaciated areas (Imankodjoeva 2009, 2015).

By 2010, the environmental justice aspects of the Kumtor mine had entered national politics during contract renegotiations, through several parliamentary commissions in which photographs of damage to the glaciers were published widely and used in deliberations. Photographs of parliamentary commission members in action, taking samples at Kumtor, helped portray government as critical and responsible. Conservation organizations used maps of mining areas to contest boundaries of concessions to be made in land abutting a nature preserve. International activist organizations made videos about Kumtor and spread these through social media. Corporate actors, business association representatives, and consultants responded with language dismissing these videos as unprofessional, nonfactual, and unscientific. Some of these commission and activist photographs and videos became iconic as they found use in national protests. Ata-Jurt (the main nationalist political party) members used placards of an image of their party MPs, standing in front of the Davidov glacier covered with waste rock, during an infamous rally for nationalization of Kumtor on October 3rd, 2012 (RFE/RL 2012; Toktaliev 2012). MPs Kamchybek Tashiev, Sadyr Japarov, and Talant Mamytov climbed the government building fence and attempted to storm the White House (the main federal government building). When I interviewed the MP Talant Mamytov, in July 2013, he showed me the poster-size photos of Kumtor's glacier damage that had been used in the Kumtor parliamentary hearings (Mamytov 2013). These political party reactions emerged at least partly in response to the ways international corporations behaved in the limited regulatory context of Kyrgyzstan, where residents felt ignored and without access to power.

Criminalization of anti-Kumtor activists in the Djeti Oguz and Karakol regions of Issyk-Kul province began again in 2013 and continue. In 2013, some youth groups organized in frustration with inaction by the national government and used confrontational tactics. These activists used anti-mining rhetoric of injustice that was simultaneously ecological and nationalistic. Some claim these groups coordinated with nationalist politicians mentioned above in developing their ideas and tactics. When videotape emerged of an exchange between a Kumtor corporate officer and two anti-mining youth leaders, Baktiyar Kurmanov and Ermek Dzhunushbayev, the two were arrested, charged with extortion, and sentenced to 7 years in jail (Nee 2013). Activists and journalists have recently spread a competing, unedited version of the conversation that calls into question these charges (Satke 2015c). Nevertheless, these arrests and the subsequent regional crackdown on anti-mining organizers contributed to another shift in justice claims. Djeti-Oguz region activists now focus on human rights ideas of access to justice combined with ecosystem justice demands and community development needs. These activists have relied heavily on videotaping conversations with KOC officials and shared photographs and videos of activists they say were beaten in police custody (Satke 2015b). In my interviews with several Djeti-Oguz activists, they spoke of themselves as the new generation building on the work of Karek and Talas mining resisters, and as providing examples for future activists to learn from their mistakes, in part through meticulously documenting their work in video.

## Imagining a Climate-Changed Future

By 2012, the most sensitive images circulating in Kyrgyzstani activist movements were of Davidov glacier movement. Because KOC placed waste rock on the Davidov glacier, the melt water beneath the glacier sped the movement of the tongue side, making the glacier and the waste rock in front of it advance as much as 4 meters per day (Colgan 2015; Jamieson, Ewertowski, and Evans 2015). The images of mining buildings at the Kumtor mine site damaged by the glacier evoked notions of uncontrollable change and distinct environmental damage. These influenced conversations about glaciers, but also about worker safety and whether the mine should operate. When I visited the mine in 2013, Kumtor managers asked me not to publish photographs of the destroyed infrastructure.

Damage to the Ak Shirak glaciers became a regular street conversation topic. The mine location is not visible even from the closest villages, so it is not proximity that makes this glacier damage resonate so widely in Kyrgyzstan. It is the centrality of drinking and irrigation water, which is dependent on glaciers, that matters most (Wooden 2013). Images of rock waste piled onto the Davidov glacier became part of everyday conversations at a time of global and national press coverage about projected climate change-driven glacier changes. These images entered the public imagination about Kumtor and resonated because they capture concerns about the country's future, also at a time when nationalism and perceived risks to sovereignty were emerging as powerful political forces.

Indeed, risks to the country's glaciers are existential threats to the Kyrgyz people. In July 2013, one acquaintance, who did not know about my work, stopped me on the street to chat after an evening she spent with a friend on the parliamentary commission. She asked, "Did you hear about what Kumtor has done to the glacier? Such a shame. It is awful, the damage is catastrophic." I asked if her friend showed her any images of this. She responded, "No, she didn't show me, she told me what she saw, and I respect and believe her. What she described was just horrible. How could they do this to our glacier." Even the unseen images entered the general public imagination about Kumtor; it was now enough that someone you know saw Kumtor. Government officials talked openly about their frustration with this damage and its future implications. At a social event in Bishkek that same summer, a government official confidentially told me of his reaction to seeing the damage to Davidov and Lysii glaciers from the air, while flying to China. Viewing it made a difference: "Why the glacier? Why did they have to do this? We are very angry about this damage."

In contemporary discussion of gold mining in Kyrgyzstan, ecological justice and ideas of productive justice—resolving the problems of mining by stopping harmful activity and not letting it dominate the country's economy—have moved beyond marginalized environmentalist ideas. Nature has become politically important, highlighting risks to endangered species but also, and perhaps more importantly to the Kyrgyzstani imagination, mountains and glaciers. Nature has also become increasingly seen not as separate from human society and activity, but is described by some research participants as "part of us," and thus also part of national identity and patriotism narratives. Glaciers—through the medium of images—have become part of representational politics, and have altered national conversations about justice in mining in two seemingly contradictory directions driven by emotional responses: national rights and ecological rights. This has led to a partial acceptance by the Kyrgyz government of environmental frames and justice concerns. The Jogorku Kenesh (parliament) organized several investigative commissions to evaluate environmental impacts from Kumtor (the latest was 2012–2013), and held several votes to nationalize the mine after each commission. On April 23rd, 2014, the Jogorku Kenesh passed a law on glaciers (authored by Imankodjoeva) that would have ended open pit mining at Kumtor. Nevertheless, the president did not sign this law and the government is still in the process of renegotiating a new contract with Centerra Gold (Satke 2015b).

## Conclusion and Implications

This chapter concerns the interacting dynamics of mining politics in Kyrgyzstan, from multiple perspectives, sites, and times, in order to better understand what discourses and tactics are changing. Imagery's role in shaping perception and in democratizing knowledge—via the common use of cellphones for photographs, social media, and DVDs for spreading information—has been to elevate gold mining resistance to national political importance. As the story of oppositional movements has shown, activism mattered in Kyrgyzstan's gold mining politics. Some activist justice framings resonated with the public nationally when the ideas aligned with climate change discourses and the larger political context. This context included frustration with the national government and cynicism about CSR approaches. Images helped shape this discursive process, either purposefully or accidentally. Residents understood CSR as hollow and not capable of compensating for environmental damage caused by mining, even as residents accepted corporate community development funding. Demanding investment in local communities was seen as a way to redistribute what foreign corporations were taking out of the country. Thus there were transitions in public discourse from first requesting damage compensation, then demanding a better permitting process, next criticizing CSR approaches, to finally pushing for nationalization and various types of mining bans.

Gold mining is divisive, especially in communities where fear of impacts is highest but where mining job opportunities also matter. Mining in rural areas is also in competition with employment in sectors potentially affected by mining, such as sheep herding. Both images and justice claims can resonate publicly although in unpredictable ways. Activists, international NGOs, and development organization staff should consider the legal value of photographic documentation, but also the limitations of relying primarily on ideas of procedural justice. Residents' frustration with government inaction and CSR approaches can lead to increasingly strident activism. Nationalism is a common way people respond to global pressures and concerns about fairness, raising questions about who benefits and who bears the costs of extraction. "Justice" ideas can also be used by powerful political actors to silence increasingly active opposition through criminalization of protests. Thus using justice claims can be a double-edged sword.

Because of gold mining, glaciers in Kyrgyzstan are now more easily imagined as threatened by both global capital actors and climate change. Glaciers have become place-making and identity-forming. Kyrgyzstanis have come to see that both gold and climate change are produced by countries that benefit the most from these processes and that the negative impacts are not accrued by those countries but rather by Kyrgyzstanis. It is not hard to imagine why mining would be so roundly contested and environmental impact elevated to national discussions. This case is important for extraction activism particularly in mountainous and glaciated places, where climate change glacier retreat may lead to expanded mining, as it already has in Greenland and other parts of the Arctic and Latin America. It provides caution in activist discourse use as defensive ideas have multiple meanings to different actors. Finally, this case highlights the constant importance of visual documentation in activism, not only for evidentiary purposes but also in helping to create a public imaginary where distant mined places become familiar and part of the community, easily seen as close and central to what is important to defend and protect.

## Notes

1 This research was funded by the 2009 ACTR/ACCELS Special Initiatives Fellowship, IREX and NCEEER short-term grants, and Bucknell University. The author thanks Sarah Beckham Hooff for conducting interviews and other research assistance, Nurshat Ababakirov, Nina Asatryan, Bekjan Japarkulov, Bermet Zhumakadyr kyzy, Morgane Treanton, Lena Perminova, Reilly Price, and Ulan Sherimbekov for assistance and transcriptions. My gratitude goes to all research participants in Kyrgyzstan, in particular Erkingul Imankodjoeva and all the Karek women who spent much time helping me understand their history.
2 All quotes and sources unless otherwise cited are from interviews conducted in Kyrgyzstan from 2009 to 2015. These interviews were conducted after Bucknell Institutional Review Board (IRB) approval of the research design and interview methods.

## References

Bagnoli, Anna. 2009. Beyond the standard interview: The use of graphic elicitation and arts-based methods. *Qualitative Research* 9, 5:547–570.

Benson, Peter, and Stuart Kirsch. 2010. Capitalism and the politics of resignation. *Current Anthropology* 51, 4:459–486.

Colgan, William. 2015. Artificial glacier surges at Kumtor mine. *Glacier Bytes* blog, July 27. http://williamcolgan.net/blog/?p=330 (accessed April 22, 2016).

Crate, Susan A. 2011. Climate and culture: Anthropology in the era of contemporary climate change. *Annual Review of Anthropology* 40:175–194.

Delicath, John W., and Kevin Michael Deluca. 2003. Image events, the public sphere, and argumentative practice: The case of radical environmental groups. *Argumentation* 17, 3:315–333.

DeLuca, Kevin Michael. 1999. Unruly arguments: The body rhetoric of Earth First!, Act UP, and Queer Nation. *Argumentation and Advocacy* 36, 1:9–21.

Downey, Kara. 2003. Deep in Kyrgyz earth: Attitudes surrounding foreign mining operations in Kyrgyzstan showcase a culture of distrust. *The Stanford Post—Soviet Post*, April 10. http://postsovietpost.stanford.edu/discussion/deep-kyrgyz-earth (accessed April 22, 2016).

Doyle, Julie. 2007. Picturing the clima(c)tic: Greenpeace and the representational politics of climate change communication. *Science as Culture* 16, 2:129–150.

Duisheeva, Tamara. 2015. Personal interview by Amanda Wooden, July 27. Bishkek, Kyrgyzstan.

Gilberthorpe, Emma, and Glenn Banks. 2012. Development on whose terms?: CSR discourse and social realities in Papua New Guinea's extractive industries sector. *Resources Policy* 37, 2:185–193.

Honkonen, Tuula. 2013. Challenges of mining policy and regulation in Central Asia: The case of the Kyrgyz Republic. *Journal of Energy & Natural Resources Law* 31, 1:5–32.

Hynes, T.P., J. Harrison, E. Bonitenko, T.M. Doronina, H. Baikowitz, M. James, and J.M. Zink. 1998. The International Scientific Commission's assessment of the impact of the cyanide spill at Barskaun, Kyrgyz Republic. *Mining and Mineral Sciences Laboratories*, May 20. www.centerragold.com/sites/default/files/final_report_of_the_international_commission_on_th_1998_cyanide_spill.pdf (accessed December 28, 2015).

Imankodjoeva, Erkingul. 2009. Personal interview by Amanda Wooden, July 28. Bishkek, Kyrgyzstan.

Imankodjoeva, Erkingul. 2015. Personal interview by Amanda Wooden, August 2. Bishkek, Kyrgyzstan.

Jakirova, Indira. 2011. Personal interview by Sarah Beckham Hooff, July 22. Bishkek, Kyrgyzstan.

Jamieson, Stewart S.R., Marek W. Ewertowski, and David J.A. Evans. 2015. Rapid advance of two mountain glaciers in response to mine-related debris loading. *Journal of Geophysical Research: Earth Surface* 120, 7:1418–1435.

Journalist (name confidential). 2013. Personal interview by Amanda Wooden, June 15. Bishkek, Kyrgyzstan.

Juris, Jeffrey S. 2008. Performing politics: Image, embodiment, and affective solidarity during anti-corporate globalization protests. *Ethnography* 9, 1:61–97.

Kirsch, Stuart. 2010. Sustainable mining. *Dialectical Anthropology* 34, 1:87–93.

Leuze, Mirjam. 2014. *Flowers of Freedom*. http://flowers-of-freedom.com/pages/en/about-the-film.php (accessed April 22, 2016).

Mamytov, Talant. 2013. Personal interview by Amanda Wooden, July 28. Bishkek, Kyrgyzstan.

Mason, Michael. 2010. Information disclosure and environmental rights: The Aarhus Convention. *Global Environmental Politics* 10, 3:10–31.

Moody, Roger. 2005. *The risks we run: Mining, communities and political risk insurance*. Utrecht, the Netherlands: International Books.

Nee, Ilya. 2013. Vymogatel'stvo vzjatki mestnymi. Kumtor, Kyrgyzstan (Extortion of bribes by locals. Kumtor, Kyrgyzstan.). YouTube, August 28. www.youtube.com/watch?v=KZm8z_DoRN8 (accessed July 5, 2016).

Paxton, Robin. 2011. Update 1: Men on horseback attack Kyrgyz mining camp. Reuters, October 10. www.reuters.com/article/2011/10/10/kyrgyzstan-mining-idUSL5E7LA23B20111010 (accessed December 28, 2015).

Radio Free Europe/Radio Liberty (RFE/RL). 2012. Anti-gold mining protest in Kyrgyzstan turns violent. Kyrgyz Service Video, October 3. www.rferl.org/media/video/24728130.html (accessed December 28, 2015).

Routledge, Paul. 1997. The imagineering of resistance: Pollok Free State and the practice of postmodern politics. *Transactions of the Institute of British Geographers* 22, 3:359–376.

Satke, Ryskeldi. 2015a. Kumtor activists after detention and torture in Kyrgyz state security prison facility. YouTube, January 27. www.youtube.com/watch?v=R9FeW6Go6oI (accessed April 22, 2016).

Satke, Ryskeldi. 2015b. Kyrgyzstan's controversial gold mine. *The Diplomat*, February 19. http://thediplomat.com/2015/02/kyrgystans-controversial-gold-mine/ (accessed December 28, 2015).

Satke, Ryskeldi. 2015c. Saruu activists meeting with Douglas Grier, Kumtor mine public relations (uncut version). YouTube, December 9. www.youtube.com/watch?v=g CRZ7YUGV5w (accessed July 5, 2016).

Schlosberg, David. 2007. *Defining environmental justice: Theories, movements, and nature.* Oxford: Oxford University Press.

Toktaliev, Mirlan. 2012. Bishkek rally held against Kumtor gold mine. Radio Free Europe/ Radio Liberty Kyrgyz Service Multimedia, October 3. www.rferl.org/media/photogallery/ bishkek-rally-held-against-kumtor-gold-mine/24727747.html (accessed December 28, 2015).

Trilling, David. 2013. Kyrgyzstan: The gold mine reports Bishkek doesn't want you to see. Eurasianet, March 25. www.eurasianet.org/node/66737 (accessed December 28, 2015).

Urgent Action Fund for Women's Human Rights. 2012. http://urgentactionfund.org/2012/ 06/justice-for-people-disabled-by-cyanide-spill/ (accessed December 27, 2015).

Volkova, Tatiana. 2011. Personal interview by Sarah Beckham Hooff, July 22. Bishkek, Kyrgyzstan.

Walker, Gordon. 2012. *Environmental justice: Concepts, evidence and politics.* London: Routledge.

Wooden, Amanda E. 2013. Another way of saying enough: Environmental concern and popular mobilization in Kyrgyzstan. *Post-Soviet Affairs* 29, 4:314–353.

Wooden, Amanda E. 2014. Kyrgyzstan's dark ages: Framing and the 2010 hydroelectric revolution. *Central Asian Survey* 33, 4:463–481.

# 12

# EL SALVADOR'S CHALLENGE TO THE LATIN AMERICAN EXTRACTIVE IMPERATIVE

*Rachel Hannah Nadelman[1]*

## Introduction

"I can mine anywhere in the world, besides El Salvador," American mining executive Robert Johansing insisted in a 2014 interview. He was home in San Salvador for a brief stopover between trips to his mining projects located throughout Central and South America. Johansing repeatedly touted the gold and silver mining industry as a "huge tool for global development and poverty reduction," explaining that he brought a simple message to those living atop gold resources: "the more money we make, the more money the communities make, the more benefits, the more everything." With gold's value steadily rising since 2002, reaching $2,000 an ounce in 2011—650% of its 1999 value—gold mining has experienced an unprecedented expansion almost everywhere. "We live here," in El Salvador, he explained. "But this is the only place where I can't work now. So I work elsewhere."

Why does Robert Johansing mine for gold anywhere "besides El Salvador?" It is not because the country lacks gold deposits, which in fact are plentiful across the country's northern territory. Rather, there is a practical reason: El Salvador has suspended all metals mining within its borders. Since 2007, three successive presidents from the rival right-wing ARENA (Alianza Republicana Nacionalista) party and the left-wing FMLN (Frente Farbundo Marti para la Liberacion Nacional) party have refused to grant or renew mining licenses. This has created a de facto moratorium, effectively immobilizing industrial metals mining in El Salvador.[2]

Why would the government of El Salvador, a low-income country that possesses domestic gold reserves, choose to forgo the "more money, more benefits, more everything" of gold mining? Inspired to find answers to this question, I conducted dissertation fieldwork in El Salvador during 2013, 2014, and 2015. I found that a determining factor influencing government decision-making was the diversity among the domestic sectors that opposed, or withheld support for, metals mining in El Salvador. In this chapter I present the El Salvador case, integrating my original findings with contemporary scholarship and sharing lessons that potentially might be utilized in other contexts by those seeking an alternate future to one reliant on extraction industries.

## Situating El Salvador and Gold Mining within the Latin America Context

El Salvador's choice to not unearth its gold resources makes it an outlier in Latin America. Jiménez In most of South and Central America, a kind of "consensus" exists that "envisions the intensification of national resource extraction as crucial for development" (ISS and CELDA 2015). Consistent with Robert Johansing's promises on behalf of the mining industry, the conviction underpinning this consensus is that extraction of domestic, sovereign natural resources uniquely generates income and employment that can then provide economic benefits across societies. What is notable is that Latin American governments of both left and right ideologies subscribe to this belief. Scholars have called this phenomenon an "extractive imperative" (Shade 2015, 3), that requires that extraction "continue and expand regardless of prevailing circumstances, be it low/high prices of commodities, protests of indigenous groups, or environmental concerns" (ISS and CELDA 2015). The metals mining industry has continued to expand even as citizen backlash escalated. According to the Observatory of Mining Conflicts in Latin America (OCMAL), as of December 2015, there were 209 active mining-provoked social conflicts throughout the region, six of which cross national boundaries. Despite this opposition, national governments across the political spectrum prioritize extraction's promised economic gains over probable negative social and environmental consequences. While conceding "some damage to the environment and even some serious social impacts are accepted as the price to be paid," those in power assert that most important are the benefits to a larger population (Acosta 2013, 72).

This consensus on extraction holds today across the majority of Latin American countries although Central and South America have starkly different extractive industry histories, particularly related to gold mining. Central America's metal resources are a fraction of South America's. Unlike global gold-producing leaders such as Peru, Chile, and Bolivia, gold has not historically provided a major source of income for any Central American nation. Yet, Central America does claim its own gold belt (Figure 12.1), which begins in northwestern Guatemala and ends in northwestern Costa Rica, crossing the length of northern El Salvador on its way (Anderson 2006). Since the late nineteenth century, foreign mining firms have intermittently engaged in Central America's mineral extraction, with domestic private sectors participating minimally, if at all. In the 1980s, crisis and war (including El Salvador's civil war from 1980 to 1992), combined with meager demand for gold in the global market, kept most commercial mining out of Central America. Yet in the post-war 1990s, Central America re-emerged as a new frontier for metals

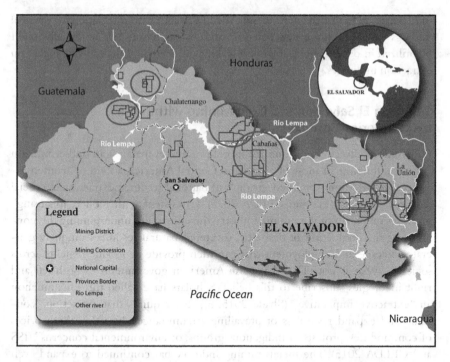

**FIGURE 12.1** The section of the Central American Gold Belt in El Salvador is represented here by mining districts and previously granted concessions that span the north of the country. Since 2007, three successive Salvadoran presidents have committed to not issue new mining permits. Pressure from across Salvadoran society based on concerns of contamination of the Lempa River and other environmental, social, and economic consequences led to the suspension of all industrial metals mining in the country. Map by Donna Gayer, Artasaverb.

mining, sparking the interest of industry as well as the post-conflict governments that sought to generate new opportunities for economic growth (Power 2005).

In the 1990s, El Salvador, too, followed this trend. Immediately after the 1992 peace accords that brought El Salvador's civil war to an end, the Salvadoran government actively courted international mining firms, like Johansing's multi-national employer, to jump-start the industry. Gold's value remained low throughout the 1990s, hovering at about $300 an ounce. Gold possessing countries became burdened with the expectation to attract companies to explore and exploit their domestic gold deposits. El Salvador accepted this challenge. Consecutive Salvadoran governments implemented strategic legal and regulatory reforms to facilitate the entry of foreign firms and expand the nascent industry. This included passing a modernized mining law in 1996 and further amendments in 2001 that lengthened mining license terms while also reducing royalties and taxes (Reyes 2012).

During this same period, Salvadoran environmental activists fought for and achieved passage of the country's first Environmental Law (1997), which established the Ministry of Environment (World Bank 2006). In the 1990s, El Salvador had already experienced extreme levels of environmental degradation, including the highest levels of soil erosion and deforestation in the hemisphere (Barry and Rosa 1995). As early as the 1970s, the World Bank called attention to the demographic strain on El Salvador's natural resources, given the small size of its territory and the high population density, predicting this would be the greatest threat to the country's economic progress (Barry and Rosa 1995). Yet developing a system of environmental governance did not derail the country's pro-extractives economic strategy that persisted through the 1990s and into the new millennium. In fact, mining proponents within and outside the government argued that the country's modernized mining law and technological advancements would allow for responsible mining practices.

In 2002, gold's value began its steady climb, eventually doubling in value to $600 per ounce in 2006. The price for gold grew to triple that amount in the ensuing years. These rising commodity prices reinforced the imperative to exploit domestic resources. El Salvador's trajectory appeared to be consistent with that of its Central and South American neighbors who had already embraced the extractive imperative. However, the "inevitability" of El Salvador's mining future, at least at present, seems to have been proven wrong.

## El Salvador's Divergence from the Regional Consensus on Extraction

The spark for El Salvador's opposition to industrial mining—what this volume has conceptualized as "extrACTION"—came from within provinces possessing gold resources, ignited by local citizens who had come to believe that their country was not suitable for metals mining. During my El Salvador fieldwork, I spent significant time in two of El Salvador's seven Gold Belt provinces, Cabañas and Chalatenango, where residents have led the community-based fight against mining. Cabañas is home to El Dorado, a formerly functioning mine licensed for re-opening in the 1990s and acquired for exploration by Canadian company Pacific Rim in 2002. Chalatenango had seven municipalities licensed for exploration, where the Canadian company Au Martinique Silver/Intrepid Minerals was responsible for the most aggressive activity. These provinces, which both share a border with Honduras, have noteworthy political and historical differences: Cabañas is a politically conservative stronghold of the ARENA party; Chalatenango is a bastion of the progressive FMLN party and center of the opposition during the civil war (Cartagena 2009).

Yet San Sebastian, in La Unión, is the only site that has experienced industrial scale mining extraction, not simply exploration, since the civil war. This made San Sebastian unique among Salvadoran towns with gold beneath their soil. Although there has been no industrial mining in San Sebastian for over two decades, each time I visited, I encountered the San Sebastian River's bright orange currents, signaling continued contamination by heavy metals and acid mine drainage. Anti-mining activists have led domestic "toxic tours" in San Sebastian and cross-border journeys to active mining sites in Honduras and Guatemala. Through these tours the Salvadoran metals mining opposition movement has sought to exhibit the negative impacts gold mining would have on the country's water sources. Antonio Pacheco, a community leader from Cabañas, guided my first San Sebastian tour in 2013. In an interview afterwards, he laid out the position of many opposed to mining for El Salvador:

> It would not matter if a [mining] company promised 100% of profits to El Salvador. The problem for us in El Salvador is not whether the community benefits. Mining "benefits" do not take into account the damage they cause at social, economic, and environmental levels. So we cannot allow it.

Diametrically opposed to the beliefs underlying the "extractive imperative," this perspective claims that no amount of economic benefit from metals mining could adequately compensate for the environmental and social damage.

El Salvador's stretch of the Central American Gold Belt covers the country's northern corridor, an area that encompasses some of El Salvador's poorest and most marginalized communities. Initially, metal mining's promises of income and employment made mining appealing for these under-developed areas. However, this declared opportunity became a liability when residents experienced the negative effects of exploration activities. In Cabañas, local farmers complained of their cattle suddenly becoming sick and even dying. Other residents spoke of wells running dry. Senator Carlos Reyes, an ARENA congressman representing Cabañas, explained to me in a 2014 interview:

> For us, the problem is that we have a tiny country. And having a tiny country means that in some way or another, wherever one starts a mining project, there are also going to be homes and this makes things really complicated for us.

Given El Salvador's population density, the territory encompassing gold deposits overlaps with residential land. This has meant that mining's negative territorial impacts could immediately affect adjacent communities.

As Broad and Cavanagh (2015a) assert, mining became a national issue when key individuals and organizations from Cabañas and Chalatenango joined with San Salvador-based organizations that had national agendas. Together they transformed "local concerns into a sophisticated, organized civil-society opposition to mining based on its environmental and social costs and lack of long term economic benefits" (Broad and Cavanagh 2015a, 421). La Mesa Frente a la Mineria, the National Roundtable against Mining, is the most prominent organizational representative of this opposition. Formally established in 2005, La Mesa encompasses a range of local and national organizations—including social service, environmental, human rights, religious, policy, and research groups. The glue that has kept the coalition together for a decade is their singular objective: a permanent, legal prohibition of mining in

El Salvador and the prevention of any cross-border mines in neighboring countries that could harm Salvadoran territory.

El Salvador's worsening environmental vulnerability, in the context of limited territory and high population density, helps to explain why a seemingly local issue would resonate nationally. Today El Salvador is the most environmentally degraded and densely populated country in Central America (UNDP 2011) and it is estimated that 90% of its bodies of surface water are polluted (USAID 2011). In the Western Hemisphere only Haiti is more deforested than El Salvador (World Bank 2011). Over half of Salvadorans access fresh water from a single source, the Lempa River. Of significant concern for many Salvadorans is that the Lempa River basin resides in the same territory that encompasses the bulk of the country's underground minerals.

"El Salvador's gold territory is in the hydraulic heart of the country," explained Dr. Sandra de Barraza, a 12-year presidential appointee on El Salvador's National Development Commission under three conservative ARENA administrations. Dr. Barraza and I discussed water's central role in the country's gold mining debates. She said, "anyone should be able to understand the people's concerns about mining in El Salvador when you look at a map," directing me to a map of the country's north, as she traced the Lempa River's course through gold country. The map revealed the stark choice for El Salvador: water or gold.

The extractive imperative acknowledges the inevitability of some environmental costs, but prioritizes the economic benefits. The anti-mining movement strategically challenged this argument by underscoring metals mining's direct dangers for El Salvador's vulnerable water sources. The perils for water are two-fold: the contamination from chemicals utilized in mineral extraction, such as cyanide, and the heavy water use in daily mining operations. Focusing on the need to protect precious water sources meant that the anti-mining movement could strategically frame their cause as "pro-water" rather than as "anti-industry" (Broad and Cavanagh 2015b). This water-protecting framing has been credited as an important factor in convincing a majority of Salvadorans that mining would be more detrimental than beneficial for the nation.

Using the pro-water framing, the opposition movement strategically showcased tangible and scientific evidence of mining's immediate and probable threats to El Salvador's territory and environment. In a 2014 interview Vidalina Morales, a spokesperson for La Mesa, explained:

> Evidence mobilizes people. I believe that one of our biggest successes has been mobilization—this has been the way that we have tried to convince others and this is how we convinced decision-makers.

Recognizing limited government capacity to deal with the issue, the movement carried out independent data collection and analysis where they had human and financial resources, and sought international partners to assist where they did not. It was a 2005 partnership with American geologist Dr. Robert Moran that catalyzed the movement's efforts to influence government policy. Enlisted by La Mesa, Moran analyzed the Environmental Impact Assessment (EIA) that the Canadian mining company Pacific Rim (now owned by Australian Oceana Gold) had submitted to the Ministry of Environment to obtain the environmental permits required to secure a mining exploitation license in Cabañas. David Pereira, from La Mesa member CEICOM, a local environmental research institute, explained that:

> Moran's work was the departure point for effective resistance in Cabañas. It gave the government evidence that enabled it to have a scientific basis to reconsider the company's environmental permit application, which would have allowed the company to begin full-fledged gold extraction (2014).

International cooperation has gone beyond targeted strategic partnership with individual experts on gold mining, like Moran. While locally led and locally backed, the anti-mining movement has also counted on strategic international partners that challenged the principles driving the extractive imperative. Large-scale international support did not immediately accompany the formation of the national coalition, but the international alliances that formed early on were crucial. For instance, community-based groups from Guatemala and Honduras that had formed in opposition to their own countries' emerging mining industries provided fundamental counsel and education for the Salvadoran movement. For international solidarity organizations, like Sister Cities, who had longstanding community relationships maintained since the civil war, the anti-mining cause was a natural extension of their existing social justice campaigns (Spalding 2014). The most strategic international partner in the early years was Oxfam America, which provided guidance and funding for the national coalition and their campaign through their El Salvador-based staff. International support did not substantially expand beyond this base until 2009, driven by the assassinations of Cabañas-based anti-mining activists and international arbitration launched against El Salvador by Commerce Group and Pacific Rim.

In 2006, in a partnership with Oxfam, La Mesa scaled up its awareness-building efforts to organize a "Week against Mining." This involved strategically planned protests and educational events hosted in June 2006 across the country, including a high profile forum featuring government officials such as the Minister of Environment Hugo Barrera, that allowed an unprecedented public dialogue between government and citizens on the issue. By 2007, a large portion of the Salvadoran public had adopted the view that mining would be more detrimental than beneficial, both for their country and for their individual lives. According to a 2007 survey, conducted by the Central American University (UCA) across the 24 municipalities for which the government had previously granted mining permits, 62.5% of those polled believed that the country did not have suitable conditions for mining (IUDOP 2007). Polling data in 2015 showed that public rejection of mining has continued to grow: 79.5% responded that El Salvador lacks suitable conditions for mining, and 77% agreed that El Salvador should permanently prohibit mining (IUDOP 2015).

## A Common Goal Without a Common Movement

There is no question that it was the community-based movement against mining in El Salvador, with some international support, that challenged the regional "extractive imperative" and ignited the local-, and then national-level, struggle that had the earliest influences on policy-makers. However, two other societal sectors were responsible for fanning the flames that forced policy-makers to further re-examine their extractive plans. In 2007, El Salvador's Catholic Church came out unanimously against mining in an open pastoral letter they called, "Let Us Care for All of Our Home" (CEDES 2007). Almost a decade before Pope Francis' groundbreaking 2015 Encyclical on climate change (Pope Francis 2015), El Salvador became the first country in which the Archbishop and his full Council of Bishops unanimously took a position against metals mining that prioritized protecting their country's environment over potential economic gain. Remarkably, Archbishop Fernando Saenz Lacalle, an Opus Dei adherent known for his ideological conservatism, had also been trained as a chemist in his native Spain. As explained to me in 2014 by Antonio Baños, the director of Caritas, the Catholic Church's international development and social service agency: "Archbishop Saenz Lacalle was not a person opposed to investment, nor could you consider him a bishop aligned with the left … But he realized immediately, as a chemist, that [the company] was lying to him."

Relying on biblical narrative and Catholic Social Teaching (Himes 2001) the Church offered a religious foundation for why protecting the environment, and water most importantly, was a responsibility one had to God. Based on this, the Church provided a moral basis for the anti-mining position, which added a new dimension to the scientific and social justifications for challenging the regional status quo (Nadelman 2015). In 2010, the El Salvadoran Catholic Church strengthened its position. Under the leadership of new Archbishop José Luis Escobar Alas, the Bishop's council reiterated its opposition to mining, condemning mining's use of cyanide and its threat to water (Rodriguez 2010).

Many among those active in the anti-mining movement believe the Catholic Church's adoption and dissemination of the anti-mining/pro-water stance enabled the mining opposition's message to reach across political ideologies and transcend entrenched economic practices. As Baños explained in our interview, the Church's position "clarified for the population that [being against mining] wasn't a political [issue] … but an issue of human and environmental consequences." This re-framing helped to transform the Salvadoran mining opposition's image and increased its political power.

Members of El Salvador's business community, known to be ferociously pro-investment, also recognized the perils that mining would pose to their country's water sources. Water, of course, is not just crucial for communities. It is also an essential resource for business. Therefore, water source contamination does not just pose risks to life, but also to private sector profit. El Salvador is not known for having robust domestic industry, but what it does have—agribusiness, ranching, juice and soft-drink production—heavily relies on water and land resources. For example, the Murray Meza family, at the top of El Salvador's infamous 14-family oligarchy, has made much of its wealth from the business of bottling sodas and juices using El Salvador's fresh water resources. The family never publically connected its members, companies, or their charitable foundations to the anti-mining fight. However, Roberto Murray Meza and the foundation he led at the time, FUNDEMAS, launched its own Lempa River protection campaign that coincided with the government's decision to stop approving mining permits (Hernandez de Lario 2014).

While advocating to protect water, the Murray Meza campaign never explicitly critiqued the metals mining industry. This is representative of how El Salvador's economic elite has appeared to largely remain outside the fray—not openly opposing metals mining, but also not defending it. El Salvador's limited mining history has meant that, when foreign firms attempted to jumpstart the industry in the 1990s, they did not have pre-established relationships with the Salvadoran business community or local elites. Foreign companies investing in El Salvador's gold resources also did not actively court or build partnerships with their natural Salvadoran counterparts. Juan Hector Vidal, formerly the executive director of ANEP, El Salvador's leading business association, noted in an interview that the Salvadoran private sector "had never been invited to dine" with these multi-national mining companies. Adding to what his predecessor had asserted, ANEP's director of economic and social issues Waldo Jiménez, explained:

> In El Salvador there is an implicit consensus around "no mining!!" No one comes out to advocate for "yes to mining!" So it would seem instead that it would be better not to get involved in these problems.

Without historical links to the industry, or the promise of making a profit—not to mention the potential threat to their existing business—El Salvador's powerful elites did not lend their political influence to the mining industry.

This lack of local business support did not change when Pacific Rim unsuccessfully applied for a mining exploitation license for the El Dorado mine in Cabañas. Pacific Rim submitted a multi-million dollar claim at the International Court for the Settlement of Investment Disputes (ICSID, housed at the World Bank) that challenged El Salvador's right to deny the company mining licenses (Reyes 2012). While openly critical of the Salvadoran government's economic policies, especially those implemented under FMLN presidencies, most of El Salvador's private sector did not support the company's multi-million-dollar claim. The private sector's overall lack of enthusiasm for the metals mining industry's attempts to penetrate the country eliminated what could have been an insurmountable obstacle for the anti-mining movement.

## Turning the Page on the Extractive Imperative

As support for the pro-water/anti-mining position congealed across distinct Salvadoran sectors, it exerted a strong influence on government decision-making. To date, there have been different analyses of who within the Salvadoran government deserves recognition for taking action that supported the anti-mining/pro-water movement's demands. Early reporting credited the presidency of Mauricio Funes (2009–2014), who led the progressive FMLN party to its first executive win after 17 years of post-war conservative ARENA rule. In 2009, at the start of his term, Funes became the first leader to solidify the government's commitment to a mining suspension in the form of a public letter. Funes' successor, Salvador Sanchez Ceren (2014–present), continues to maintain the mining stoppage in an open alliance between the FMLN and the public civil society organizations that had become the face of the Salvadoran mining opposition and the international publicity following the ICSID lawsuit.

However, there are important policy continuities between the FMLN presidents and their conservative ARENA predecessor, Antonio Saca (2004–2009). Initially Saca's cabinet leadership took the first steps to slow, and then halt, mining activity, with his first Minister of Environment, the businessman Hugo Barrera at the fore-front of these initiatives. Records from the Ministry of Economy show that the end of gold mining effectively dates back to mid-2006 when, without fanfare, the two Ministries stopped approving mining exploration licenses even as company requests continued (MINEC 2014). Later that year Barrera, who had no prior environ-mental background, rescinded the exploitation license for San Sebastian and, while never rejecting Pacific Rim's application, simply never approved it.

In an interview with me, Barrera explained his actions by saying the govern-ment could not grant the environmental permit because Pacific Rim never dem-onstrated its operations would "guarantee protection of water, land, and human health" required by law. Per Broad and Cavanagh (2015a), this was a "conscious act of disapproving by not acting." In 2007, following the recommendations of a government commissioned study on mining's feasibility for El Salvador, these Ministries announced they would formally stop granting the environmental per-mits required for mining licenses until the country undertook a strategic EIA and made changes to national regulation and oversight (De Gavidia 2014). With these actions, this conservative, pro-investment, administration responded to the grow-ing community-based mining opposition, as well as the parallel campaigns by the Catholic Church and actors in the private sector, to protect El Salvador's water sources.

In early 2009 Saca became the first sitting president to speak out publically in opposition to mining. Pacific Rim had already made its international arbitra-tion intentions clear, yet Saca insisted in a radio interview that he preferred for El Salvador "to be forced into international arbitration and face those consequences" rather than allow mining (Lopez Piche 2009). In my interview with Funes' first Minister of Economy, Hector Dada, he explained that, "If Saca had not already decreed the 'moratorium', for the FMLN to have decreed it first would have elicited a furious attack about the state violating the rights of private enterprise" (2014). Therefore, because an administration seen as a friend to business halted all metals mining activity, the moratorium had enough credibility to be sustained by progressive leadership.

Today, La Mesa, other anti-mining civil society actors, and the Catholic hierarchy continue advocating for the government to take legally binding action against mining. El Salvador's Congress has yet to prohibit mining via legislation that overrides, revises, or limits the extant 1996 mining law. Therefore, while the suspension has stopped the industry, anti-mining activists argue that the lack of decisive legislation leaves room for a future reversal. Yet, even without legislative certainty and in the face of international arbitration, support for the suspension of mining by three consecutive presidents keeps metals mining outside of El Salvador's borders.

## Lessons for an Alternative Future

El Salvador is a nation that chose to forestall mining activities even while neighboring countries like Guatemala and Honduras, all of whom also have limited histories with mining, have bound their economies to extractive imperatives. These countries have accepted risks to the environment and their people by conforming their policies to a regional and international "consensus" on the benefits and importance of mining for national growth and social stability. El Salvador's story suggests that alternatives to the extractive imperative are possible.

What can we draw from El Salvador's experience to be instructive to opposition movements elsewhere in the world? Despite El Salvador's unique economic, environmental, and social circumstances, there are generalizations that may be applicable to other countries. The first is that there can be various paths to achieving a similar goal. El Salvador's rejection of the extractive imperative did not come because of the influence or actions of one societal sector. Instead, different sectors, with at times overlapping interests and at other times parallel trajectories, provided multiple modes of influence on government decision-making processes that together shaped policy actions. All actors did not have to collaborate, or even have the same interests, as long as they were working toward a consistent goal. This is not to undermine the power of coalition building, however. In El Salvador, the strength of community-based anti-mining efforts lies in both their developing and sustaining networks built throughout the movement. Yet, this case does demonstrate that having one movement coordinator is not necessarily as critical as is identifying the common goal. Powell (Chapter 14) found similar occurrences in her research on the Navajo transition movement.

This leads to a second lesson we can draw from El Salvador's story: the importance of strategic framing. By situating the opposition message as pro-water rather than anti-mining (Broad and Cavanagh, 2015b), the Salvadoran mining opposition adopted a tactical strategy that allowed the cause to be relevant across Salvadoran society. A pro-water focus made extraction's dangers significant for people outside of mining-affected areas, thus launching the issue from the local to the national and enlarging the constituency that could have electoral impacts. The broad focus on water also enabled sectors with distinct perceptions of water's central importance—for example, as a human right or a commodity to be sold for profit—to advocate for its protection (and to different degrees against mining) without having to align their motivations. Finally, a pro-water focus provided positive messaging about the importance of protecting an essential resource rather than being against a particular industry or mode of economic growth.

A third lesson relates to the transcendent nature of moral authority. In El Salvador, the Catholic Church's advocacy of the anti-mining/pro-water position gave the movement a moral authority that helped it rise above political partisanship. In the context of Pope Francis' Encyclical and the Catholic Church hierarchy's focus on environmental justice, we see that Catholic Social Teaching provided a faith-based justification for preserving "God's creation" and therefore a faith-based questioning of the extractive imperative. In this case, faith and science were mutually reinforcing. This is particularly salient in a country like El Salvador, where the institution of the Catholic Church commands significant respect, even among non-Catholics. However, alignment of principles between faith, science, and justice is far from guaranteed in El Salvador and elsewhere in the world. In public debates on contentious social and political issues, like women's reproductive rights or sexuality, they often clash. Yet, on environmental issues, particularly related to extraction, religious teachings may give a higher meaning to the environment, and can be utilized to bolster societal support for policies that choose sustainability over short-term economic benefit.

A final point I wish to make is that business interests, nationally and globally, are not monolithic. Even when there appear to be natural allies for foreign-led extraction industry in the domestic private sector, there can be other more dominant interests that prevent supposedly obvious partnership. Domestic business can be reliant on natural resources for their existing industries. Preserving profitmaking that already exists can trump the potential for other, less certain, revenue. Therefore, when facing extraction industries' threats to natural resources, activists and the private sector can find common ground on the need for environmental protections.

## Conclusion

It is important to recognize that El Salvador's ability to enact and sustain the de facto moratorium comes in large part because the nation's mining industry had not yet been fully operationalized. In many ways El Salvador happened to be situated in a particular temporal, ecological, and political climate that allowed for advocating to ban metals mining. While it is necessary to acknowledge these differences in El Salvador's circumstances, compared to countries like Guatemala and Honduras that have actively operating metals mining industries, it does not reduce the power of this case study's lessons.

Since mining eventually exhausts finite resources, the industry is forced to continually expand by moving into untapped territories—often into areas that have not yet been exploited because of environmental, social, and other vulnerabilities. This is one possible future for El Salvador's people. However, in this chapter I have sought to illustrate how a robust community-based movement anchored domestic opposition to metals mining by basing their case on environmental, pro-water based, arguments. The oppositional movement was later bolstered by sectors not typically in agreement with activist movements, most significantly the Catholic Church and key actors within the domestic private sector. These stakeholders often followed parallel paths in their opposition to metals mining without direct collaboration, but together succeeded in moving public opinion and influencing electoral politics and policy, thereby bucking the prevailing regional economic trends that demanded extractive pursuits despite environmental consequences. Therefore, one could find relevant parallels between other extractive settings and El Salvador, even where mining already exists; finding common ground, building coalitions, and leveraging common interests, without requiring direct collaboration across diverse stakeholder groups, may be the key to protecting the country's natural resources over economic gain.

## Notes

1 I am indebted to Herbert Vargas for research and transcription assistance, Anthony Lauren and Alice and Manny Nadelman for editorial (and emotional) support, editor Kirk Jalbert for his guidance and patience, Dr. Robin Broad, for her foundational research on El Salvador and the metals mining struggle, and for her wisdom and support for my own work on these topics and to all those in El Salvador who shared their time and knowledge.
2 On March 29, 2017, after the finalization of this chapter, the Salvadoran legislature voted overwhelmingly to make legal the de facto moratorium. This new law makes El Salvador the first country in the world to ban metals mining nationwide.

## References

Acosta, Alberto. 2013. Extraction and neoextractism: Two sides of the same curse. In *Beyond development: Alternative visions from Latin America*, edited by Miriam Lang and Dunia Mokrani, 61–86. Quito, Ecuador: Transnational Institute.

Anderson, Stephen. 2006. The mineral industries of Central America Belize, Costa Rica, El Salvador, Guatemala, Honduras, Nicaragua, and Panama. *U.S. Geological Survey minerals yearbook 2006*, 6.1–6.11. Washington DC: US Department of the Interior and US Geological Survey.

Barry, Deborah, and Herman Rosa. 1995. *El Salvador: Dinámica de la degradación ambiental*. San Salvador, El Salvador: Programa Salvadoreño de Investigación sobre Desarrollo y Medio Ambiente (PRISMA).

Broad, Robin, and John Cavanagh. 2015a. Poorer countries and the environment: Friends or foes? *World Development* 72:419–431.

Broad, Robin, and John Cavanagh. 2015b. El Salvador gold: Toward a mining ban. In *Ending the fossil fuel era*, edited by Thomas Princen, Jack P. Manno, and Pamela L. Martin, 167–192. Cambridge, MA: MIT Press.

Cartagena, Rafael E. 2009. Origenes del movimiento de oposicion a la minería metalica en El Salvador. *Estudios Centroamericanos* 64, 2:497–524.

Conferencia Episcopal de El Salvador (CEDES). 2007. *Cuidemos La Casa de Todos: Pronunciamiento de la Conferencia Episcopal de El Salvador sobre la explotación de minas de oro y plata*. May 3.

De Gavidia, Yolanda. 2014. Interview by Rachel Nadelman. Personal Interview. Guatemala City, Guatemala, September 19.

Francis (Pope). 2015. *Encyclical letter "laudato si" of the Holy Father Francis: On care for our common home.* Vatican City: Libreria Editrice Vaticana.

Hernandez de Lario, Silvia. 2014. Interview by Rachel Nadelman. Personal Interview. Ministry of Environment: San Salvador, El Salvador, September 10.

Himes, Kenneth R. 2001. *Responses to 101 questions on Catholic social teaching.* Mahwah, NJ: Paulist Press.

Institute of Social Studies (ISS), and Centre for Latin American Research and Documentation (CELDA). 2015. *The political economy of the extractive imperative in Latin America.* Workshop notes, Netherlands, April 10.

Instituto Universitario de Opinión Pública (IUDOP). 2007. *Conocimientos y percepciones hacia la minería en zonas afectadas por la incursión minera.* San Salvador, El Salvador: Universidad Centroamericana José Simeón Cañas.

Instituto Universitario de Opinión Pública (IUDOP). 2015. *Opiniones y Percepciones hacia la Minería Metálica en El Salvador.* San Salvador, El Salvador: Universidad Centroamericana José Simeón Cañas.

Lopez Piche, Keny L. 2009. No a la minería: Saca cierra puertas a explotación de metals. *La Prensa Grafica*, February 28. www.laprensagrafica.com/economia/nacional/20190-no-a-la-mineriasaca-cierra-puertas-a-explotacion-de-metales#sthash.0ffcMSZJ.dpuf (accessed February 1, 2015).

Ministerio de Economía (MINEC). 2014. *Solicitudes de licencias de exploración 2000–2014.* Generated in response to a freedom of information request submitted by Rachel Nadelman. Received November 28, 2014.

Nadelman, Rachel. 2015. "Let us care for everyone's home": The Catholic Church's role in keeping gold mining out of El Salvador. *CLALS Working Paper Series No. 9.* Washington, DC: American University Center for Latin American & Latino Studies. http://ssrn.com/abstract=2706819 (accessed February 1, 2015).

Power, Thomas M. 2005. *Metals, mining, and sustainable development in Central America: An assessment of benefits and costs.* Washington, DC: Oxfam America.

Reyes, Josué. 2012. El Salvador. In *Latin American investment protections: Comparative perspectives on laws, treaties and disputes for investors, states and counsel,* edited by Jonathan C. Hamilton, Omar E. Garcia-Bolivar, and Hernando Otero, 293–316. Boston, MA: Martinus Nijhoff Publishers.

Rodriguez, Carmen. 2010. Conferencia Episcopal vuelve a rechazar la explotación minera en El Salvador. *La Pagina*, November 10. www.lapagina.com.sv/ampliar.php?id=42718 (accessed October 15, 2015).

Shade, Lindsay. 2015. Sustainable development or sacrifice zone? Politics below the surface in post-neoliberal Ecuador. *The Extractive Industries and Society* 2, 4:775–784.

Spalding, Rose J. 2014. *Contesting trade in Central America: Market reform and resistance.* Austin: University of Texas Press.

United Nations Development Programme (UNDP). 2011. *Paving the way for climate-resilient infrastructure: Guidance for practitioners and planners,* 8 & 96. New York: United Nations Development Program.

United States Agency for International Development (USAID). 2011. *El Salvador country profile: Property rights and resource governance,* 11. Washington, DC: United States Agency for International Development.

World Bank. 2006. *Republic of El Salvador country environmental analysis improving environmental management to address trade liberalization and infrastructure expansion, March 20.* Report No. 35226–SV. Washington, DC: World Bank.

World Bank. 2011. The global facility for disaster reduction and recovery. In *Disaster risk management in Latin America and the Caribbean region: GFDRR country notes—El Salvador,* 19. Washington, DC: The World Bank.

# 13

# UNCONVENTIONAL ACTION AND COMMUNITY CONTROL

## Rerouting Dependencies Despite the Hydrocarbon Economy

*Tristan Partridge*

In recent years, extractive industries have expanded operations by developing technologies to mine unconventional fossil fuels, leading to further investments in infrastructures to support the industry. Exploiting the apparent abundance of unconventional fossil fuels, thus, not only contributes to the very real risk of runaway climate change; it also creates global futures where dependence on extraction products and practices is deepened. By contrast, there are innumerable initiatives and struggles to create alternative futures that work toward lessening the role played by subsurface hydrocarbons in meeting everyday needs, especially at the community level. This chapter looks at examples of collective action now underway to reduce present and future dependency on fossil fuel extraction. It focuses on the importance of community control over land and political processes, and on the concerns and commitments that motivate alternative visions for the future.

There are few places that are not implicated in one way or another in the fossil fuel industry, and these connections vary dramatically across geographies and social circumstances. Indeed, the two case studies considered in this chapter occupy very different locations, with distinct social histories, political realities, and cultural identities. The Isle of Eigg is a small island located 10 miles off the west coast of Scotland (Figure 13.1) with a population of about 100. There has never been any connection between the island and the UK mainland electricity grid. In 2008, an island-wide electricity micro-grid based on renewable sources was completed, altering how residents used and depended upon fossil fuels. Over 5,000 miles away, in the Ecuadorian Andes, the indigenous community of San Isidro (Figure 13.2) is engaged in struggles for land rights, water justice, and political participation. It is marked by labor migration: most of the 92 households there are home to someone who makes the day-long journey to the country's Amazon regions for work in the oil industry. As this source of income becomes increasingly precarious, collective initiatives have developed new forms of community support.

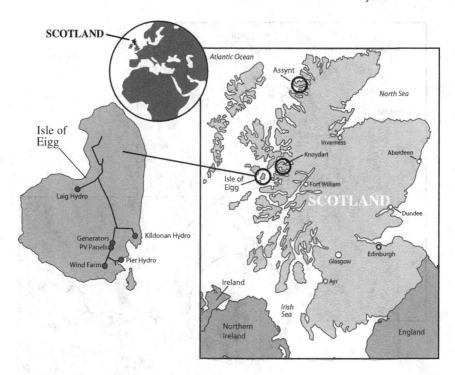

**FIGURE 13.1** The electricity micro-grid on the Isle of Eigg in Scotland is a shared infrastructure project managed by the resident community. It uses a mixture of energy sources (including Hydro, Wind, and Solar PV) to provide a dependable energy supply and to reduce everyday dependency on fossil fuels. The project highlights the importance of localized control over land and political processes in developing alternatives to extraction. Map by Donna Gayer, Artasaverb.

Previous anthropological work has illustrated how diverse place-based struggles for social and ecological sustainability have responded to historical dispossession by "reclaiming community control over land and over their political processes" (Kenrick 2011, 195). Arguing that these dynamics make critical contributions to the creation of alternative futures, I bring attention to how communities reassess and redesign relations with the fossil fuel industry, challenging the underlying imperatives of contemporary extractive economies. By revising social organization and resource relations that attend more closely to local concerns, such actions might also be described as "unconventional" insofar as they disrupt, however slightly, the dynamics of fossil fuel dependence.

## Within and Beyond the Hydrocarbon Economy

The term "hydrocarbon economy" denotes not only financial concerns but also the diverse social and environmental relations bound up with processes of

**FIGURE 13.2** Local implementation of a commons irrigation system to promote agriculture in the indigenous community of San Isidro in highland Ecuador supports alternatives to oil-industry labor, representing a collective effort to reduce dependency on fossil fuel extraction and create sustainable futures. Map by Donna Gayer, Artasaverb.

extraction. It is the seemingly all-encompassing web of supply-chains, technologies, and social systems that both deliver and depend upon relatively affordable energy (Jasanoff and Kim 2013). Although the individuals, institutions, and practices involved vary across space and time, the hydrocarbon economy can be thought of as shorthand for the political economy of extraction, in which privatized, market-based, and extractivist initiatives dominate to the extent that they become "naturalized" and are assumed to be inevitable (Boykoff et al. 2009). Enacting alternatives to these economic practices is thus discouraged or deferred by the institutions that depend on them, or is seen as unrealistic, despite the fact that doing so is a necessity for many remote or marginalized populations. Any attempts to move beyond the hydrocarbon economy take place largely within the structures and systems it perpetuates: as such, alternatives are not created *outside* these networks and their influences but *despite* them.

The basis of the global hydrocarbon economy has hitherto been defined by reserves of conventional fossil fuels. Today, these are running out; exhausted by the appetite of the economic arrangements they have fueled—systems of mass production, high consumption lifestyles, and the push for endless growth on a finite planet (Chatterton and Cutler 2008; Graeber 2011). Extractive industries have responded to this exhaustion by finding ways to remove oil, coal, and gas from "unconventional" sources—exacerbating social inequalities and ecological degradation—and redirecting technological futures to facilitate the expansion, rather than the contraction, of the hydrocarbon economy (Gordon 2012). Meanwhile, climate scientists warn that the world needs to leave unconventional fossil fuels in the ground and move to a post-fossil fuel era (Short et al. 2015). There is an urgent need for action toward creating alternative futures.

## Relations of Dependence

Collective action that seeks to reassess a community's relations with fossil fuels occurs within complex relations of dependence on systems that have negative impacts for those communities, such as through exposure to environmental pollution or hazardous working conditions. Early attempts in international development to theorize "dependence" between individuals, regions, and nations established hierarchies between different actors as stable or constant. Such theories were later modified to highlight instabilities and the possibility that hierarchies and relations of dependence could be overcome, changing across time and space (Edelman and Haugerud 2005; Gledhill 2000). This work recognized the power of communities to reshape at least some of their political interactions and economic exchanges (Bebbington 1993) but did not deny power asymmetries between smaller groups and others who dominate state political structures and economic systems (Leys 2005). To address such inequalities, many successful community initiatives have worked toward "strategic dislocations" from within the more unequal networks they have been bound to politically, economically, or historically (Mason and Whitehead 2011, 505; Dobson 2003).

The "alternative" initiatives described in this chapter are characteristic of such strategic dislocations: rearrangements of communal activities to selectively choose the outside agencies and systems that everyday life depends on, and reducing reliance on those deemed to be unsustainable. This might be done by changing patterns of energy generation and consumption (as in Eigg) or supporting localized agriculture and employment (as in San Isidro). Such initiatives are deliberately place-based; designed to respond and contribute to particular local conditions (Rennie and Billing 2015). They are neither wholesale "solutions" nor specific models for action to be replicated. They do, however, reflect the roles and possible powers that collective organizing may have in reengineering the social and material bases of community life—away from a dominant dependency on fossil fuels, and tailored to specific social and historical contexts. Despite the significant cultural, historical, socio-economic, and geographical differences between these contexts, the actions undertaken in each share some similarities. Of particular interest is how action has been enabled (and significant social change facilitated) in both locations following processes of land reform and through revived political organizing within, and between, communities.

## Eigg, Land Reform, and Electrification

In June 1997 the residents of Eigg purchased the island they called home, bringing an end to years of insecure relations between the 60–70 residents and the individual who had been the sole owner and landlord. In collaboration with supporters and activists from other highland and island communities in Scotland, as well as with financial support from thousands of donations, a community Trust was formed to buy out the previous owner. Following the buy out, a residents' association and the Trust board members would have decision-making powers. Their vision was to establish community control over island planning, infrastructure, and development—effectively to guide the future of Eigg (Braid 1996; McIntosh 2003).

Eigg was not the first example in the region of collective organizing to localize governance. In Assynt, local crofters who were farming the land set an important precedent by forming a Trust in 1992. The following year, they took a privately owned estate into community ownership by mounting an "open market bid" with outside financial support—the same model that was adapted by Eigg in 1997, and subsequently Knoydart in 1999 and Gigha in 2002 (Hunter et al. 2013). Community buy-outs emerged as a Scottish land reform movement, but one that preceded institutional change—Scotland's official Land Reform Act wasn't ratified until 2003 (Kenrick 2011). It is a movement that has been pushing back against drastic inequalities in land ownership. For instance, in 2009, just 0.025% of Scotland's population owned 67% of privately held rural land (Warren 2009). Morgan's ethnographic analysis of the Eigg buy-out provides a range of insights into the process. Two aspects underscored are the influence of the Assynt success and Eigg's innovative strategy of building a partnership to purchase and manage the island, where islanders joined with the Scottish Wildlife Trust and the regional Highland Council (Morgan 1999). Cases like Eigg illustrate how localized action has initiated political changes both within and beyond local legal structures.

Today, islanders participate in the partnership via the Eigg Residents' Association (ERA). Four ERA directors, elected by the community, meet every three weeks with responsibility for day-to-day management. In addition, there are three subsidiary companies of the Isle of Eigg Heritage Trust (Eigg Trading Limited; Eigg Construction Limited; Eigg Electric Limited) each with a board of directors appointed by community members (IEHT n.d.). The emphasis on management here is critical: collectively designing and governing island infrastructure has been the key to Eigg completing a micro-grid electrification project.

As a small island (five miles by three) with a population of about 100 (and growing since the buy-out), planners found that the costs involved in potentially linking

Eigg to the UK mainland electric grid were prohibitive. For many years, electricity on Eigg came from individually owned diesel-fuel generators dotted across the landscape. Following the buy-out, plans for an alternative system were developed between islanders, renewable energy specialists, and outside technicians with support from public agencies and charitable organizations. In 2008, following extensive community campaigning and fundraising, construction was completed on an island-wide electricity micro-grid based on renewable sources. The old household generators were replaced as the primary source of electricity and, as one resident put it, "we heard silence again." Electricity now came from three hydroelectric generators (totaling up to 119kW), four 6kW wind turbines, and a 30kW solar array—with two 80kW diesel generators remaining in place in emergencies, or to meet demand peaks. Island estimates put the supply from renewables at about 95%. Residents have also found this new energy supply more reliable and sustained, and less dependent on the delivery and fluctuating prices of barrels of diesel sourced from the mainland. This transition not only represents a vital shift in how energy needs are met on Eigg, it has also strengthened the island's reputation as a leader in local and national environmental action.

The transitioning away from diesel generators to the micro-grid has not created isolation, however. Electricity may now be island-based, and more appropriate to the needs of residents, but its generation still requires maintenance, components, and expertise sourced from different parts of the UK and the world, as well as the small amounts of backup diesel. Daily life is also largely dependent on medical, food, and other provisions ferried in from off-island locations. These are some of many examples where communities remain deeply linked with distant places and projects. Entanglements with extraction dependencies are still present. By creating the micro-grid, relations of dependence on fossil fuels were lessened and rerouted, but not entirely severed.

Rearranged dependencies can also come as a result of collective reassessments of use and need. For example, the electrification project also addressed patterns of consumption. Generator maintenance on older properties had revealed disproportionate levels of electricity use across households of a similar size, due mainly to aging and inefficient appliances—a problem planners felt the new grid could solve by regulating or "sharing" available supply, effectively limiting the number of appliances that can be used at any one time. Residents and project designers calculated a 5kW-per-household limit (a higher limit is set for commercial properties). Building the micro-grid from scratch made it possible to install "owl meters," electricity monitors that track usage and govern the power limit at each property. The 5kW limit also made it cheaper to lay cabling for the micro-grid itself. Aluminium wire could be used in place of more expensive copper. This measure saved on construction costs and has also enabled residents to manage and reflect upon their personal dependencies on electricity consumption. Meeting energy needs thus invited critical reassessment of the island's energy use.

Eigg's story of reassigning property ownership through land reform has had consequences beyond those quantified in economic terms, and these changes continue to enable the pursuit of an alternative energy future. Deeper personal investment of time, money, and effort in these projects has increased motivation and support for future actions as those involved gained awareness of their relationships with others. These dynamics are witnessed elsewhere in the world. If land reform "empowers people to settle more deeply into their geographical place," and enables people "to make decisions about the habitation, resource use and amenity enrichment of their own place," as McIntosh (2015, 3) suggests, it does so by creating communities that are democratically accountable to their own residents. Changes to how people on Eigg accessed electricity were intricately bound to projects and possibilities enabled by the community buy-out.

Rather than offering a replicable model for change, the recent history of Eigg reflects an understanding of resilience and pathways to change that is geographically and socioculturally specific. For many communities, organizing to create alternative futures requires developing localized capacities to withstand and respond to unwanted change often driven by external influences and events. Rennie and Billing (2015, 35) note that this resilience is found by "utilizing the human and natural resources of [an] area in a manner that sensitively exploits the ability of these resources to adapt to and benefit from change." This understanding of resilience creates a basis for alternative futures that are locally relevant, responsive, and appropriate.

That being said, implementing such "strategic dislocations," and reducing dependencies on the fossil fuel economy, were actions that were enabled by three key factors, each reinforcing one another: (i) collective decision-making, (ii) direct control of land and other resources, and (iii) forms of social organizing developed in dialogue with similar communities elsewhere. These are dynamics that have played a critical role amidst other collective efforts working toward alternative futures; among them, the struggles of indigenous communities such as San Isidro in the Ecuadorian Andes.

## San Isidro, Water and Labor Migration

Older residents in San Isidro, those who remembered life there before 1964, would talk about the watershed moment when "yerak" ("IERAC") arrived in their communities, after which everything changed. Families acquired title-deeds to the small plots of land they had been living and farming on, ushering in a new era of freedom and local decision-making that had been suppressed for generations. IERAC was the Ecuadorian Institute of Agrarian Reform and Colonization, a federal agency responsible for implementing land reform. Previously, residents were considered "bound laborers" under the Spanish colonial regime. The land was claimed by Las Madres Agustinas (a sect of Catholic nuns) and a tenant farmer governed life in San Isidro. Similar structures of land dispossession were in place across highland Ecuador until state measures changed these relationships in the 1960s. This marked a pivotal moment in the growth of Ecuador's Indigenous Movement, a movement that San Isidro has been an active part of for decades. In 2009, the community formally registered as a legally recognized "*comunidad*" and that same year secured government funding to build an irrigation water pipeline. This project radically improved conditions for small-scale agriculture in the community since previously irrigation water was administered and rationed by the estate owner. Irrigation continues to both support and demand cooperation among the community's approximately 450 residents.

Despite gains in local land ownership following land reform, San Isidro remained heavily dependent on income from migrant labor. Based on field research in 2010–2011, virtually every household in the community was found to have at least one resident who regularly left San Isidro for work. Oil companies operating deep in the Amazon jungle employed almost two-thirds of these migrant workers. The journey would take a whole day, sometimes longer: a couple of bus rides to get to Quito, from where the oil companies would usually arrange flights to take employees to the Amazonian city of Coca. Depending on the location of the rig, workers would often then be helicoptered on site. Depending on education and experience, jobs ranged from technical and maintenance positions directly involved in extraction operations, to supporting roles such as in providing transportation and catering services. Nearly all work was scheduled in standardized "14–7" shifts: a cycle of two weeks at work followed by one week off. Most San Isidro oil workers and their families arranged their lives around these recurrent cycles.

Even though extraction industry jobs were becoming increasingly scarce, this work generated important income and time at home for migrant laborers. These resources made significant contributions to community projects to reduce local dependence on widespread labor migration. At the heart of these efforts were community-wide investments in an irrigation pipeline project. Prior to the pipeline, San Isidro's agricultural economy was limited by minimal access to water and unreliable patterns of seasonal rainfall. With the construction of the pipeline, which was maintained collectively by the community, a sustained flow of 25 liters per second was shared among nearly 90 participating households (almost all of San Isidro). Access to regular water improved agriculture production in San Isidro, increasing earned incomes from farming for most families and reducing dependence on food purchased at regional markets. Irrigation also facilitated the formation of a community food cooperative, promoting a robust exchange economy within San Isidro itself.

Additional income from agriculture was not sufficient to replace the need for income earned through labor migration and the oil industry. However, the number of initiatives aimed at consolidating the potential for local growth and resilience were boosted by the organizational systems put in place to coordinate the pipeline project. For instance, plans emerged to set aside an area of land for a community garden large enough to employ two to three young residents. This and other projects were designed to create viable pathways for generations of children and grandchildren to continue living in San Isidro. Young adults in San Isidro who were starting families of their own were faced with an unprecedented mix of "promise and poverty" (Comaroff and Comaroff 2000). This generation was familiar with regular migratory work in the oil industry, but also with the move toward strengthening community-based resources and systems of cooperation.

Freddy Chancusi, formerly employed by the oil industry, told me that work was so scarce in local communities that young men had only three options when looking for jobs: join the police, join the military, or join the oil industry. Many San Isidro migrant workers recognized that the concentration of employment within the oil industry was unsustainable. Such labor uncertainty undermines the capacity for developing long-term stability in a region, and has characterized the experiences of marginalized populations elsewhere in the world wrapped up in an economy where wage-labor is said to make "no promise for the future and expects none in return" (Crawford 2008, 16). The pipeline project sought to reverse this course—to increase the promise of both near- and long-term futures in San Isidro.

For some San Isidro residents, there were also ethical motivations for extricating themselves from work in the oil industry. A number of the migrant workers I spent time with were acutely aware of how the industry contributed to the destruction and dispossession of the lands and lives of indigenous peoples throughout the Amazon region. They described the tensions they felt between the need to earn income and support their families, and their concern for the well-being of people affected by the oil industry in those regions.

In other instances, ethical dilemmas about working for the oil industry created tensions within the community. For example, Milton Guamán—who was elected president of San Isidro at the age of 26, and whose father and elder brother both worked for oil companies—faced opposition when he publicly criticized the oil companies for endangering the well-being of both Amazonian peoples and the world at large. Others, however, agreed with Milton's belief that the extraction and exploitation of subsurface minerals was too destructive to be justifiable, or puts the health of too many people at risk.

In communal efforts to reroute dependencies, San Isidro had both learned from and inspired the work of communities across the region. Just as Eigg had drawn on previous models for community-based land reform in Scotland and had informed subsequent efforts in other places, San Isidro also participated in an extensive politically engaged network through Ecuador's national Indigenous Movement, adopting a model of collective organizing found across the Ecuadorian highlands. San Isidro's residents elected a community council every two years and strategic decisions were approved by popular vote. In alliance with other community members within regional branches of the Indigenous Movement, San Isidro successfully campaigned against local plantations using their water, against land grabs, and for more stringent regional legislation governing the use of agrochemicals on large-scale farms. These alliances and actions highlight how revising relations with the fossil fuel industry was only one component of a broader range of engagements to envision alternative futures. Land reform had initiated certain opportunities, but sustaining these gains required confronting ongoing threats to the social and ecological relations at the root of those initiatives.

## Chains of Extraction

As on Eigg, initiatives such as the pipeline project undertaken in San Isidro cast new light on how collaborative action can create social and physical relations that move away from the hydrocarbon economy—redirecting the ties of dependence that run between places, practices, and natural resources. In San Isidro, the "rerouting" was less direct than replacing fossil fuels with renewables as the source for electricity generation. The rerouting does, however, share a similar long-term perspective: addressing the stability of life as it can be lived in that particular place, and reducing the extent to which day-to-day needs are met through the fossil fuel industries and their products. Another thematic link between the two cases concerns their different "locations" in relation to the fossil fuel industry as workers, consumers, and citizens. Entangled dependencies on fossil fuels in places such as Eigg and San Isidro take many forms, involving links to trans-national corporations and national interests, but also stemming from how particular needs are met and how resources are used. This reaches beyond the tools put in place to power the lights. Dependencies extend to questions around work, income, and planning for the future, and are mediated by different positions within chains of production.

Fossil fuel industry language favors the idea of production—producing fields, productive plays, productivity wells—but the term needs to be used with caution. The notion that extraction is a process with effects limited to the location and time of removing subsurface materials is misleading. It implies an impossible containment of extraction and its consequences, obscuring the many inputs that extraction depends on, among them labor. Production thus overlooks the caused ecological damage and the subsequent activities of moving, modifying, and burning minerals within the fuel cycle, a chain of processes that also includes consumption and disposal (Allen et al. 2011; Fischer-Kowalski 2000; Willow and Wylie 2014).

Perhaps a better concept is "chain of extraction," which takes many different forms according to mineral type, mining location and conditions, and the types of end products that are manufactured and consumed. In this sense, our two case communities may be said to occupy different ends of the chain of extraction that influence life in their locales: San Isidro, where residents are physically involved in the labor of extraction; and Eigg, where daily life—through the provision of electricity—had previously been highly dependent on the availability of diesel fuel. Workers and consumers at either end of chains of extraction also face an uneven distribution of their social, economic, and environmental costs. People living near sites of extraction clearly face the worst impacts from pollution, ill health, and dispossession but, by looking at these two cases together, we can identify key strategies and establish shared infrastructures of support to counteract these inequalities and reroute dependencies, despite the persistent hydrocarbon economy.

## Conclusion

Alternative ways of life and forms of social organizing aimed at improving the environment are all too often suppressed by those in positions of power who deem such alternatives to be running counter to national interests or against established ideas of progress (Blaser 2004). Thus, the significance of struggles in places like Eigg and San Isidro is not limited to their abilities to meet local community needs and change historical relations of dependence. They also embody vital resistance to the otherwise unilateral flows of a global hydrocarbon economy. There are, however, questions about the scale and broader impact of such localized struggles. Community initiatives in places like Eigg and San Isidro raise issues about the nature of power, responsibility and social change (Kenrick 2013). What are the politics of place-based struggle, as distinct from activism that focuses on structural change? Is action that reduces or reroutes dependency on the fossil fuel industry doing enough, if anything at all, to address the root causes of global inequality, environmental collapse, and climate change? Is it possible to change the world without taking power?

Even without directly addressing these broader questions, we can read the lived examples of Eigg and San Isidro presented here as reflecting how bottom-up processes of organization and design might address vulnerabilities experienced within current social and economic structures, and work to counteract them by meeting community needs through locally attuned means. They are actions that emphasize how diverse resources—relationships, perspectives, purposes, and values—can be utilized and reconfigured in order to avoid some of the social, economic, and environmental costs of extraction, to build strategies to withstand them, and to respond to different forms of uninvited change. The futures that such localized projects initiate are alternative in that they contrast the directions of extractivist economies.

And yet no singular blueprint or solution exists here. Instead, Eigg and San Isidro reflect how basing future-oriented action in the resources and realities immediately at hand can inform strategies for redesigning how the products and practices of fossil fuel extraction are avoided or integrated into everyday life. By rerouting everyday dependencies and increasing their control over land and political processes, these communities have achieved greater resilience and pursued projects that work against the apparent inevitability of the hydrocarbon economy.

## References

Allen, Lucy, Michael J. Cohen, David Abelson, and Bart Miller. 2011. Fossil fuels and water quality. In *The world's water, volume 7*, edited by Peter H. Gleick, Lucy Allen, Juliet Christian-Smith, Michael J. Cohen, Heather Cooley, Matthew Heberger, Jason Morrison, Meena Palaniappan, and Paul Schulte, 73–96. Washington, DC: Island Press.

Bebbington, Anthony. 1993. Sustainable livelihood development in the Andes: Local institutions and regional resource use in Ecuador. *Development Policy Review* 11, 1:5–30.

Blaser, Mario. 2004. Life projects: Indigenous peoples' agency and development. In *In the way of development: Indigenous peoples, life projects and globalization*, edited by Mario Blaser, Harvey A. Feit, and Glenn McRae, 26–44. London: Zed Books.

Boykoff, Maxwell T., Adam Bumpus, Diana Liverman, and Samual Randalls. 2009. Theorizing the carbon economy. *Environment and Planning A* 41, 10:2299–2304.

Braid, Mary. 1996. Between a rock and a hard place. *The Independent*, February 26. www. independent.co.uk/news/between-a-rock-and-a-hard-place-5626845.html (accessed March 23, 2016).

Chatterton, Paul, and Alice Cutler. 2008. *The rocky road to a real transition: The transition towns movement and what it means for social change*. Leeds: Trapese Collective.

Comaroff, Jean, and John L. Comaroff. 2000. Millennial capitalism: First thoughts on a second coming. *Public Culture* 12, 2:291–343.

Crawford, David. 2008. *Moroccan households in the world economy: Labor and inequality in a Berber village*. Baton Rouge: Louisiana State University Press.

Dobson, Andrew. 2003. *Citizenship and the environment*. Oxford: Oxford University Press.

Edelman, Marc, and Angelique Haugerud. 2005. Introduction. In *The Anthropology of Development and Globalization*, edited by Marc Edelman and Angelique Haugerud, 77–86. Oxford: Blackwell Publishing.

Fischer-Kowalski, Marina. 2000. Society's metabolism: On the childhood and adolescence of a rising conceptual star. In *The International Handbook of Environmental Sociology*, edited by Michael R. Redclift, and Graham Woodgate, 119–137. Cheltenham, UK: Edward Elgar.

Gledhill, John. 2000. *Power and its disguises: Anthropological perspectives on politics*. 2nd edn. London: Pluto Press.

Gordon, Deborah. 2012. Understanding unconventional oil. *The Carnegie papers: Energy and climate*. Washington, DC: Carnegie Endowment for International Peace.

Graeber, David. 2011. *Revolutions in reverse: Essays on politics, violence, art, and imagination*. New York: Minor Compositions.

Hunter, James, Peter Peacock, Andy Wightman, and Michael Foxley. 2013. *432:50—Towards a comprehensive land reform agenda for Scotland*. London: Parliament of the United Kingdom, Scottish Affairs Committee.

Isle of Eigg Heritage Trust (IEHT) n.d. *The structure of the Isle of Eigg Heritage Trust: subsidiary companies*. www.isleofeigg.net/eigg_heritage_trust.html (accessed March 23, 2016).

Jasanoff, Sheila, and Sang-Hyun Kim. 2013. Sociotechnical imaginaries and national energy policies. *Science as Culture* 22, 2:189–196.

Kenrick, Justin. 2011. Scottish land reform and indigenous peoples' rights: Self-determination and historical reversibility. *Social Anthropology* 19, 2:189–203.

Kenrick, Justin. 2013. Emerging from the shadow of climate change denial. *ACME: An International E-Journal for Critical Geographies* 12, 1:102–130.

Leys, C. 2005. The rise and fall of development theory. In *The Anthropology of Development and Globalization*, edited by Marc Edelman and Angelique Haugerud, 109–125. Oxford: Blackwell Publishing.

Mason, Kelvin, and Mark Whitehead. 2011. Transition urbanism and the contested politics of ethical place making. *Antipode* 44, 2:493–516.

McIntosh, Alastair. 2003. The precious burden: 4 stages of land reform—Scotland. *The Hebridean*, October 2. www.alastairmcintosh.com/articles/2003-hebridean3&4-4stages. htm (accessed March 23, 2016).

McIntosh, Alastair. 2015. *Consultation response to the future of land reform in Scotland*. Govan, Scotland: Centre for Human Ecology. www.alastairmcintosh.com/articles/2015-McIntosh-Land-Reform-Consultation.pdf (accessed March 23, 2016).

Morgan, Daniel Rhys. 1999. *The Isle of Eigg: Land reform, people, and power*. PhD Thesis, University of Edinburgh.

Rennie, Frank, and Suzannah-Lynn Billing. 2015. Changing community perceptions of sustainable rural development in Scotland. *Journal of Rural and Community Development* 10, 2:35–46.

Short, Damien, Jessica Elliot, Kadin Norder, Edward Lloyd-Davies, and Joanna Morley. 2015. Extreme energy, "fracking" and human rights: A new field for human rights impact assessments? *The International Journal of Human Rights* 19, 6:697–736.

Warren, Charles R. 2009. *Managing Scotland's environment*. Edinburgh: Edinburgh University Press.

Willow, Anna, and Sara Wylie. 2014. Politics, ecology, and the new anthropology of energy: Exploring the emerging frontiers of hydraulic fracking. *Journal of Political Ecology* 21, 12:222–236.

# 14

# TOWARD TRANSITION?

## Challenging Extractivism and the Politics of the Inevitable on the Navajo Nation

*Dana E. Powell*

This chapter explores how longstanding extractive legacies and discrepancies of energy access in the Diné (Navajo) Nation are being challenged through transition efforts in the early twenty-first century. Among Diné people, an emerging critical politics exposes the longstanding environmental and social exposures shouldered by Diné people dwelling on the Navajo reservation. This politics further challenges the assumed inevitability of large-scale extraction, "extractivism," as the necessary, collateral damage of the modern world. However, what transition means in theory and social practice remains unsettled in Navajo energy politics. Convergences and clashes among different modalities of energy activism since the 1960s have situated these extractive legacies within the ongoing conditions of colonialism, where colonialism is not a single, historical event, but rather an unfolding process and structure (Wolfe 2006). Yet perhaps transition too, like colonialism, is not a rupture or event, but a process. This chapter explores the politics and implications for the social practice of such a possibility.

Political visions compete and diverge regarding how the future ought to be differently (infra)structured on the Navajo Nation to reduce environmental and social harm and, at the same time, generate robust tribal sovereignty. Recent activism regarding extraction on the Navajo Nation makes political ecological claims in the language of transition, with some nongovernmental groups like the Just Transition Coalition (among many others) pushing the Nation to transition away from coal, due to its political risks and social-ecological damages, while other entities like the Navajo Transitional Energy Corporation (NTEC) advocate to maintain coal dependency, while transitioning to include a diversified portfolio of energy resources and toward Navajo ownership (following nearly a century of external ownership) of Navajo coal production. The tension inherent in these contradictory deployments of transition raises the problem of inevitability: that which is considered utterly unavoidable and so certain to happen as to become predictable in nature. Extraction has become just that in Navajo energy and economic development. Although transition discourse tends to imply a break or rupture in history enacted through a move beyond extraction, the future pathway remains unresolved. This central question regarding competing energy futures is, of course, not only a question about the kinds of infrastructural worlds Diné people strive to build in a strictly technical sense, but is also a question about how Diné people, and others, are actively, critically rethinking their socio-natural worlds and tribal policies to overcome decades of extraction-driven colonialism.

## Legacies of Extraction

Only in the last few years has the Navajo Nation in the American Southwest begun to articulate and enact an independent and strategic tribal energy policy, despite nearly a century of intensive natural resource extraction on Diné lands. For one hundred years, the Nation has been in a reactionary position, responding to non-Native initiatives to extract and develop Navajo energy mineral reserves. Extractive ambitions quite literally formed the modern political body known as the Navajo Nation: Standard Oil Company began prospecting for oil in the US Southwest in the early twentieth century, resulting in the federal government reorganizing customary forms of Diné governance into a recognizable, "legible" political leadership, assembled specifically to broker the extraction of Navajo energy resources, under new gendered norms of leadership (Curley 2014a; Denetdale 2006). This neocolonial formation is now part of the Navajo Nation's official political origin narrative: "In 1923, a tribal government was established to help meet the increasing desires of American oil companies to lease Navajoland for exploration," states the Nation's website (Navajo Nation n.d.). By all accounts, the story of the formation of the Navajo Nation as such evokes a legacy of enabling extraction.

Subsequent decades followed this energy mineral-dependent pathway, establishing a development model of exporting extractive resources to fuel regional economics and fortify national security. The initial oil rush of the 1920s and 30s gave way to intensive uranium mining from the Grants Uranium Belt, underlying much of the Navajo Nation and neighboring Pueblo Nations (Figure 14.1), supplying the United States' nuclear weapons arsenal during the Cold War (Johnston 2007; Masco 1999). The radioactive contamination of open-pit uranium mines and residual un-reclaimed tailings piles haunts the Nation and is the subject of many other important studies (Benally, Brugge, and Yazzie-Lewis 2006; Heisinger 2010; Johnston 2007). The uranium era was followed by a turn to mining and processing Navajo coal in the 1960s to fuel the emerging "Sunbelt" urban centers of the Southwest (Needham 2014; Redhouse n.d.).

While the new coal-fired power plants fueled modernity, so to speak, in cities like Phoenix, many Navajo homesteads on the largely rural reservation remained without power throughout the late twentieth century. Many homes continue to be un-electrified and lacking in infrastructure today: 32% of Navajo households

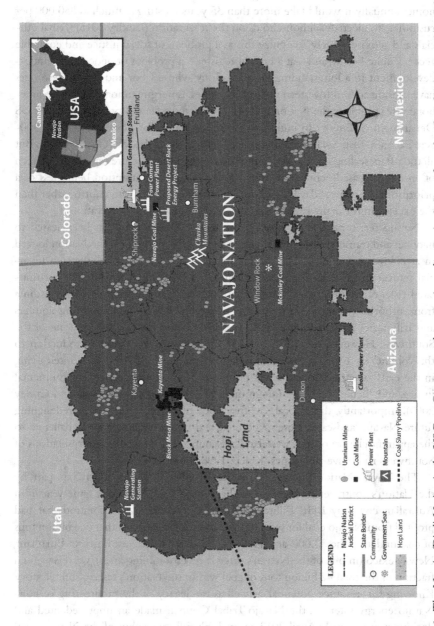

**FIGURE 14.1** The Navajo (Diné) Nation in the US Four Corners area has experienced extensive impacts from decades of uranium and fossil fuel extraction. Some tribal citizens are calling for an alternative energy future based on renewable power and environmental justice. Map by Donna Gayer, Artasaverb.

lack any source of electricity, 31% lack indoor plumbing, 38% lack water services, 86% lack natural gas, and 60% lack telephone lines, with the Navajo Tribal Utility Authority estimating that, following the current rate of electrical installment at 700 homes annually, it would take more than 35 years (costing as much as $50,000 per customer) to electrify all households on the reservation (Landry 2015). Tribal officials and activists widely recognize this as a problem of social justice and equitable access, public health, and—at a critical register—a problem of neocolonial under-development in a longstanding energy colony whose labor and natural resources have subsidized Southwestern urban economies. Emerging initiatives seek to ame-liorate this problem: the Nation in 2015 completed a feasibility study with the US Department of Energy to build its first utility-scale solar power project, 22,000-acre Paragon-Bisti Solar Ranch in northwestern New Mexico (OIEPP 2015). But all too often, scaling up or diversifying the energy infrastructure repeats the pattern of an export-based economy, with local access and consumption being less of a priority. In short, everyday life without basic infrastructure is the norm rather than the exception for many residents of the 24,000 square mile reservation.

Navajo territory, held in trust by the federal government, has been leased to national and transnational energy corporations with royalties for the Nation locked in at below-market rates. The shining promise of "development" through finan-cial returns from extractive industry remains a false summit, while the accumu-lated risks of environmental contamination became increasingly evident. Asthma from airborne pollution, cancer from residual radiation, and vanishing aquifers and tributaries reshaped Diné landscapes and bodies into a sacrifice zone of the Southwest. However, extrACTIVISM (a distinction made in the introduction to this volume) has been on the rise among Diné citizens since the 1960s, intensifying in the early twenty-first century as questions of good governance, environmental justice, and "being" Diné are foregrounded in energy politics (Powell and Curley 2009). Importantly, the critical, creative labor of citizens engaged in redesigning future Navajo landscapes poses a pointed and under-acknowledged challenge to the apparent closure of the "wasteland" discourse that dominates interpretations of Southwestern Native landscapes (Kuletz 1998; Voyles 2015).

The Navajo Nation Energy Policy established in 2013 was spurred, in part, by the Nation's controversial purchase of the Navajo Coal Mine that same year from Australian company BHP Billiton, a multinational energy corporation that had profited from Navajo coal for several decades. Estimates suggest that one billion tons of coal underlies the 33,000-acre area of the Navajo Mine, just north of Burnham, New Mexico (in one of the Nation's three large coal mining areas), yet this is just a fraction of the total 42 billion tons of coal within the Nation's reservation territory. Knowing this resource potential, as well as the legacy of the profiteering of non-Navajo energy interests, the Navajo Tribal Council made an unprecedented and decisive move in early April 2013 to establish full ownership of the Navajo Coal Mine by forming NTEC. This was a watershed moment in Navajo energy politics: since 1957, the Navajo Coal Mine had been under lease to BHP Billiton to provide the sole source of coal for the Four Corners Power Plant in Fruitland, New Mexico, on land inexpensively leased from the Navajo Nation.

Thus after nearly 60 years of external ownership, the Navajo Nation now owns this highly productive coalmine and is poised to expand its operations. But a contradiction emerges. NTEC's explicit mandate is "to manage, protect, and put these resources into production" (Woods 2014). A mission to put coal "into production" seems at odds with the transformative politics implied in the term "transition" in NTEC's name. There is friction, too, among these coexisting temporalities of Navajo energy politics: past legacies of extraction, present impetus by tribal leadership to increase mining, and active grassroots citizens groups arguing for investments in solar and wind technology, all contribute to rampant ambiguities and shifting meanings of transition. These shifting meanings and histories are further complicated by a global discourse of transition, widely interpreted as a future-oriented, moral project aimed at moving *beyond* a dangerous present (Hopkins 2008). With the Navajo Nation, the "allegorical package" (Tsing 2005) known as transition cannot be taken for granted: it resonates with global environmentalism yet it departs from the script, taking on situated and contested meanings due to the particular legacies of extraction haunting the Nation.

## The Colonial Critique of Energy Development: The Emergence of Navajo ExtrACTIVISM

The footprint of the burgeoning energy industry became increasingly visible on Navajo territory in the latter half of the twentieth century, with coal mine expansions, oil well proliferation, new above- and below-ground transport infrastructure, more substations and, most recently, the emergence of shale gas fracturing. As early as the 1960s, tribal citizens organized to challenge this trend. Historian Andrew Needham's (2014) analysis of this period of articulation between energy development and Navajo nationalism deeply informs my understanding of the evolution of Navajo collective action around energy development infrastructure, or extrACTIVISM. Activists situated the extraction-based, export-driven model as a distinctive practice of colonialism, an ongoing structure of violence that continues to affect Native nation-building and self-determination in the twenty-first century. As Needham notes, midcentury decolonization movements in the global Third World along with the national American Indian Movement (AIM) heavily influenced activists' perspectives. Targeting their struggle against major multinational energy corporations, such as Peabody Coal (owner of the mines at Black Mesa, in the Western region of the reservation), these activists began interviewing tribal members, becoming increasingly militant, and mounting a critique against coal development as economic "progress." Their work helped launch networks of community-based alliances that would emerge as robust, globally connected environmental justice movements in the late 1980s and early 1990s.

Several years later, when AIM members conducted an armed occupation of Black Mesa Mine No. 1 and then, six months later, when they staged an armed occupation of a semiconductor plant in Shiprock, New Mexico, the infrastructures of energy development became visible as "political machines" (Needham 2014). As such, the rising tide of Diné nationalism and the broader pan-Indian movement through which it was articulated were situated within specific debates over extractive industries and were increasingly mobilized. Yet, youth activists' critique of the tribal government's embrace of extractive industries cut both ways: it set the stage for a change of power in tribal leadership, making way for Peter MacDonald to become Tribal Chairman in 1971 on a platform of "anti-colonial populism" and self-determination defined as control over natural resources. However, it also led to conflict between these youth activists and MacDonald's new administration. MacDonald expanded energy development on the reservation, launching new networks such as the inter-tribal Council of Energy Resource Tribes (CERT). This contrasted with the position of activists who wanted natural resource development halted altogether.

For example, a proposal for coal gasification technology in the Diné community of Burnham became a defining event in the rupture of meaning between the colonial critique of Diné youth activists and the colonial critique of MacDonald's tribal administration, perhaps foreshadowing the rupture in meanings of "transition" that struggle for dominance in contemporary Navajo energy politics. Proposed in 1972, El Paso Natural Gas and WESCO approached the Nation about leasing land for coal gasification plants, which would convert coal into a crude form of methane and then into synthetic natural gas to meet a growing need in Southwestern cities. Forty miles south of the border town of Farmington, New Mexico, the Burnham Chapter (one of 110 local governance bodies on the Navajo Nation) had no running water or electricity apart from two generators. Yet Burnham did have community members interested in secure employment in a landscape that offered few formal economic opportunities. Capitalizing on this desire, WESCO and El Paso agreed to a "Navajo hiring preference" policy, claiming that, over time, the plants' employees would be majority Diné.

During the five years of debate over coal gasification, two narratives of Navajo "tradition" were constructed against one another: tribal government energy activists pushed for coal gasification with a narrative of tradition based on the Navajo method of thinking, planning, and strategizing for change; at the same time, youth activists and Burnham residents resisted energy technologies, deploying a narrative of Navajo tradition grounded in the historical connection between people and the landscape, arguing that to disrupt this connection was to fundamentally disrupt Navajo culture. As Denetdale and other Diné scholars have noted, the deployment of "tradition" carries a politics of its own, deeply entangled with Western frameworks of time, space, epistemology, and subjectivity (Denetdale 2006; Lee 2014). Another key point in the debate centered on youth activists' critique of the relationship between the Nation and energy companies. Rather than the joint venture development model promoted by MacDonald, the eventual plan would lease land in exchange for paying royalties to the Navajo Nation. Despite MacDonald's characterization of the coal gasification plants as a "necessary evil" for the advancement and development of the Nation, and despite the companies' promises of employment, new infrastructure for the community, and mitigations to minimize environmental impacts, residents of Burnham voted three times to reject the plants. In fact, the Burnham Chapter went so far as to issue a letter to MacDonald, demanding that he recall the proposal for coal gasification and to cease any future negotiations with the company.

This very brief retrospective of Navajo activism around energy infrastructure acquires meaning and momentum when understood as the predecessor to the Diné environmental justice movement in the late 1980s and energy justice in the early 2000s. I turn to this more recent history, below, to consider extrACTIVISM on the Navajo Nation through diverging interpretations of "transition."

## Risk and Action at the Grassroots

The Burnham controversy is crucial background for understanding more recent controversies surrounding the Desert Rock Energy Project, a 1500-megawatt coal-fired power plant proposed for the same Burnham area, nearly forty years later. John Redhouse, a prominent youth activist during the 1960s–70s coal wars, emerged as one of the leading critical intellectuals writing against Desert Rock. In an unpublished report, titled "Desert Rock: 1953–2003," Redhouse draws out the complex history of energy proposals and tribal members' critical responses to the project, noting the generational ramifications in the Burnham struggle (Redhouse n.d.). He describes how the parents of area resident Lucy Willie—now an elder herself—were at the forefront of recent struggles against Desert Rock. In particular, Redhouse notes their filing a complaint with the Federal Power Commission to stop proposed coal gasification plants. The work of these elders (Willie's parents and others) prefigured the contemporary energy activism that their children would take up decades later.

Contemporary critics reject coal development while also promoting alternative forms of energy production, strategically deploying the discourse of "transition" to usher in what appears to be a changing vision for integrating energy development into narratives of Navajo sovereignty. Technology is no longer monolithically "colonial," as once imagined, though it has long been a modality of politics in Diné political ecology (Powell 2015). Nevertheless, the hamlet of Burnham remained in the minds of Desert Rock developers as an ideal location for coal power due to the imagined absence of human life and the visible abundance of easily accessed sub-bituminous coal, coupled with a proposed expansion of the nearby Navajo Coal Mine and extension of electrical transmission lines to move the power to urban centers. The 1972 debate over coal gasification barely shimmered beneath the surface of public debates over Desert Rock in the summer of 2007 and was rarely present in the personal accounts of local residents, regional activists, and tribal leaders. This apparent absence of memory, however, is supplanted by the recollection of more recent histories of energy activism among current grassroots leaders.

The story of the emergence of one energy activism group, in particular, helps to illustrate these points. In the late 1980s, on the opposite side of the reservation from Burnham, residents of Dilkon, Arizona, found out about a plan concocted by Navajo Chairman MacDonald and Colorado-based Waste-Tech Corporation, which would bring tons of medical and toxic waste from all over the United States to a treatment facility in their community. The $40 million offer sounded appealing to some residents, and certainly to many tribal leaders spearheading the project. But by 1987, with the surge of a new kind of environmental movement redefining "nature" through a critical analysis of race, gender, and place (Bullard 2000; Checker 2005; Di Chiro 1996) the disproportionate siting of hazardous wastes in low-income neighborhoods and communities of color was under attack by scholars and activists as a new formation of structural violence.

Rejecting the idea that this euphemistic "regional landfill" would benefit the Dilkon community, area residents resisted the proposal. As one longtime activist (and tribal employee) recalled, "the matriarchs in Dilkon came forward, and talked about life in its entirety," (Tulley 2008). They rejected the proposed treatment facility by moving the discussion away from a strict discussion of tribal revenue and toward a conversation about livelihoods, the maintenance of relationships, and long-range planning for the future. These were values tied to governing ethical principles set forth in Navajo Fundamental Law, which would continue to shape this Diné environmental movement as it grew. This group of Dilkon women, authoritative as decision-makers regarding land customarily under their control in Diné matrilineal descent also allied with other residents as Diné "Citizens Against Ruining our Environment" (CARE). They worked locally to convince voting members of the Dilkon Chapter to reject Waste-Tech's proposal, which they achieved two years later, in 1989.[1] Stopping the toxic waste dump planned for their community garnered the attention of indigenous activists from other nations, catalyzing the first of many trans-national Protecting Mother Earth gatherings in 1990. The initial gathering, held in Dilkon, also launched the formation of an international grassroots group called the Indigenous Environmental Network, which has emerged in recent decades as a leading voice against intensive extraction in Native territories, from the Alberta tar sands to biocolonialism in Latin America. The rural town of Dilkon thus became a crucial trans-local site in the emergence of a new global environmentalism.

Local leaders of Diné CARE expanded work beyond the lava butte landscape of Dilkon, responding to requests from other Diné communities working on similar issues related to environmental contamination and energy extraction. They formed alliances with tribal members active in the eastern part of the Nation who were working to protect the forests of the Chuska Mountains—550 square miles of dense, high alpine forest along the northeastern Arizona and northwestern New Mexico borders. Much of the organization's work in the 1990s focused on the commercial logging practices of the Nation's own Navajo Forest Products Industries, calling for a stop to the harvesting of timber for processing and export to regional markets (Sherry 2002). Throughout these efforts CARE pushed for a consideration of extraction's impacts to "life in its entirety," challenging the politics of inevitability informing tribal policies that promoted Waste-Tech in the west, deforestation in the northeast, uranium mining across the reservation, as well as alcoholism and enduring racism along the Nation's border towns.

Following a sharp increase in their visibility as a political force on the Navajo Nation—largely due to their 1994 success in passing a tribal moratorium on logging in the Chuskas—Diné CARE expanded its network and became involved in a number of projects to halt extractivism. Approached by survivors of uranium exposure and other Navajo community members working on the radioactive legacies of Cold War uranium mining, Diné CARE helped build momentum for a reservation-wide grassroots movement to reform the 1990 Radiation Exposure Compensation Act (RECA), which they felt discriminated against Navajo miners and their families through bureaucratic mandates that were a mismatch with Diné cultural practices (such as requiring marriage licenses which many Diné do not obtain and decades-old pay stubs to prove employment). With the internet now making it possible to expand their work beyond the previous door-to-door methods of community organizing, Diné CARE organizers connected with radiation exposure movements across the United States and around the world, including activists in the Marshall Islands. In 2000, Diné CARE took a leading role in the passage of a bill reforming RECA (originally passed in 1990 and amended in 2000 and 2002). This activism reached (at least a temporary) victory, with the Diné Natural Resources Protection Act of 2005, a new tribal law placing a moratorium on any new uranium mining on reservation territories.

In 2016, Diné CARE remains an informal network of elder and youth tribal activists run by a community-based board of advisors with no central office and minimal paid staff. Its leading organizers partner with other energy and environmental groups across Diné and Hopi territories, including the Black Mesa Water Coalition, the C Aquifer for Diné, the Black Mesa Trust, the Eastern Navajo Against Uranium Mining, Toh'nizhoni Ani (Beautiful Water Speaking), and the Just Transition Coalition, among others. Many of these groups are still actively building a transition movement across the reservation, pressuring their government to move away from a reliance on extractive industry as economic development and toward alternative energy technologies, such as wind and solar. Their vision is of a different kind of energy landscape: smaller scale, decentralized, not necessarily export-driven, and built into the environment through wind farms and solar troughs, local food movements, and alternative economic livelihoods (Ecos and Diné CARE 2008; Eldridge et al. 2014).

Although adversaries in terms of their politics of coal, these grassroots groups' vision of transition aligns with NTEC's vision in one crucial way: a belief that Navajo citizens ought to regain, and then maintain, ownership and control of Navajo resources as a prerequisite for robust tribal sovereignty. This belief has surfaced poignantly in recent debates over a Navajo water rights settlement with the state of Arizona, in which extraction (or "selling off") of Navajo water resources is understood within the broader historical critique of settler colonialism. In sum, their register of transition is about a disruption of the status quo—a shift toward specific energy technologies—but also about putting an end to the longstanding Navajo subsidy of the urban Southwest.

## Alternative Logics of Transition

Compared to the historical development and contemporary state of the movement against fossil fuels and other intensive extraction of Navajo natural resources, NTEC is a barometer of the Navajo Nation's fledgling energy policy. But it is also, much like all other energy extraction debates on the Navajo Nation, an indicator of the contested opinions, shifting circumstances, and hybrid social formations that constitute Diné energy activism. Coal development remains front and center for the Navajo Nation, through NTEC, which has in fact recently "doubled-down on coal" (Curley 2014b); this is perhaps most visible in 2017, as tribal leaders try to forestall the closure of the Navajo Generating Station, one of the region's oldest, and dirtiest, coal plants. This pathway continues the Nation's longstanding economic development model, literally grounded in its rich reserves of fossil fuels, despite the crescendo of resistance among Diné citizens to this environmentally and financially perilous pathway.

NTEC's weak investment in renewable energy underscores coal's continuing importance in the Navajo Nation, as well as its many difficult social, political, and ecological entanglements (Dennison 2012). One of NTEC's leading public spokespeople, Sam Woods, is a former commissioner with the Navajo Nation's Green Economy Commission, tasked under an earlier tribal administration with advancing renewable energy and "green jobs" for the Nation. Curley argues that this green jobs movement, for all of its radical and utopian visions among grassroots advocates, was undercut by neoliberal interests only very roughly disguised (Curley forthcoming). To this point, in 2014, Woods reported that NTEC is committed to reinvesting 10% of net profits into renewable energy, to include what he called, "clean coal." When publicly challenged by a community member at a public hearing to justify the paltry fraction dedicated to renewables, Woods stiffly replied: "that was what the Board decided." Such a statement anchors the authority of closed-door decision-making and a politically veiled process not easily swayed to public demands for transparency. Notably, in a public speech in early 2014, Woods added that at least one of the NTEC Board members holds several patents in hydro-fracking.

NTEC's own economic estimates hover at $2.5 billion in revenue over 25 years and seemingly secure employment for Diné youth, calculated (by NTEC) as 42,574 "job years" of employment. The project will "engage our youth and bring our students back to the Navajo Nation," Woods argued at a public forum of primarily Diné citizens near the reservation town of Shiprock. This position conjures the well-worn "jobs versus the environment" standoff, yet falls flat for many Diné people whose non- or informal-wage livelihoods and other modes of care-based laboring go unrecognized in official employment measures.

In this way, the Navajo Nation's fledgling energy policy emerges after more than thirty years of urging by academics, activists, and policymakers of the Tribal Council to establish an independent energy policy for mineral development on the reservation.

This widely recognized structural failure to manage energy minerals sustainably and strategically has been a topic of intensive discussion for decades.[2] Former Navajo Nation President Ben Shelly, during his service as Vice-President to Joe Shirley in 2008, acknowledged the complexity of developing a sound policy. He related the need to the longstanding inter-tribal movement embodied by CERT, the inter-tribal group formed in 1975 involving 10% of Native Nations, in profitably developing their energy resources. In an interview, Shelly criticized CERT's extractivism:

> There is also another energy policy, which is CERT's. Now this is a Native American Indian policy—they have a group, CERT. It's still around. But I went to their meeting in Las Vegas and I sat in and when they are talking about their energy policy, it's back in the coal, coal, coal days—coal and gas. Nothing to do with alternative energy. So I seen some old faces, they all know each other. They all been in there too long. That's the way I look at it. New young people, the ones that look to the future, I sense that is what needs to be done ... I told them, we have to update a new Native American energy policy, a new one, to represent all of us Indian Native Nations that have energy resources ... Right now, Indian energy people are just spectators in a ball game. That's the analogy. I want to have a Native American team playing big energy. I said if you [CERT] don't do it, Navajo is going to go forward by itself.
>
> *(Shelly 2008)*

With former Chairman Peter MacDonald as one of its founders, CERT had Navajo leadership from the beginning, and has frequently been invoked as the pan-Indian referent for a Navajo-based, yet globally influential, energy policy. CERT was designed in 1975 during the heyday of Diné nationalism (noted above) to intervene nationally in the global "oil crisis" of the day, modeled after the Organization of Petroleum Exporting Countries, or OPEC, founded in Iraq. And while NTEC is a very recent tribal corporation tasked primarily with the takeover (and potential expansion) of the Navajo Coal Mine, its global ambitions are perhaps not so geopolitically distant from CERT's, as the vision of intensified coal extraction includes possible westward railroad export of Navajo coal to Pacific ports and on to China.

MacDonald brought his experiences managing one of the most mineral-rich nations into this new platform for inter-tribal advocacy, critiquing the US Carter administration for not only failing to include leaders of Native Nations at the pivotal energy policy talks held at Camp David, but also for ignoring altogether that 20% of the United States' mineral resources lie beneath Indian territory (Ruffing 1980, 49). MacDonald understood the Navajo Nation's mineral wealth to be of great historical significance, harboring the "power to control power" in the greater Southwest region, thus affecting emerging SunBelt cities like Phoenix and Los Angeles, as they boomed and bloomed (Needham 2014). He was aware of how the advancement of non-Native urban centers was subsidized by Navajo labor and resources, resulting in underdevelopment on the Navajo reservation. However, given the variety of mineral resources CERT members held, CERT's power to have any real effect on prices was limited (Ruffing 1980). Moreover, lacking independent legal status, such as the nation-state based sovereignty enjoyed by OPEC member countries, Native Nations that were members of CERT were limited in legal recourse for transforming the exploitative nature of existing leased tribal land. MacDonald's proposal for "joint ventures" with stipulations favoring Navajo sovereignty became the method that CERT hoped would transform colonial relationships between Native Nations and energy corporations (Needham 2014).

The direct challenge posed by CERT leaders to the US government is a recognition of what I consider to be entangled *landscapes of power*, in which different registers of force (material, aesthetic, figurative) shape the politics and ecology of energy in the Navajo Nation. Elsewhere, I argue that multifaceted and shifting landscapes define Navajo energy politics, such that the seen and unseen, affective and discursive, technical and figurative worlds of extractive industry in Navajo territory produced new articulations of tribal sovereignty, expert knowledge, and cultural production (Powell 2015; Powell forthcoming; Powell and Long 2010). CERT was significant as a model of trans–local collective action, despite mounting critiques of the politics of fossil fuel inevitability it embraced and advanced. Today, CERT continues to operate as a voice for more than fifty mineral-rich Native Nations in addressing Congress and collaborating with industry to mobilize Native Nations to control and protect their interests in energy development, from coal to biofuels. Although contemporary leaders like Ben Shelly—not to mention a vast network of green energy activists—view CERT as lacking the political vision needed to bolster alternative energy development due to its favoring the status quo of settler government, CERT's energy activism advanced collective action by advancing trans-national solidarity for managing fossil fuel resources.

As Shelly's reflection above suggests, CERT figures as a benchmark against which Native Nations can evaluate and implement their own policies, and even "form their own teams," to use Shelly's competitive metaphor, if they feel CERT's stance is not aggressive enough. CERT's contemporary visions to restructure the federal–Indian relationship and to assist Native Nations in building self-sufficient economies are by all measures radical goals, extending the founding Council's anti-colonial position. By other accounts, CERT is culpable for putting Native Nations in precarious positions financially and environmentally by working to secure bids for US Department of Energy disposal sites for toxic and radioactive waste (LaDuke 1999).

Yet even as Shelly critiques CERT's leadership and urges the Navajo Nation to go forward on its own, the history of CERT is intimately entangled with Navajo landscapes of power, especially along the question of historical rupture and transition. Even now, as Diné citizens wrestle with their Nation's decades-long dependence on a fossil-fuel based economy, NTEC moves forward, posing the question of a tribal-based CERT for the twenty-first century, with its own signature brand of transition—one that intensifies extraction, while at the same time working to intensify self-determination. The ongoing debate among Native Nations, non-governmental groups, states, and the federal government, as well as *within* Native Nations is, however, about *which* infrastructures, technologies, processes, and voices hold the solutions to sovereign futures.

Likewise, what it means to transition from the past to the future, by way of a contested present, belies competing theories of temporality, risk, and change, which in their inchoate formations underlie—and often undermine—meaningful dialogue in Diné energy politics. If fossil fuels are perhaps *not* inevitable—meaning, their extraction is not the foregone conclusion of modernity, itself the other side or "underside" of coloniality (Mignolo 2000)—then what might transition look like for the Navajo Nation? Diné grassroots groups, filmmakers (Lempert 2014) and visual artists, intellectuals, and other collectives are hard at work to articulate an environmental politics in which transition *away* from large-scale extraction of natural resources can go hand-in-hand with a transition *toward* a more autonomous, self-reliant, sovereign Native Nation. This is a political, environmental, and economic argument; one requiring, at a minimum, a rethinking of the complex meanings of transition and sustainability in the particular political-ecological context of extraction-derived exposure, and of Native citizenship and self-determination.

## Back to the Future: Beyond Extractivism?

If transition is not a rupture but a process, and, likewise, if settler colonialism is not an event but a process (Wolfe 2006), then we are called upon to dwell within, and interrogate, the contradictory experiences and discourses of "post-extractivism" (Gudynas 2014). That which might appear inevitable can then be situated and historicized. When extraction can be seen as the product of particular social formations and historical actors, we might first imagine and then design different kinds of machines, engendering different kinds of politics—politics that might better sustain Native economies, ecologies, and polities. When global energy extraction struggles are emplaced, as ethnography aims to do, we see how "transition"—much like "sustainability"—has traction in some, but not all, conversations. Transition, to many Diné grassroots activists, means something different than transition for NTEC. Both argue for a new ethics of energy production, yet their visions of the process and infrastructure of change dramatically diverge. Designing alternative energy and more flourishing futures demands that researchers and activists take seriously the analytic categories and critical metaphors emerging from activists, artists, intellectuals, and leaders in tribal and grassroots politics who have engaged this issue under the banner of anti-colonialism and nation-building over the last half century—even when these actors have been at odds with one another. Nadelman (Chapter 12) notes similar discoveries in her study of El Salvadoran fights against metals mining.

One of the goals of this piece has been to briefly chronicle some of the vast internal differences among Diné people engaged in energy activism. Another goal has been to pose the question of the politics of inevitability in extraction-based economies. We work against the popular sense that history unfolds along a predetermined pathway, the philosophical residue of a teleological, divine ordering of life. The term "transition" is slippery as an analytic category or critical metaphor. Could transition yet shift, to become a matter of common interest, where activists on either side of the great fossil fuel divide could creatively engage the difficult question of the future in the language of transition, grounded in their common concern over tribal sovereignty and Navajo control of natural resources? I believe this is possible, though it requires a profound realignment in the terms of the debate. At stake is a crucial, under-examined concept of justice embedded in each group's different deployment of the term. For NTEC, justice is embodied in full tribal control and execution of energy development. For grassroots groups, justice concerns a set of broader relations, and "the entirety of life" (to return to the movement founders in Dilkon).

If these conversations can sidestep the riddle of whether or not "transition" implies an inherently post-extractivist rupture, and move toward a discussion of what justice looks and feels like for Navajo people and how it might be designed into the human-built environment, there may yet be an opening for the clarity and creativity needed to redesign the future. To be sure, on both sides of the debate, the language of transition galvanizes support for a future-oriented energy strategy that, implicitly or explicitly, recognizes a toxic history of contamination and dependency, and the urgent need for change. This is a slow, yet hopeful process of departure from a past scarred by the violence inherent in subsidizing development elsewhere.

## Notes

1 In the political structure on the Navajo Nation, any development project planned for a community must be approved through a Chapter Resolution by the local chapter. Thus, much of the debate over energy development, as well as other land use issues, takes place at the chapter level, with high stakes in passing resolutions, as the Tribal Council in Window Rock must then take these decisions seriously.

2 At least as early as 1980, Lorraine T. Ruffing's important critique of the uneven development of mineral resources among American Indian Native Nations, and the Navajo Nation in particular, stands out as a thorough analysis of the problem as well as agenda for action to increase tribal sovereignty vis-à-vis control over its energy resources. Her analysis focuses on the power of transnational corporations, American contract law, Indian mineral dependency, federal mismanagement, and effects of a misunderstood "energy crisis" in shaping how Native Nations manage—or fail to manage—their energy resources through tribal policy change (see Ruffing 1980).

## References

Benally, Timothy, Doug Brugge, and Esther Yazzie-Lewis. 2006. *The Navajo People and uranium mining.* Albuquerque: University of New Mexico Press.

Bullard, Robert D. 2000. *Dumping in Dixie: Race, class, and environmental quality.* 3rd edn. Boulder, CO: Westview Press.

Checker, Melissa. 2005. *Polluted Promises: Environmental Racism and the Search for Justice in a Southern Town.* New York: NYU Press.

Curley, Andrew. 2014a. The origin of legibility: Rethinking colonialism and resistance among the Navajo People, 1868–1937. In *Diné perspectives: Revitalizing and reclaiming Navajo thought,* edited by Lloyd L. Lee, 129–150. Tucson: University of Arizona Press.

Curley, Andrew. 2014b. Navajo Nation doubles down on coal. *Navajo Times*, January 16.

Curley, Andrew. Forthcoming. A failed green future: Green jobs and the limits of hybrid neo-liberalism in the Navajo Nation. *Geoforum*.

Denetdale, Jennifer. 2006. Chairmen, presidents, and princesses: The Navajo Nation, gender, and the politics of tradition. *Wicazo Sa Review* 21, 1:9–28.

Dennison, Jean. 2012. *Colonial entanglement: Constituting a twenty-first-century Osage Nation.* Chapel Hill: University of North Carolina Press.

Diné Policy Institute. 2014. *Diné Food Sovereignty: A Report on the Navajo Nation Food System and the Case to Rebuild a Self-Sufficient Food System for the Diné People.* Report, April 2014. Tsaile, AZ: Diné Policy Institute. www.dinecollege.edu/institutes/DPI/Docs/dpi-food-sovereignty-report.pdf (accessed March 23, 2016).

Di Chiro, Giovanna. 1996. Nature as community: The convergence of environment and social justice. In *Uncommon ground: Rethinking the human place in nature*, edited by William Cronon, 298–320. New York: Norton & Company.

Ecos Consulting and members of Diné Citizens Against Ruining our Environment (Diné CARE). 2008. *Energy and Economic Alternatives to the Desert Rock Energy Project.* Report, January 12. Durango, CO: Ecos Consulting. www.dine-care.org/pages/Coal/pdfs/Alternatives_to_Desert_Rock_Full_Report.pdf (accessed March 23, 2016).

Gudynas, Eduardo. 2014. *Derechos de la naturaleza y políticas ambientales.* La Paz, Bolivia: Plural.

Heisinger, Margaret A. 2010. The house that uranium built: Perspectives on the effects of exposure on individuals and community. In *The energy reader*, edited by Laura Nader, 113–131. Hoboken, NJ: Wiley-Blackwell.

Hopkins, Rob. 2008. *The transition handbook: From oil dependency to local resilience.* Cambridge, UK: Green Books.

Johnston, Barbara Rose, ed. 2007. *Half-lives and half-truths: Confronting the radioactive legacies of the Cold War.* Santa Fe, NM: School of Advanced Research Press.

Kuletz, Valerie. 1998. *The tainted desert: Environmental ruin in the American west.* New York: Routledge.

LaDuke, Winona. 1999. *All our relations: Native struggles for land and life.* Cambridge, MA: South End Press.

Landry, Alysa. 2015. Not alone in the dark: Navajo Nation's lack of electricity problem. *Indian Country Today*, February 11. http://indiancountrytodaymedianetwork.com/2015/02/11/not-alone-dark-navajo-nations-lack-electricity-problem-159135 (accessed March 23, 2016).

Lee, Lloyd L, ed. 2014. *Diné perspectives: Revitalizing and reclaiming Navajo thought.* Tucson: University of Arizona Press.

Lempert, Michael. 2014. Decolonizing encounters of the third kind: Alternative futuring in Native science fiction film. *Visual Anthropology Review* 30, 2: 164–176.

Masco, Joseph. 1999. *Nuclear borderlands: The Manhattan Project in post-Cold War New Mexico.* Princeton, NJ: Princeton University Press.

Mignolo, Walter D. 2000. *Local Histories/Global Designs: Coloniality, Subaltern Knowledges, and Border Thinking.* Princeton, NJ: Princeton University Press.

Navajo Nation. n.d. *History.* www.navajo-nsn.gov/history.htm (accessed March 23, 2016).

Needham, Andrew. 2014. *Power lines: Phoenix and the making of the modern southwest.* Princeton, NJ: Princeton University Press.

Office of Indian Energy Policy and Programs (OIEPP). 2015. *Winning the future: Navajo-Hopi Land Commission leverages DOE grant to advance solar ranch project*, October 22. Washington, DC: United States Department of Energy. http://energy.gov/indianenergy/articles/winning-future-navajo-hopi-land-commission-leverages-doe-grant-advance-solar (accessed March 23, 2016).

Powell, Dana E. 2015. The rainbow is our sovereignty: Rethinking the politics of energy on the Navajo Nation. *Journal of Political Ecology* 22:53–78.

Powell, Dana E. forthcoming. *Landscapes of power: Energy politics on the Navajo Nation.* Durham, NC: Duke University Press.

Powell, Dana E., and Andrew Curley. 2009. K'e, Hozhó, and non-governmental politics on the Navajo Nation: Ontologies of difference manifest in environmental activism. In *World Anthropologies Network E-Journal No.* 4, edited by Marisol de la Cadena and Mario Blaser. www.ram-wan.net/html/journal-4.htm (accessed March 23, 2016).

Powell, Dana E., and Dáilan J. Long. 2010. Landscapes of power: Renewable energy activism in Diné Bikeyah. In *Indians and energy: Exploitation and opportunity in the American southwest,* edited by Sherry Smith and Brian Frehner, 231–262. Santa Fe, NM: School of Advanced Research Press.

Redhouse, John. n.d. *Desert Rock: 1953–2003.* Unpublished report.

Ruffing, Lorraine Turner. 1980. The role of policy in American Indian mineral development. In *American Indian Energy Resources and Development,* edited by Roxanne Dunbar Ortiz, 39–73. Albuquerque: Institute for Native American Development Native American Studies, University of New Mexico.

Shelly, Ben. 2008. Interview by Dana Powell. Personal Interview. Window Rock, AZ, October 20.

Sherry, John W. 2002. *Land, wind, and hard words: A story of Navajo activism.* Albuquerque: University of New Mexico Press.

Tsing, Anna L. 2005. *Friction: An ethnography of global connection.* Princeton, NJ: Princeton University Press.

Tulley, Earl. 2008. Interview by Dana Powell. Personal Interview. Chinle, AZ. February 15.

Voyles, Traci Brynne. 2015. *Wastelanding: Legacies of uranium mining in Navajo country.* Minneapolis: University of Minnesota Press.

Wolfe, Patrick. 2006. Settler colonialism and the elimination of the Native. *Journal of Genocide Research* 8, 4:387–309.

Woods, Sam. 2014. NTEC public forum at Operating Engineers Union Hall, April 9. Kirtland, NM.

# AFTERWORD

## An Open Letter to ExtrACTIVISTs

### Jeanne Simonelli

In 2007, I changed the name of my Applied Anthropology seminar to Development Wars. It was not just an opportunistic switch to a sexy title in order to lure reluctant students; it was a fundamental shift in the underlying logic of the course. During the semester, we explored the immediate and long-term impacts of competing social and economic development ideologies on the lives of those subject to them. As an avenue to understanding the ways that water, land, and mineral rights are held and lost in the United States, we watched the film version (1988) of the New Mexico-based novel *The Milagro Beanfield War*. *Beanfield* tells the story of powerless people searching for power. As author John Nichols wrote, "People are bitter over how they lost their land and their water rights. And this sort of act, small as it may seem, could touch off something bigger" (Nichols 1974, 42). The film also features a hapless New York sociology student intent on doing cultural research. Presented with gentle humor, these two threads allowed the class to question whether there is anything inherently useful or helpful in what we, as social scientists, learn and do. We asked: *can we help without hurting?*

Also in 2007, an incipient development war was brewing in New York, where I had a home. In the Northeast United States natural gas drilling had begun in the Marcellus Shale. Representatives of international and US gas exploration companies began knocking on doors in rural New York State and Pennsylvania starting in 2002, asking to buy underground mineral rights. Industry observers claimed that, "The hottest natural gas boom in the world isn't in Russia, Canada, or even the Middle East. It's right here in the U.S. ... the Marcellus formation may contain up to 1,300 trillion cubic feet of natural gas!" (Energy and Capital 2009). Many of my neighbors signed contracts. Integrating the topic of shale gas drilling into the Development Wars seminar, I searched the literature and the Internet for scientific studies for my class to read, but there was little to be found. Much that was available had been commissioned by the industry.

In 2012, I taught Development Wars again. Students did in-depth projects on myriad aspects of oil and gas development all over the USA. Their bibliographies were richer in some respects, but research on health and social impacts was limited in scope and guarded in its claims. Critical data and insight sometimes get caught between urgency and the validation process required by scientific methodology. As Stephanie Paladino and I have observed:

> In the face of an avalanche of uncritical electronic information, with its twin threads of fetishization of scientific process/science, on the one hand, and complete misunderstanding and mistrust of it on the other, social science is particularly vulnerable … the institutional responses and supporting science continue to come long after the damages have been done and many have suffered.
>
> *(Paladino and Simonelli 2013, 2)*

Following a series of interviews concerning the health effects of fracking on children, one student in the seminar concluded that "the actual studies on this topic are shockingly slim … People have given up. Researchers are tired" (Bendas 2012). In fact, it was the shortage of health related studies that kept New York's 2008 moratorium on shale gas drilling in place until the State passed a ban in 2015 (Simonelli 2014).

In the latest turn of events, eminent domain has been used to claim large segments of land for laying pipe and building compressor stations tied to the proposed Constitution Pipeline route in New York and Pennsylvania. With this bitterly contested process of seizing private land for the "public good," local activists saw the struggle morphing into something bigger. In their continuing campaign to encourage the State's Governor Andrew Cuomo to direct the environmental watchdog agency to deny needed water quality certificates, landowners were explicit:

> It is war all right! Many of us are pushing your plan to go 50% renewable energy by 2030 … a modest but necessary first battle in the war. But we already have the 50% of fossil fuel and nuclear power to make up that part of our energy mix. So we really need to be saying "NO" to any and all fracked gas infrastructure.
>
> *(Higgins 2016)*

The Constitution project began with open "informational" presentations along the pipeline route. While lip service is constantly given to the need to consult with local communities, it is only in rare instances that voices are heard. Mainstream Americans are not protected by concepts and agreements like Convention 169 of the International Labor Organization's Article 7, which states that indigenous and tribal peoples have the right to "decide their own priorities for the process of development as it affects their lives, beliefs, institutions and spiritual well-being and the lands they occupy" (ILO 1989). Even for people for whom these articles do apply, they are weak at best and more often than not we fail.

But when we do win, as occurred with the Constitution Pipeline on Earth Day, April 22, 2016, it is groundbreaking. "We are the first group to stop a FERC approved pipeline since fracking started in the US," said attorney Anne Marie Garti (2016). "That is a major accomplishment, and we should all be proud of it." As Sandra Steingraber (2016) noted concerning an earlier, unexpected triumph: "the third lesson from the Shell No! victory in Painted Post, New York? Surely, it's the power of unflinching citizen activism."

As the chapters in this book illustrate, information about extraction and the interest in learning about it are growing. The weapons that are being used by activists in today's development wars include the studies and collaborations reported in this volume, as well as the burgeoning literature that they cite. These are tools emerging from the work of communities and advocacy groups around the world who are concerned about extraction, as well as a language acquired during this great awakening. But these chapters are just fourteen contributions to a body of research that needs to reach the public and policymakers before additional damage is done. Keeping a critical mass of people working on gathering, compiling, and analyzing the breaking news of the extraction industry is what grassroots groups and citizen scientists do for those of us who translate data into "science." We have skills and methods that can contribute to direct and ethical attempts to solve human problems. Our credentials can make what activists do in community meetings and formal motions "credible"; compiling and translating the data so that it resonates with those with the power to make policy.

For academics, building direct links between research and activism may not be the road to tenure. Those of us who have already made the journey, received our promotions, and now contemplate retirement, must take the lead in the public arena and in showing younger colleagues how to negotiate the institutional highway while still remaining activists. Those working for governmental and nongovernmental agencies face a similar dilemma concerning when to act, speak, and push against the stated mission of those who employ you. The chapters in this book reinforce the adage that the local is the global. Where activism is concerned, the individual is the collective: "struggle is collective, but the decision to struggle is individual, personal, intimate, as is the decision to go on or give up" (Marcos 2014). In the final analysis, yours is a personal decision to act for the public good; to exercise eminent domain over the social landscape of our shared environmental future. Collectively, we can be the architects of socially just solutions for lasting change.

# References

Bendas, Yasmin. n.d. The impacts of hydraulic fracturing on the health and well-being of children. Unpublished paper prepared for Development Wars, Department of Anthropology, Wake Forest University. Copy in author's possession.

Energy and Capital. 2009. *The Marcellus gas formation: Welcome to the next natural gas boom.* www.energyandcapital.com/aqx_p/10779?gclid=CMfN_obj6JgCFQMQswodY-mAw2A (accessed March 24, 2009).

Garti, Anne Marie. 2016. Birthday message to Stop the Pipeline. Stop the Pipeline email list serve, June 28.

Higgins, Dennis. 2016. New York under siege by pipelines, and our own legislators, February 12. Letter to New York Governor Andrew Cuomo. Copy in author's possession.

International Labor Organization (ILO). 1989. *Convention concerning Indigenous and tribal peoples in independent countries.* Indigenous and Tribal Peoples Convention, Number 169, Geneva.

Marcos, Subcomandante. 2014. *EZLN communiqué: "When the dead silently speak out". Text via enlace Zapatista.* English translation by Dorset Chiapas Solidarity. The Chiapas Support Committee. http://roarmag.org/2014/01/subcomandante-marcos-ezln-anniversary-communique/ (accessed March 1, 2016).

Nichols, John. 1974. *The Milagro beanfield war.* New York: Ballantine Books.

Paladino, Stephanie, and Jeanne Simonelli. 2013. Hazards so grave: Anthropology and energy. *Culture, Agriculture, Food and Environment* 35, 1:1–3.

Simonelli, Jeanne. 2014. Home rule and natural gas development in New York: Civil fracking rights. *Journal of Political Ecology* 21, 1:258–278.

Steingraber, Sandra. 2016. The people win over Shell in fracking water withdrawal case. *EcoWatch*, January 7. http://ecowatch.com/2016/01/07/people-win-over-shell/ (accessed March 1, 2016).

# INDEX